SCALE
OPEN | CLOSE

SCALE

OPEN | CLOSE

WINDOWS, DOORS, GATES, LOGGIAS, FILTERS

EDITORS
ALEXANDER REICHEL
KERSTIN SCHULTZ

AUTHORS
ANETTE HOCHBERG
JAN-HENRIK HAFKE
JOACHIM RAAB

Birkhäuser
Basel · Boston · Berlin

EDITORS' FOREWORD

There is plenty of literature about outstanding architecture and its creators, usually accompanied by illustrations showing the end results. But how does high-quality architecture come about? What sets it apart?

The *SCALE* series focuses on the design process, illustrating the development and fleshing-out of design approaches and architectural concepts. Importantly, it includes their detailed implementation. The series also provides illustrations at various different scales and with various degrees of abstraction, which demonstrate the interrelations of space, design and construction.

The architectural grammar of design and construction studies mainly deals with the individual components. Although this is useful as a standard classification providing a clear structure, it largely ignores the high number of new and constantly evolving techniques for expressing ideas, as well as new, wider ranges of materials, technologies, guidelines and standards. Publications mention the different levels of abstract presentation, but they do not comprehensively demonstrate how to work with them. Readers do not get the opportunity to follow the development from the abstract idea to the specific details. Yet this is an essential part of high-quality and sustainable architecture.

This new series of books aims to fill this gap. Intended both as an inspiration and as a practical tool, it demonstrates the complex and integrative process of building from the first design idea to the tender documents. It does this in terms of abstract design principles, but, crucially, includes specific details. This continuous reciprocal relationship within design is the starting point for a representation of architectural and spatial ideas—the basis of any building project. The series uses project examples to show the consequences of different construction techniques, and the critical influence of materials and construction details.

The series is titled *SCALE* because of the way that good, fully detailed plans develop by passing through different levels of abstraction, at different scales. The title reflects the integrative and process-based way an architect must work, and the need to combine design and construction intimately. Building is a continuous process; the combination of design and implementation is its essence.

This is the first book in the series. Its title is *Open | Close*, and it examines architectural openings, from idea to implementation. Openings connect the exterior and the interior. In doing so, they define the relationship of people with their surroundings, which in turn shapes the character of the building.
A catalogue, grouped by opening type, is used to demonstrate ways of changing the atmosphere of a space using openings. In the process, the book also looks at the technical aspects of openings, with a section for each structural component: windows, loggias, skylights, doors and gates. The individual elements are arranged, described and fleshed out in both design and construction terms. Recently built

projects are illustrated as examples; these are both practical and generally applicable. The projects are not chosen for their homogeneous architectural language, but for the architectural quality of their treatment of openings and for their practical construction.

The other volumes of this series will examine the design-based construction process of other individual building elements in a particular sequence. The books in the series each deal with two linked concepts (linked in design, construction and associative terms). Taking each individual architectural element separately, the series shows how different visual representations relate to each other.
The second title in the series, *Enclose | Build*, deals with the design and implementation of a building's outer shell.

Our intention in publishing this series is not to give prominence to individual architectural approaches, but to show our readers design situations with an internal coherence and logic. A wide range of very different architectural personalities were involved from the very start, helping us to retain a broad enough basis in the design field to do justice to the varied tasks involved in construction. This book uses up-to-date examples coupled with historical, traditional architecture to present these architects' experience of varied building construction themes in an easy-to-understand way, reflecting the available architectural solutions in all their variety and all their different stages of development.
The presence of architecture and the impression it gives define our built environment and our society. This series is intended as a contribution to a functional and sustainable architecture, and therefore to the quality of our constructed environment.

We would like to thank Birkhäuser Verlag, and especially Andrea Wiegelmann, for giving us the opportunity to work on this series of books.

Basel, 30th September 2009
Alexander Reichel, Kerstin Schultz

OPEN | CLOSE
INTRODUCTION

THEORETICAL FOUNDATIONS

Openings are central to our overall impression of a building design, and to its interior ambience. The interplay of closed and open surfaces and of mass and space, and the way the specific details—materials, forms and shapes—interact with its interior and exterior all influence a building's appearance, just as the interior's ambience is affected by openings' proportions and dimensions, and the light and shadows they create.

The basic function of a building's enclosing components is to exclude climatic and social influences by creating an interior and an exterior. Solid floors, walls and ceilings satisfy our need for security, for a protected habitation. In contrast, the relationship between interior and exterior space is defined by openings. They connect the two, creating links and providing rooms with daylight and fresh air. Openings provide contact with the outside world, so that residents know where they are and can observe their surroundings and communicate with those outside. They satisfy our basic needs for light, ventilation and orientation, and are a means of 'seeing in' as well as a means of 'seeing out'. Specific kinds of opening, each with a different size, form and position within the enclosing components, fulfill different requirements. These include the Windauge or "wind's eye" (window), the skylight and the access opening (which has a longer architectural history.

The act of making an opening raises the question of how to close it—an opening enables connections, but does not prevent them, so protective or filtering components such as doors, gates, windows, shutters and sun control elements are created to do this. These allow the opening's function, form and the impact it has on a space to be altered.

Doors and gates are components used to close or open a passage through a wall. They allow rooms to be closed off from other rooms or from the outside area, while allowing people to pass through. The difference between doors and gates is a matter of dimension: while a door approximates to the size of a human being, gates are used to close off larger openings. Doors and gates can be constructed to permit entry to certain users and to exclude others.

A window is a component that closes an opening in a wall. To light the building's interior and to permit views in and out of the building, it is transparent, while an opening mechanism allows for ventilation. Occupants can therefore keep wind and rain, for instance, out of the interior without obstructing sunlight or blocking the view in or out.

Filters can modify the external influences that interiors are exposed to by openings. Their efficiency can be improved using controls. Effective closure of an opening is impossible without a filter.

Social and technological developments during the twentieth century changed the prevailing characteristics of windows. It could even be said that modernism practically

1 Schaulager, Basel, 2003, by Herzog & De Meuron.

2 Salk Institut, La Jolla, 1959–1965, by Louis I. Kahn.

3, 4 Residential buildings on
the former Junghans site,
Venice, 2002, by Cino Zucchi.

led to an abhorrence of windows. Improved construction techniques led to open ground plans and fewer restrictions on the design and format of openings. The architecture of today offers a veritable plurality of possible opening shapes, from a vertical slit to a horizontal strip, or a transparent wall. The construction of lintels, reveals and parapets, the arrangement of windows in the wall structure and the deployment of sun control elements all offer plenty of possibilities for design. The number, size and arrangement of the openings can be varied so as to give the building's facade a structure and regular pattern, determining the sense of scale. Cino Zucchi's residential buildings in Venice, for instance, have openings that hint at the diversity of the interiors by their playful arrangement and positioning, their different sizes and formats, their light-colored surrounds and their colorful design. ➘ 3, 4

Construction industry standardization is rapidly turning windows and doors into prefabricated standard products. The range of models on offer is immense and generally of high technical quality. As a consequence, windows are often left out of serious design and construction considerations. And yet, to produce an opening with a harmonious design, it is not enough to use prefabricated standard products. A mass of products and new technologies bring with them increased user expectations and the requirements of very different building types when choosing and designing openings, plus economic and energy-related issues. How can a design idea be developed from drafting through to construction without losing the intended architectural effect? What are the factors to be taken into account in designing an opening? The first of these is the opening's relationship with the enclosing wall, ceiling and floor elements: a structural frame allows types of opening that a masonry wall, timber studding or cross-wall construction would not. Then there is the choice of construction materials—wood, stone or steel—and whether the building has a single-layer or multilayer envelope. Architectural design criteria such as the size, position, proportion, shape, number, materials and construction of openings must be taken into account, as must each opening's inner structure, the type and (depending on the material) the thickness of the frame, the color of any glass and the direction of opening. Put together, these construction and design specifications give the typology of openings for the building. To understand this great variety of openings and associated components, one has to know their significance and origins. Openings greatly affect the impression a building makes, and are crucial to its exterior form and interior atmosphere.

ATMOSPHERE

A building's openings affect its form. The eye as a window that allows us to see out into the world—and the world to look back in at us—is a familiar poetic image. If, like Aristotle, we consider the eyes to be the mirror of the soul, then it is only a short step to believing that a building's openings reveal its character, showing us its architectural essence. They are a sign of accessibility, with a social, public character. Where openings are less generous, there is no direct connection between the interior and the surroundings. The design of access elements determines whether a building has a welcoming or forbidding attitude, so public buildings usually have extensive, open-plan foyers and ground floor areas.

Special door constructions such as revolving doors or a porch can be used to emphasize entrances. In the Doge's palace in Venice, as with many grand buildings, the type and function of the window openings demonstrate wealth and power, in this case of the ruler of the Venetian empire. The loggia, for instance, was the place where death sentences were pronounced. There are seven openings in the upper section of the wall above the arcades, the central one of which incorporates a balcony for public appearances.

Openings can be a form of decoration, making a building into a status symbol, enhancing the prestige of its occupants and expressing their relationship with the public sphere. ↘1 Splendid entrance portals show the owner's wealth and carry a demonstrative and symbolic weight, with proportions, format and size all expressing a certain meaning. For instance, sacred buildings and meeting places, despite their communal function, are seldom easy to see in or out of.

A connection with the outside world would distract the group within, or attract unwanted observers.

Neither result would be appropriate to meetings or religious services. Instead, the openings of such buildings make clear that contact with the outside world is incompatible with the building's purpose. At the same time, daylight can be directed in churches so as to highlight elements of the interior that serve liturgical purposes and accentuate the spatial composition.

The chapel of Notre-Dame-du-Haut in Ronchamp, by Le Corbusier ↘2 shows how a space can be shaped by means of different openings and different designs for reveals. This building has an otherworldly atmosphere orchestrated by light, which heightens the effect of the space itself.

Creating a private sphere involves a careful arrangement of thresholds, entrances and windows. Expanded spatially, an entrance area can become an intermediate space between private and public territory. Windows can be specially arranged or fitted with 'filters' so that one can look out of them without being seen.

In contrast to private windows, the display windows used to show off products are intended to be seen into. Private openings may also be display windows, symbolizing the openness of the occupier and allowing a glimpse into his or her private territory. The studio of artist Lino Bardill has a sliding gate opening onto the village square. When the gate is open, the locals can look inside, while the village square can be seen from indoors. When it is closed, the studio is connected to the outside world solely by a large atrium, making it a small sheltered space in the middle of the village.

A closing element adjusts the degree of communication with the outside world in a way that can be understood by anyone viewing it from the outside.

1 The Doge's palace in Venice, 14th–15th century. Public and grand buildings often have balconies for public appearances, for political announcements and shows of power. Today, they are often used in festivities.

2 The chapel of Notre-Dame-du-Haut in Ronchamp, 1955, by Le Corbusier: Impenetrable by looking in from the outside, it excludes the secular world. The interior is given a religious atmosphere by the design of the openings and the management of daylight.

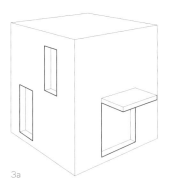
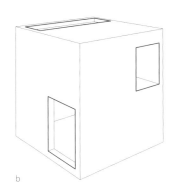
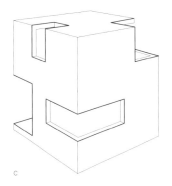
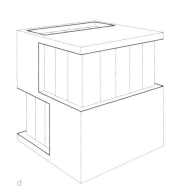

3a   b   c   d

3 The opening's position in a build-ing's structure changes the impres-sion that the building makes:

Is the opening well within the wall, ➚ a or does it have a more unusual position at a corner ➚ b

Openings around corners ➚ c are expressive and open up the volume's geometry.

Large-area openings ➚ d dissolve structures, creating a sense of openness.

4, 5 Atelier Lino Bardill, Scharans, 2007, by Valerio Olgiati: The build-ing as a mirror of the occupant's needs. The artist opens the gate to allow people to see in, and closes it when he needs peace.

Constructing a space means defining a particular part of the environment, enclosing it and giving it a certain role. A border creates an inside and an outside, a "before" and an "after". All fixed locations—territories, private open spaces, houses or rooms—are marked out by boundaries. Passages—the most primitive form of opening—define the transition between these defined areas. A built boundary must both separate the inside from the out-side and, by means of architectural design, create a har-mony between them. Elements that open up, connect and enclose spaces all go towards creating a spatial intersec-tion. The access opening is the meeting point between the two spheres—the inside and outside—that creates the relationship between public and private space.

4

5

PASSAGEWAY, THRESHOLD AND ENTRANCE

The opening is a threshold that both unites and separates. A threshold is an element that creates two distinct zones while providing a transition. It stands both for a break and continuity, a boundary and access. Thresholds and transitional spaces—steps, open staircases, porch roofs, portals, doors, windows and balconies—can also be locations in their own right. They emphasize two zones' separation while offering a chance to overcome it by creating a visual or spatial connection.

Thresholds announce the character of the place they provide access to or which they are the public face of. Consequently, there is nothing random about the design of thresholds. A direct transition can be created from the street into a living space; however, for many people this does not provide the necessary artificial boundary between themselves and the public world—that is to say, a transitional area that tells people whose territory they are presently in, welcomes guests and dissuades unwanted visitors from entering.

A step or a different flooring material helps to mark a threshold, while doorbells, letterboxes and locks are features usually to be found at the threshold of a private space.

A door forms an access point, creating connections between the inside and the outside. As a protective element, it controls admittance; there is a significance to going through a door. The threshold's construction reveals the character and values of the inner world. In poorer countries, in particular, thresholds are not merely serviceable—a great deal of attention is often paid to the entrance space. The threshold is also often used to express prosperity or social status. Bible quotations, coats of arms, dates—a decorative setting can be an architectural expression of a high social standing. The architect must create a design combining all the desired qualities for the threshold and transitional spaces. For the heavily glazed Farnsworth House, Mies van der Rohe created a transition to the house area using only the height difference between the tiered terraces. ⤷ **6**

The new entrance to the Gelbes Haus in Flims by Valerio Olgiati ⤷ **7** was created as an element of the existing building—with its own formal vocabulary and materials,

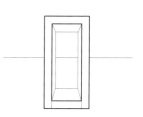

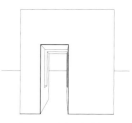

Access and threshold

1 Stones forming a boundary. The different territories are not apparent from the landscape. A gap created by the simple means of leaving a stone out marks the transition.

2 Public opening: In an urban structure, passages can lead through houses—without allowing passersby to see into the private sphere.

3 A triumphal arch marks the beginning of a path through a territory—and symbolizes the power of the builder and owner. The structure's design matches the opening's form.

4 A view into a Japanese garden. A finely differentiated transition has been created, from the garden to the house.

5a Simple entrance: Slightly raised surrounds and the use of recesses provide emphasis.

b   All the elements of the entrance—door, platform, roof, steps—are enclosed within a box.

c   The porch roof, jambs and door-step, with the bells and letterboxes, are condensed into a single element.

d   Like a loggia, a recessed entrance provides protection. The landing and steps can be integrated into the design.

e   Extensive diagonal entrance area.

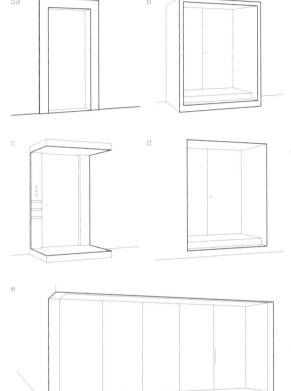

6 Farnsworth House, Plano, 1951, by Ludwig Mies van der Rohe.

7 Gelbes Haus, Flims, 1999, by Valerio Olgiati.

8, 9 Storefront Gallery, New York, 1993, by Steven Holl.

but with a design suitable for this high-profile community building, making it an appropriate marker for the entrance. Steven Holl's Storefront Gallery in New York → **8, 9** can be entirely closed off or extended into the street by an expressive facade feature. The gallery opens up to display its art like a shop front, or a market stall, thereby becoming both an exhibited object and a place to linger. The threshold becomes a location and the openings become the gallery.

ORIENTATION, LIGHT AND AIR

Orientation is the alignment of a building and its openings in relation to the surrounding environment: the points of the compass, the position of the sun, the region's climate, topography, vegetation and, of course, the man-made environment—surrounding buildings, with reference to their massing and functions. In urban contexts, an ideal orientation (in terms of light, air and view) is often impossible given existing emission levels, the exclusion of sunlight and obstructed views, meaning that case-by-case design solutions are required. The Klampenborg living units by Arne Jacobsen are staggered so that each apartment commands a view of the water through a glazed corner. An energy-efficient construction must pay special attention to the building's orientation in general and the orientation of its openings in particular. Large apertures to the south, east or west facilitate passive heat gains, but the need for sun and heat control devices should be considered. Openings on the side of the building that faces the prevailing weather must be protected; it is also a good idea to minimize the size of openings on the north side of buildings.

The archetypal window opening is an opening to provide light and air, once known as a "windauge". Its geometry and position are different from those of an opening intended to allow people to see out. Skylights can be used as light sources to highlight certain areas of the interior. Thanks to the stack effect, they can provide a whole building with natural ventilation if properly constructed as a shaft-like opening. ⤸2 An architectural space changes with the time of day and with the season, in a process governed by its openings, its alignment with the sun and its geographical location. A room that receives lateral sunlight all day has a different atmosphere to one with a skylight facing east; a skylight tones down contrasts, giving a different appearance to spaces that are the same geometrically. Natural light sources facilitate human well-being and human activities. Places designed to live in or to linger in need openings that are different to those of working and production premises, exhibition spaces or meeting places. Careful deployment of openings controls the intensity and evenness of light; apart from size, the opening's position is crucial. Skylights are suitable where plenty of light is required, because they have a high zenith light yield. In the case of wall openings, lintels reduce zenith light. ⤸6 Openings are planned on the basis of room height, opening size and room depth. As its distance from the opening increases, a given point receives a lower proportion of zenith light and a higher proportion of the light reflected from the enclosing surfaces, which is less direct and has a different color and texture.

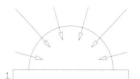

1

2

3

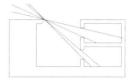

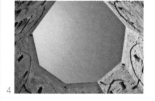

4

5

1 A window set into the wall receives only half of the full light strength. Neighboring buildings restrict the light. The light gain for an opening of the same size decreases constantly floor by floor as one goes down.

2 Traditional wind towers in Yazd, Iran use the stack effect to regulate temperature. They also dominate a building's appearance.

3 Holiday apartments, Bellavista, Klampenborg, 1934, Arne Jacobsen: Every apartment has a view of the sea and a sheltered outdoor space of its own.

4 Castel del Monte, Andria: The courtyard provides natural ventilation and a basic level of daylight for inmost parts of the building without reducing security.

5 Holiday apartments Can Lis, Majorca, 1971, Jörn Utzon: Carefully positioned openings concentrate the sunlight and offer a view of the sea.

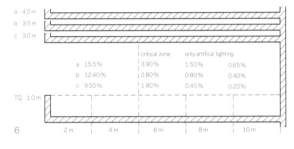

		critical zone	only artifical lighting	
a	15.5%	3.90%	1.50%	0.65%
b	12.40%	2.80%	0.80%	0.40%
c	9.50%	1.90%	0.45%	0.20%

6 The daylight yield of openings on horizontal surfaces can be measured using the daylight quotient. It is particularly high in the case of zenith light.

7 Bruder-Klaus-Kapelle, Mechernich-Wachendorf, 2007, by Peter Zumthor: The archaic atmosphere of the space is reinforcedby zenith light.

8 Gothic rose window with leaded glass in the cathedral of Notre Dame de Paris.

9 The skylight in the Neue Wache, Berlin, 1818, by K. F. Schinkel, converted 1931, by H. Tessenow. This opening is the only light source in the room, creating an atmospheric play of light on the walls that enclose the space.

VIEWS IN AND OUT

Openings define the relationship with the location. They emphasize particular views or, if widened, offer a more immediate experience of the surrounding landscape. Openings, therefore, can enable or prevent interaction between inside and outside, with the design of any window looking onto outside space inevitably focusing on the public-private relationship and the relationship of human beings to nature. Apart from providing light and air, one of the functional advantages of the window is that one can communicate through it. A window facing the street addresses someone; it faces onto, and also towards, public life. A window provides a view out, a prospect. The display window is a special case—rather than serving as an accessory to the private world, it allows people to see in. A private window is principally a way of observing the outside world from inside an enclosed space. It was not only improved technology that turned peepholes into broad windows—it was also a response to changes in the way human beings see the world. A need to keep a lookout, based on fear, was succeeded by the pleasure of observation, and a window on the outside world became a metaphysical architectural location. Careful arrangement of windows can create lines of sight with the outside world, and their construction can reinforce these. Some kinds of window make the outside world look like a picture, giving the viewer an impression of a radical division between the interior and exterior space. The Haus am Luganer See by Wespi De Meuron ⬎ 2, 3 responds in a remarkable way to its geographical position and topography. The panoramic view of the lake is framed by an opening in a loggia, a significant part of the building's form which provides a protected outdoor space. This is located in an extension to the residential rooms on the upper storey. The height makes it impossible to see in from outside.

2

1

3

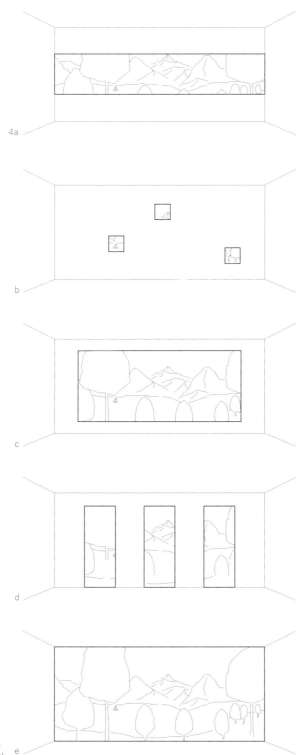

4a

b

c

d

e

1 House in Sent, 2006,
Hans-Jörg Ruch.

2, 3 Haus MÜ, Morcote, 2003,
by Wespi De Meuron.

4 Window shapes:

a   Long window
b, c Picture window
d   French window
e   Glazed wall

*Le Corbusier (²2001), Feststel-
lungen zu Architektur und Städtebau, p. 124 ff. (translation: Michael
Robinson)

The long window matches the horizontal sweep of human vision—nothing may interrupt our view. On the main storeys of the Villa Savoye, Poissy-sur-Seine, 1931 and the Petit Maison on Lake Geneva, Corseaux, 1925, by Le Corbusier managed to approximate to this ideal. All the intermediate elements between indoors and outdoors are suppressed. The parapet and lintel conceal the closer-lying parts of the landscape and the line of the sky, so that the field of vision is restricted to the far distance. The outer world appears to be at a distance, like a picture on the wall. "A single window, 11 m in length, connects and illuminates all these rooms; it also reveals a magnificent and wonderful landscape: the moving surface of the lake and the light on the mountains. [...] The 11 m long window invites the vast nature in all its authenticity and its unity—the storm-wracked lake and the radiant, peaceful landscape."* ➔ **4a**

In this it is similar to the modern picture window; a refinement that makes reality look virtual. The picture frame becomes synonymous with the window frame. Picture frames also have a dual role. They both demarcate and connect, creating both distance and unity. The frame is a two-way portal for the picture and the outside world. It cuts the vista off from the wall, sharply and absolutely. The size of the picture window plays no part in this effect, but large windows can dominate the room, making it subordinate to the picture. The house in Sent, 2006, by Hans-Jörg Rucj, whose opening provides a particular view of the alps, is an example of this. ➔ **1, 4bc**

The upright rectangular shape of the French window matches human proportions. This diagrammatic perspective shows the whole interior, from the viewer's standpoint to the image. The French window, like a door, is a transitional element. The light that penetrates the room without any parapet to block it reinforces this aspect. A bay window with a niche is similar to the French window, as it is set back from the floor upwards. ➔ **4d**

A massive wall gives way to a glazed wall, merging inside and outside. This creates the impression of a two-way spatial continuum between inside and outside. ➔ **4e**

SPATIAL OPENINGS AND INTERMEDIATE SPACES

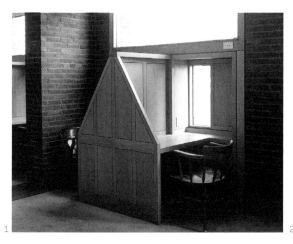

1, 2 In the library of Exeter, New Hampshire USA, 1972 and in Fisher House, Philadelphia, 1960 Louis I. Kahn created a unity of openings and furniture.

3   Opening design with offset window planes at a girls' boarding school in Disentis, 2004, by Gion Caminada.

4   In Christoph Mäckler's residence an opening is a place to study, read and work.

THREE-DIMENSIONAL WINDOWS

One can enter an intermediate space between inside and outside by simply stepping into the niche of a French window. A bay window or a deeper window niche intensify this effect, creating a "habitable" window and an in-between space. The window area becomes a special area within the room, as its form, together with light and even sunshine, allows particular activities such as looking out of the window and cultivating plants or work requiring a high level of light. The way the space in the window is formed varies. If furniture is incorporated to fill the opening, as in the designs by Louis I. Kahn, ⌐ 1, 2 a place specially designed for a specific function can be created without any alterations to the building's shape or structure. If the walls are deep enough, as in the converted residence of Christoph Mäckler, ⌐ 4 useable spaces can be created within the wall plane.

If the frame is placed within the depth of the wall, then the position of the glazing is critical. If the glass is posi-tioned at its outer face, a useable place is created inside it, where, for instance, one can sit. If the pane is placed further inside, a deep niche is created on the outside of the building.

Changing the relationship of inside and outside for each opening ⌐ 1, 2, 3 creates distinctive and diverse spatial effects. The plane of the glazing within an opening can be positioned further inwards or outwards, creating a space on the inside or a plastic depth on the outside, while reflecting both the polarity of the different window planes and the intermediate spaces they create.

If the opening goes beyond the wall plane and protrudes outward (a bay window), it changes the building's architectural form. ⌐ 6 In the building regulations, bay windows are considered extra areas and require extra authorization. Like conservatories, bay windows primarily constructed of glass can act as a kind of energy barrier. The use of glass, however, also impinges on the user's private sphere; something which must also be taken into account

5   Spatial openings can be on the outside, projecting from the facade, within the depth of the wall, or within the building. They may serve many different functions.

a   Verandah
b   Spatial window
c   Bay window
d   Balcony
e   Loggia
f   Internal courtyard

6   The bay windows alter the appearance of whole streets in Valetta, Malta's capital.

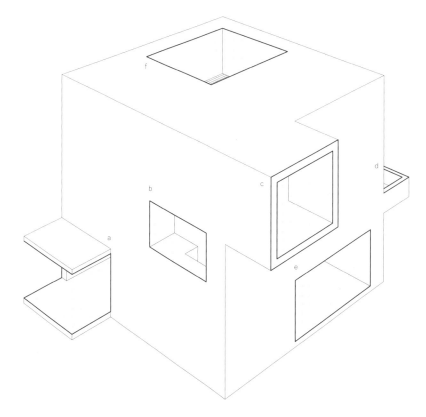

5

when planning a balcony or a verandah. Loggias are outdoor spaces integrated into the building's shell and lying within the building's volume. They provide a sheltered outdoor area, but also restrict the light to the rooms lying behind them.

A wealth of regional variation on these opening types has developed in response to the particular character of their environments, with designs subject to cultural influences, social norms and climatic conditions. This can be seen, for instance, in the elaborate decorated latticework of the mashrabiyas used for bay windows in the Islamic world. These allow residents to look out on the street without being seen from the outside.

6

CLOSURE AND PROTECTION

Openings make interiors useable by answering a basic human need for light, air and contact with the outside world. In physical terms, however, an opening represents a structural weakness in the building's shell. Depending on the situation, human beings seek refuge from bright light, cold and damp air, or an inquisitive outside world, meaning that the required thermal properties of a building's shell and openings depend on the climatic and regional situation. On the one hand, we require natural light, ventilation and solar warmth, but on the other hand, we need protection from weather, heat, cold, sun, glare, view and noise.

HEAT
The indoor climate will often be required to be different to the outdoor climate and, as openings are a weak point in the building's insulation, this imposes certain restrictions on their size and the properties of the materials used in their components. Even in temperate regions, rising raw material prices and climate concerns make it vital that the materials and construction used for an opening be energy-efficient. Heat loss becomes more acute, for instance, as the opening's size increases; on the other hand, any passive heat gain from sunlight is increased. The relationship of openings and warmth is dialectical. In winter, the aim is to prevent loss of warmth through openings while encouraging passive heat gain through openings, while a summer climate demands openings that provide protection from the sun, preventing excessive direct sunlight and heat gain while ventilating and

moderating the internal climate. The intensity and duration of direct exposure to sunlight and the angle at which it hits the facade are important. Direct sunlight can be regulated to some extent by adjusting the size of the opening or its position within the wall. If the wall is thick enough, deeper-lying openings can protect against excessive sunlight exposure. Elements that limit sunlight, glare and views are part of the typology of openings. They are matched to the position of the window and the size of the opening, and may be positioned either on the inside or on the outside.

COMFORT
As openings can be places to linger ➚ p. 18, the temperature on the inner face of the window is important. Someone seeking out a well-lit window as a place to work during the winter may be put off by a cold temperature. In summer, an interior space should ideally be cool and shady. What is meant by comfort here is the creation of a comfortable room temperature, although this is, despite the prescribed temperature range of 23–25 °C, a subjective feeling which will be influenced by factors like clothing or regional climates. Our sense of warmth comes from both the air temperature and the temperature of surfaces, and is influenced by humidity and air movement. We generally think it is slightly less warm than it actually is. A difference of not more than 3–4 °C is felt to be comfortable. Heat reaches the interior space in the form of sun rays, without any carrier medium. As glass is somewhat permeable to radiation, further heat can

1   The interior of the Curtain Wall House can be screened by curtains, Tokyo, 1995, by Shigeru Ban.

2   Room-high curtains form the interior of Hakama House, Kyoto, 1998, by Jun Tamaki.

be created through the greenhouse effect. Sun control measures prevent overheating. The structural, opaque components of windows and doors absorb light radiation as heat; depending on their material and color, this may subject them to considerable forces (heat expansion). Thermally decoupled panes, or insulating glass, were developed to counteract the high thermal conductivity of glass and metal. The panes are fixed in insulating frames of extruded plastic sections, ensuring a warm inner surface regardless of the temperature of the outer face. Wood does not need any inserts to create a thermal break, as it has some insulating properties and to a certain extent does not conduct heat. Air currents, leaks in and around openings, and manual ventilation all cause heat exchange, meaning that appropriate ventilation behavior and well-fitting windows can limit heat loss. Heat convection occurs between the internal rebates of the frame and at the joint between the frame and the structural shell, as well as between the sun blind and the window (shutter case). These components must therefore be insulated specially.

VENTILATION

Ventilation creates an exchange of air, allowing moisture to pass from the inside to the outside, and consequently reducing the relatively high humidity of the interior. A lack of insulation can lead to condensation on cold objects and, as the pane is the coldest surface in a single-glazed window, this causes visible precipitation to develop on window panes. Providing indoor spaces with fresh air is one of a window's most basic functions. Leaving aside the possibilities of mechanical ventilation, the position of the window in a room is essential to good ventilation. Getting this right involves ensuring cross-ventilation and ventilation around corners, choosing appropriate types of opening with the right alignment and the right kind of catch, and making sure the dimensions of openings and the geometry of rooms have a positive impact on ventilation. The need to avoid draughts should be taken into account.

WIND, RAIN AND AIR

A building will always have one side facing the wind and one side turned away from the wind. This creates areas of high air pressure and low air pressure on the facades. Where the house is not wind-tight, this can lead to an undesirable air exchange. If openings are correctly positioned, however, the effect can be deliberately used to provide ventilation. In windy locations, the window frames are fitted at the outer edge of a house's walls, and their casements open outwards. Wind load presses the window against the house wall, increasing the security of the seals and thus preventing drafts and uncontrolled air exchange.

Wind can drive rainwater against gravity upwards into joints in the facade. In strong wind and rain, large expanses of glass can be distorted, causing the seals to leak. In regions where heavy precipitation is encountered, it is important to construct components of openings with rainproofing in mind. This can be done through the position, the use of exceptionally corrosion-resistant materials and the shape of the construction, and thus has implications for the design of the facade.

3 The facade of this apartment building in the Madrid suburb of Carabanchel, 2007, by Foreign Office Architects can be completely closed when necessary using folding/sliding shutters.

3

Thermal insulation:
Openings are weak points in the insulation of a building. This imposes requirements on the size of openings and on the properties of their constituent materials.
Openings should be arranged so as to ensure heat control in the summer. This may involve filter or shade components and depend on the opening's position in the building shell. Le Corbusier's sketch for the facade of the St. Die factory demonstrates how the brise soleil works. (DIN 4108)

Weatherproofing:
Closure components have two functions in this context: to protect the inside of the building from penetration by water (rain) and by air (wind) in order to prevent energy from being lost through permeable parts of the building shell.

Noise reduction:
Completely soundproofed spaces are uncomfortable. Nevertheless, noise emissions from outside have to be reduced to create a comfortable level of background noise in the interior. In this respect, openings, particularly windows, are the building envelope's neuralgic points. The best way to deal with noise pollution is to avoid large openings. Owing to their construction, windows and doors do not have the mass that is needed to absorb sound. Beyond this, the construction's function determines the tolerances and the clearance spaces that allow sound to penetrate. (DIN 4109)

Fire safety:
Openings are often escape or rescue routes, and therefore need specific shapes and dimensions depending on the type, size and use of the building. This should be taken into account during planning, as it may mean that certain formats and proportions are not possible. The construction of windows and doors should also be checked.

Intrusion prevention:
Openings that are not in public view tend to invite burglary. The fact that the living space and the garden are often connected by large openings at the back of the building means that these doors and windows must either satisfy special requirements or have special filters (e.g. shutters).

FILTERS

A filter is a component that helps an opening to function by modifying it to cope with external influences and internal requirements. Depending on what is needed, the filter may be a simple cloth drape. ⤳7 Filters mainly control light influx and the interior climate, possibilities of communication between the interior and exterior and, in the case of solid filters, increased protection against intrusion. Many filters can be adjusted to perform several functions. A distinction is made between fixed filters (filter masonry or brise soleils) and moveable filters (wooden sliding shutters or metal folding shutters). ⤳**chapter 3**

DESIGN POSSIBILITIES
External filters affect the building's shape, partly because of the way they are constructed, their materials and their geometry, and partly because of the arrangement of several of them across the whole surface. If the filter is moveable, the facade changes depending on external influences such as the position of the sun and how the user adjusts the filters—especially if the facade consists

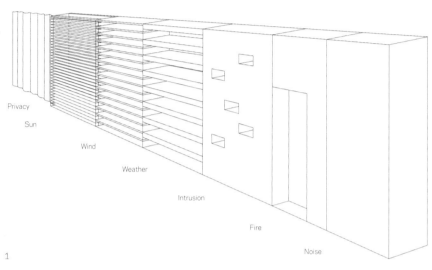

1

2 A filter made up of planks in a simple barn in the Alps creates an elementary spatial effect. Direct light is substantially filtered without preventing ventilation. The filter and the wall structure are a single unit.

2

3

4

5

1 Diagram of fixed and moveable filters.

2 A filter made up of planks in a simple barn in the Alps creates an elementary spatial effect. Direct light is substantially filtered without preventing ventilation. The filter and the wall structure are a single unit.

3 Combination of construction, space and filter in Tenerife Espacio des las Artes, Santa Cruz, 2008, by Herzog & de Meuron.

4 In the Arab world, the mashrabiya acts as a light filter and climatic filter, and also prevents unwanted attention.

5 A skylight ceiling made from loadbearing exposed concrete elements in Centro de Estudios Hidrográficos, Madrid, 1960, by Miguel Fisac.

6a Fixed filters: Loggia, brise soleil, filter masonry, slat support.

b Rigid moveable filters: sliding shutters, folding shutters, slat frame.

c Light, moveable filters: blinds, external blinds, drapes, roller blinds.

6a

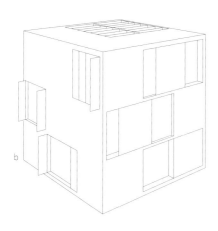

b

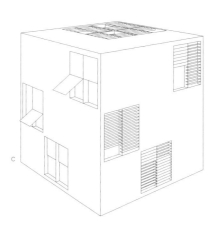

c

entirely of filters. ⟶ p. 21 At the other end of the scale, it is possible to make the filters out of the same material as the facade, integrating them into the design so that the openings and the facade look like a single component ⟶ School in Vella-p. 146–49. Regional climate may lead to filters becoming a major architectural design element for a whole community or all the buildings in a certain location. ⟶ 7

SPATIAL EFFECT

Filters can significantly influence the atmosphere of an interior. Apart from allowing rooms to be opened or closed off, their format and the degree to which they can be opened allow fine nuances to be created. As well as being a fascinating sight in itself, an Arabic mashrabiya creates a fascinating play of shadow that gives the interior a mysterious character. ⟶ 4 Even a simple construction of planks interlocking at the corners to create gaps is enough to form an elementary interior, characterized by the alternation of solid and void in the outer wall and its linear silhouette. ⟶ 2

The relationship between the opaque and transparent areas of filters determines their effect. Translucent filters let light through evenly, but cannot be seen through. Filters with particularly fine perforations (such as the mashrabiya) can only be seen through at close quarters. If the open and closed areas are widely spaced, on the other hand, they can be seen through from a distance, creating a more permeable structure.

7 The drapes of the colonnade in Venice may be considered the original example of an unsubstantial filter altering the form of a construction and the appearance of a place.   7

THE GEOMETRY OF OPENINGS

A ROOM IS DEFINED BY FLOOR, WALLS AND CEILING AND BY THE POSITION AND TYPE OF ITS OPENINGS.

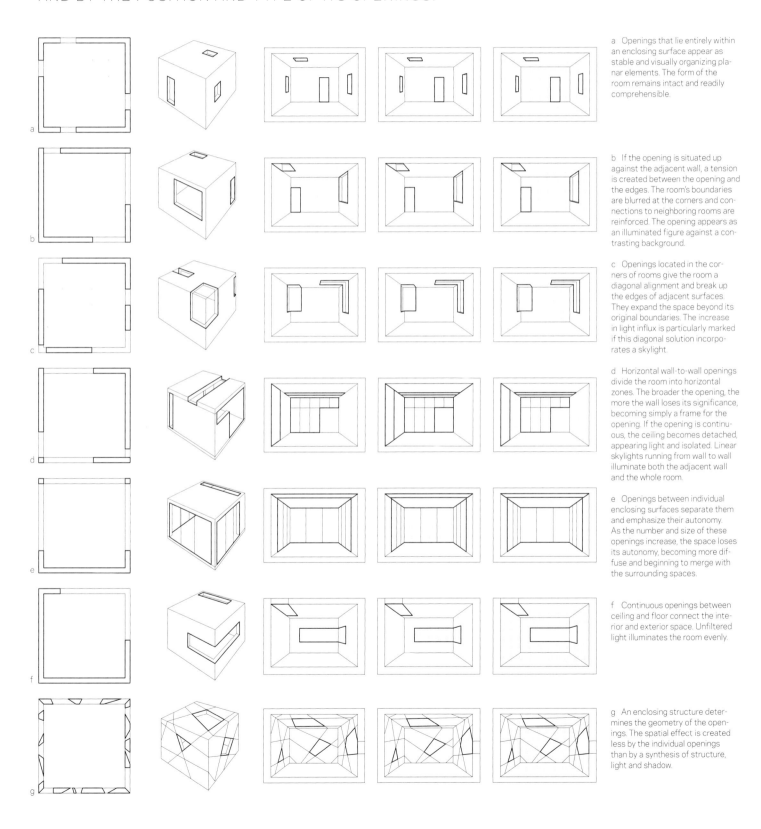

a   Openings that lie entirely within an enclosing surface appear as stable and visually organizing planar elements. The form of the room remains intact and readily comprehensible.

b   If the opening is situated up against the adjacent wall, a tension is created between the opening and the edges. The room's boundaries are blurred at the corners and connections to neighboring rooms are reinforced. The opening appears as an illuminated figure against a contrasting background.

c   Openings located in the corners of rooms give the room a diagonal alignment and break up the edges of adjacent surfaces. They expand the space beyond its original boundaries. The increase in light influx is particularly marked if this diagonal solution incorporates a skylight.

d   Horizontal wall-to-wall openings divide the room into horizontal zones. The broader the opening, the more the wall loses its significance, becoming simply a frame for the opening. If the opening is continuous, the ceiling becomes detached, appearing light and isolated. Linear skylights running from wall to wall illuminate both the adjacent wall and the whole room.

e   Openings between individual enclosing surfaces separate them and emphasize their autonomy. As the number and size of these openings increase, the space loses its autonomy, becoming more diffuse and beginning to merge with the surrounding spaces.

f   Continuous openings between ceiling and floor connect the interior and exterior space. Unfiltered light illuminates the room evenly.

g   An enclosing structure determines the geometry of the openings. The spatial effect is created less by the individual openings than by a synthesis of structure, light and shadow.

In this residence in San Pedro, Chile, 2007, by Pezo von Elrichhausen, some of the square openings in the wall plane are located at the corners. They differentiate the storeys on the outside and create interesting contrasts in the interior. ➔ 1, 2

Openings' position and format significantly affect the interior's atmosphere. The large strip windows of this school building in Paspels by Valerio Olgiati ➔ 3, 4 create even lighting and provide a horizontal view of the surrounding landscape. The parapet and lintel, however, separate the learning space and the outdoor space. From the outside, the recessed strip windows show where the classrooms are, while the rectangular openings in the circulation areas lie flush with the facades. Their low parapets provide benches to sit on next to the window.

Owing to their geometry and position, differently formatted openings give rooms and facades a different atmosphere: the access opening (French window or door), the hole-type opening, the strip window, the room-sized opening (window wall), and other variations on these types, plus corner openings (which neutralize the edges of the room) like in the Gipsoteca del Canova in Possagno, 1957, by Carlo Scarpa. ➔ 5, 6

1

2

3

4

5

6

OPENING GEOMETRY
AND BUILDING TYPOLOGY

The geometry of openings responds to human needs, and is therefore mainly based on the human form. For doors, the size and the breadth of the doorway are important, while eye height is important for windows. For both kinds of opening, the operation of catches and the function of the adjoining spaces are important. Handles should be comfortable to hold, with a non-slip surface that can be easily cleaned and a suitable pressure point. The distance between the grip and the mounting, for instance, must be sufficient to prevent any injuries. An accessible handle makes it easier to open and close the element, as well as to clean and maintain the handle.

The position of openings depends on the height and breadth of the room. The level of the parapet and the lintel, as well as the depth of the reveals in horizontal section, are crucial to the design of a window. Rebates and the depth or angle of reveals all affect the quality of outlook and light influx. ⤳ **chapter 2**

The position and shape of openings are defined by moving and resting activities such as walking and standing still (doors or French windows), sitting, lingering, eating or working (long windows or high small windows) or lying down or crawling (horizontal formats). The size of the user may also be a factor—kindergartens, for instance, may have lower openings.

The way a building is used creates specific requirements for openings, depending on its type. In residential buildings, different areas (for living, sleeping etc.) each have their own type of opening, depending on the required degree of privacy and the outside context.

Office workspaces need even illumination with no glare. This can be directly implemented as a part of the building's form by creating a uniform perforated facade, a strip facade or glass facade. This involves taking into account the fit-out grid, the arrangement of partition walls and any continuous filler components for openings, together with sun control devices. Filter systems that channel light can keep work spaces free of glare while directing light into inward areas and minimizing overheating problems caused by large aperture surfaces.

Industrial buildings and production facilities require uniform lighting and do not need any view of the outside. The demand for indirect, no-glare lighting for these spaces has created special types of opening—including large shed constructions or skylight lanterns on the roof and horizontal openings in the wall with filters and sightproof screening. These are among the elements that give these building their distinctive appearance.

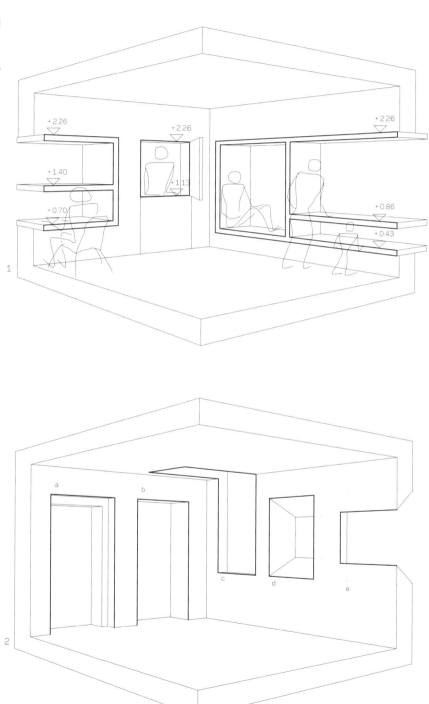

1 Important reference heights for openings:
sill height, lintel height, height of transoms and glazing bars, lower edge of the glass pane. These are important criteria when designing a window to accommodate specific user needs and day-to-day necessities. The dimensions listed in the drawing correspond to Le Corbusier's Modulor system. These examples show the basic correlation between the geometry of the opening and its use, or users, which means that it varies depending on the specific situation.

2 Geometries of openings:
a Opening with rebate: the opening looks bigger from the inside than from the outside. The component filling it is partially concealed.

b Openings with straight edges: if walls are thick, light penetration will be low.

c The smaller the lintel and the higher the opening, the better the depths of the room are illuminated. A diagonal corner solution or combined window and skylight provides an even higher proportion of zenith light.

d Increased light penetration with a relatively small opening. The window is flush with the wall's external surface. The window's edges are not useable, and the view is restricted.

e Reveals slanted outwards: this suggest a small aperture surface for the opening on the outside, allowing for a directed view.

3 Residential building on Auguststraße, Berlin, 2004, by Jörg Ebers.

3

AMBIENCE AND MATERIALS

An architectural space is given much of its character by the nature and materials of its enclosing surfaces, the objects within it and their brightness. We comprehend it through its sounds and smells and by touching its component parts. Our perception of a space depends directly on the type and amount of light it receives, its light incidence. The type of opening chosen and its design create a particular lighting ambience in the space and on the facade to match the function of the room and the building. A gradual transition from a lit to a shaded surface gives a body three-dimensionality, meaning that when an object is lit from one side, the contrast is hard, and our level of information about it is reduced. Glancing sunlight intensifies the surface modeling of facades, producing deep shadows from bay windows and in recesses (as with the Rauch house). Where light comes from more than one side, contrast is reduced and object's plasticity is increased. Light and shadow are as important to users of a room as its form. Terms like 'slit', 'opening' or 'corner window' describe certain formats and functions. Of course, it is not just the format of individual openings, but also their overall composition that affects the building's form. In the Rauch house ⌐ 1, 2, a caesura is created by offsetting the structure. The arrangement of two neighboring, almost square openings in the front

part of the building and a recessed door lower down create a dynamic equilibrium between both sections. Not only the proportions, but also the colors and materials used for the edges of openings have a strong presence in the interior. If, for instance, they are dark-colored, the degree of reflection is reduced, but their dominance in the room is increased. Closing elements (windows, doors) generally have fixed frame constructions, sometimes with moveable frames for each section. The inner structure of these frame elements and their proportions, colors and materials have as much effect on the opening's form as the construction of the opening's actual edges. Thick moldings reduce the aperture's surface area, thereby reducing the light influx and view. On the other hand, the appearance, silhouette and materials of the frame molding pattern may contribute to the room's atmosphere. Narrow profiles create an understated frame construction. This helps to make openings—particularly corner openings—more expansive. Seen against the light, windows with fine moldings create lines of shadow, while the strips of shadow created by more pronounced moldings increase the three-dimensionality of the window plane. A tooled joint between the wall and the wood of the frame—the shadow gap—marks the line of separation.

1

2

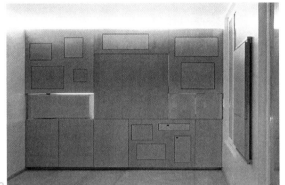

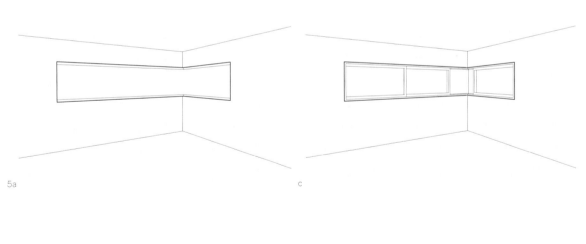

1, 2 House in Schlins, Austria, 2008, by Roger Boltshauser/ Martin Rauch.

3, 4 Apartment in Paris, 2007, by Marchi Architectes, Adélaïde Marchi, Nicola Marchi: Both the materials and the design and construction influence the object's effect and its surrounding space.

5a, b Two rooms with corner openings without filling elements, one horizontal and one vertical; their atmosphere, light penetration and spatial impression are very different, owing to the different formats.

c, d The same openings with rudimentary window frames: The windows' subdivisions and frame thickness wchange the way we experience the space, affecting light influx, silhouette, visual impression, color, material and structure.

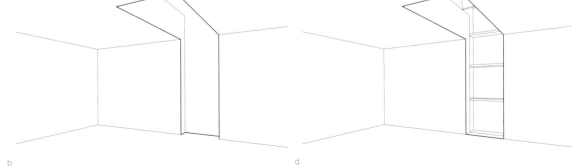

DESIGN AND CONSTRUCTION

The "evolution of the opening", from the archetypal hole or slit to a complex architectural element, is inseparable from changes and innovations in material processing and construction technology. The slanted reveals of this archaic opening in Nizwa, Oman, ➘2 offer maximum protection together with a good outlook and good temperature control. In the residential and studio building in Monthey by Bonnard+Woeffrey, ➘1 only glass separates nature and domesticity. A desire for safety and protection gave way to the need for people to feel connected to their environment. With the focus on its beauty, the opening becomes part of a living concept that unites personal living space with the outside world, and brings the sights of nature into the living room.

1

2

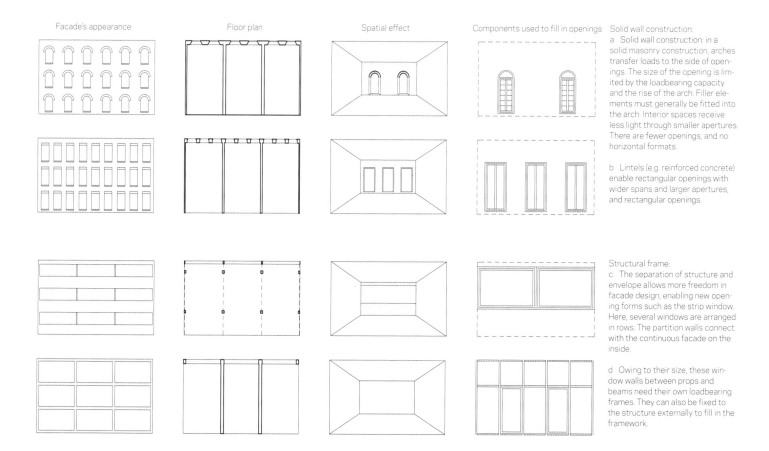

Facade's appearance	Floor plan	Spatial effect	Components used to fill in openings	

Solid wall construction:

a   Solid wall construction: in a solid masonry construction, arches transfer loads to the side of openings. The size of the opening is limited by the loadbearing capacity and the rise of the arch. Filler elements must generally be fitted into the arch. Interior spaces receive less light through smaller apertures. There are fewer openings, and no horizontal formats.

b   Lintels (e.g. reinforced concrete) enable rectangular openings with wider spans and larger apertures, and rectangular openings.

Structural frame:

c   The separation of structure and envelope allows more freedom in facade design, enabling new opening forms such as the strip window. Here, several windows are arranged in rows. The partition walls connect with the continuous facade on the inside.

d   Owing to their size, these window walls between props and beams need their own loadbearing frames. They can also be fixed to the structure externally to fill in the framework.

1 Residential and studio building, Monthey, 2002-2003, by
Bonnard + Woeffrey.

2 Archaic opening with deep,
chamfered reveals in Nizwa, Oman.

3 Different possible designs for
use with brickwork/masonry construction:

a Single-block window
b Series of upright round arch
   openings
c Opening constructed solely in
   masonry: round arch, parapet
   or ledge, reveals
d Opening with lintel
e Filter masonry

4 The town hall of Murcia, 1998,
by Rafael Moneo: The reinforced
concrete ceilings act as lintels
and allow an irregular arrangement
of openings on each storey.

5 Church of St. Bonifatius,
Wildbergerhütte, 1981, by
Heinz Bienefeld. Here we can see
the design possibilities of masonry
construction, offered by arrang-
ing the bricks in decorative courses and by different shapes of the
relieving arch and use of larger
bricks to emphasize the reveals.

For masonry structures with loadbearing exterior walls, perforated facades are the most common approach. Doors and windows create openings. They may be an access point, a framed picture of a landscape, or a source of light and air. The arrangement and relative sizes and shapes of these openings structure the space, giving it an alignment and providing information on the nature of the outer shell.

Masonry structures offer limited possibilities for creating openings in walls, owing to their structural properties and the weight of the material. Lintels or different kinds of arch (round arches, lancet arches and jack arches) can be used to distribute the weight. Arches divert the vertical loads in the wall, making it possible to create an opening in the area that has been relieved of load. The larger the opening, the higher the arch's rise. This means that the size of openings is dependent on the space's height. Rectangular openings generally require lintels made from tension-resistant materials, such as wood, steel or steel-reinforced concrete. Sometimes large blocks of natural stone are used. In masonry structures, the shape of a building is created by courses made from individual modules. The edges of openings are always architectural constructions—with regular modular courses being interrupted by the different shape and fit of an arch, an upright masonry course forming a sill, or the change of material created by a concrete lintel. Edge work—masonry rebates and tapering reveals—also affects lighting and

the positioning of the window plane. Checker brickwork (created by regularly leaving out individual bricks) constitutes a special kind of opening that uses perforations integrated into the masonry course system to create indirect lighting.

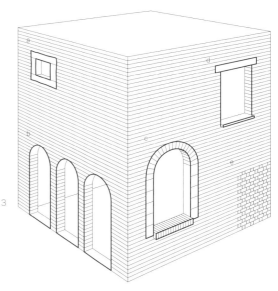

3

4

5

1 Casa del Fascio, Como, 1936, by Giuseppi Terragni.

2 Facade detail, Bauhaus Dessau, 1925, by Walter Gropius.

3 These axonometric representations exemplify how openings changed in Modernism, with the line between indoors and outdoors blurring as the facade and the loadbearing structure became separated.

Frank Lloyd Wright

De Stijl

Le Corbusier

Le Corbusier, one of the most influential architects of the 20th century, emphasized the importance of openings in architecture thus: "The history of architecture is the history of the window." He also actively contributed to the demise of traditional forms of window. The twin drives behind this upheaval were modernism and technological progress. Innovations in steel, glass and reinforced concrete construction around the end of the 19th century made greater spatial freedom possible. The invention of structural frames separated the facade from the loadbearing structure, allowing it to become completely transparent. The transparent wall was the new boundary between inside and outside; the window became a wall—or the wall became a window. The conventional relief modeling with a frame and surrounds was deliberately avoided in favor of a purist transparent shell, with its light, bright and airy atmosphere. The new mastery of these techniques is demonstrated by the large spatial creations of the early 20th century.

Modernist architects used autonomous surfaces to define spatial zones that were part of a boundless, fluid space. In conjunction with the elimination of decorative detail from buildings, this led to a redefinition of the window and its architectural character.

By removing the dependency of openings on the loadbearing structure, reinforced concrete, steel and glass have certainly expanded the expressive possibilities. Structural systems no longer impose any limitation, while rooms and facades can be freely articulated. Panoramic windows,

strip windows, bay windows and glass walls, elements that add a new spatial dimension, are the hallmarks of this kind of architecture. Without the improvements made in glass manufacture, the separation of facade and structure would not have been possible, as it was float-glass technology that paved the way for much larger window formats. Full-length openings and glass facades have their own loadbearing structures. One example is the post-and-rail facade: the horizontal rails provide stiffening and the posts take up the vertical load. The fill elements, such as the casements of the opening, are secured to the posts and rails by snap-in channels. In construction terms, the window is no longer a wall opening, but rather a modular facade and envelope.

This apparent freedom in positioning and formatting the opening means that openings can be treated as part of a design concept for the whole facade. Where this is the case, the individual opening, its construction and proportions 1-p. 30 is less important than the tectonic effect of surfaces and openings, projections and recesses 1 as well as the overall composition and pattern of openings of different sizes within the facade. 2, 3 The same is true where openings are integrated into geometrically complex building envelopes: openings represent negative spaces in the enclosing structure and are part of an interplay of solid and void. 4

It is a fact that the design possibilities of today are almost limitless. There are openings for every function, satisfying very diverse user requirements. Some of them have

STRUCTURAL FRAME

4 Design options for frame structures:

a Geometrically free openings can be created within the bays of the structural frame, using various types of infill.

b Facade systems such as post-and-rail construction are situated in front of the loadbearing structure. They make it possible to close multi-storey openings, and to build fully glazed facades.

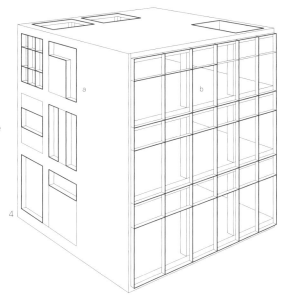

a special importance, as part of the character of a building. Dealing with all these different design parameters, however, requires a precise knowledge of the structural and building physics requirements of openings in general and of the specific properties of windows ⌐chapter 2, filters ⌐chapter 3, and doors and gates. ⌐chapter 4 This book uses selected projects ⌐chapter 5 to illustrate this process at the design, detailing and construction stages.

5 Conference hall, Leon, 2003, by Mansilla Tuñón.

6 Pavilion, Serpentine Gallery, London, 2002, by Toyo Ito.

7 Business School, Zeche Zollverein, 2006, Essen, by SANAA.

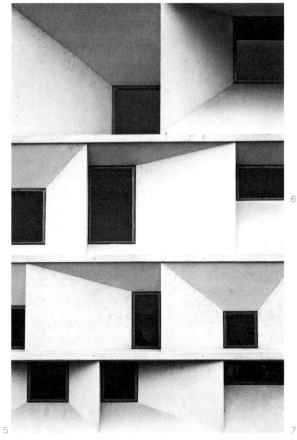

OPEN | CLOSE
WINDOWS

CHAPTER 2

POSITION OF THE WINDOW IN THE BUILDING ENVELOPE

The position of a window within the standard construction and the geometric space of the enclosure, taken in conjunction with the rebate detail, influence the architectural appearance of a building. Where windows are flush with the facade surface, the effect of their openings remains in the background, without distracting from the overall form of the building. The construction of deep window reveals or bay windows breaks up the building envelope. The design and choice of materials for the closure components influence the expression and character of an opening through their distribution and profile dimensions. The figure opposite shows closure components installed in various positions in typical wall constructions. Window control climatic processes in buildings. Depending on their requirements and wishes, building users can prevent or allow the passage of light, air, heat, cold, sound or views in and out. Window are not barriers; on the contrary, they form the external closure element of openings that regulate all the relationships between the inside and outside spaces. The technical requirements of windows are set out in standards, guidance documents and building regulations and are described in the following sections.

The decision on the constructional form of windows must take into account a series of formal, technical and economic requirements:
– Requirements relating to form and shape: Size, format, surface division, color and surface treatment.
– Functional requirements: Opening type, ventilation requirements, sunshading, convenience of operation.
– Technical and constructional requirements: Overall safety relating to balustrade and fall heights, protection against incorrect operation, watertightness of joints and in driving rain, thermal insulation.
– Special requirements: Fire protection, sound insulation, intrusion protection.

1, 2 Apartments in Zurich, 2003,
Andreas Fuhrimann /
Gabrielle Hächler Architekten.

1

2

inside

outside

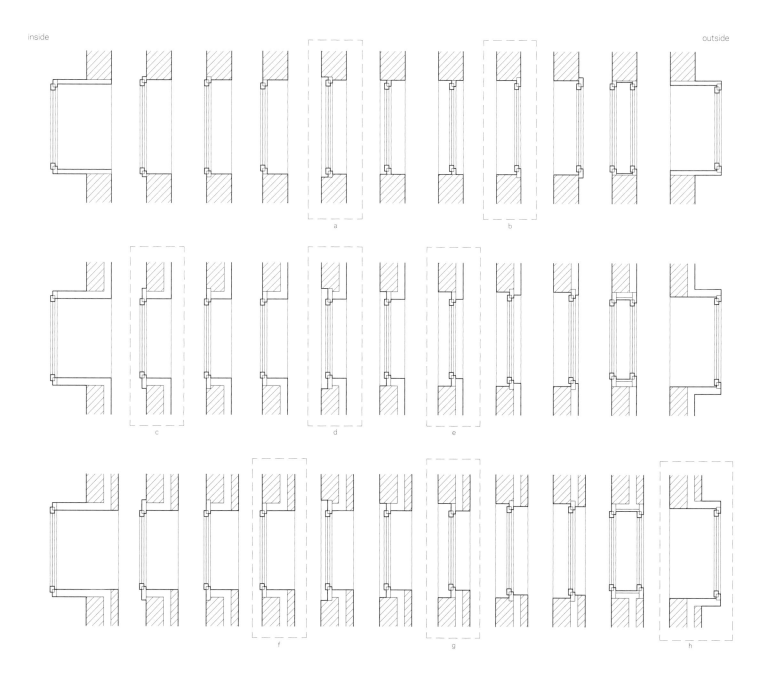

a

b

c

d

e

f

g

h

WINDOW REBATES

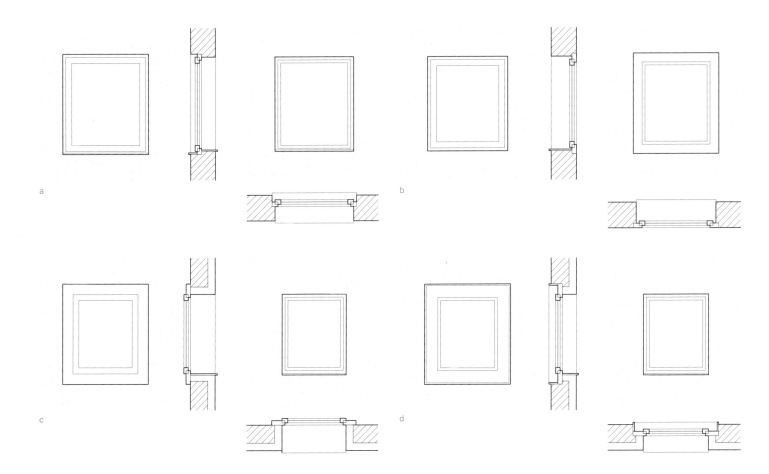

a

b

c

d

Window rebates can be traced back to traditional methods of fixing a wooden frame into a masonry wall. To make the joint as impermeable to the passage of air as possible, an internal corner into which the frame would fit exactly was formed in the masonry. This is described as an internal rebate. As a general rule, a window may be positioned anywhere within the thickness of the wall construction. The most common arrangements are windows with an internal rebate, no rebate or an external rebate. Depending on the weatherproofing, thermal insulation, seals and sunshading requirements, not every window position is advisable or feasible due to complexity of construction and associated costs.

INTERNAL REBATE ⟶ p. 37-39
The window is installed from the inside of the room. The erection of a facade scaffold is not normally necessary. The external reveal shelters the window from the weather and its depth depends on the position of the window within the thickness of the wall. The position of a window in a building envelope has an effect on its energy performance. The plane of insulation must always be continued right up to the window, if necessary into the reveal.
Possible construction details:
– The window sits in the reveal, the wall construction is monolithic with a solid rebate. ⟶ a
– The window sits in the reveal, the insulation is continued into the reveal to the window and conceals the window frame. The frame is fully exposed on the inside. ⟶ d
– The window sits flush with the line of the inner wall. Insulation and cladding are continued to the window and conceal much of the frame. ⟶ f
– The window sits in front of the inner line of the external wall. Insulation and cladding are continued into the whole reveal to the window and conceal much of the frame. The window protrudes into the interior as a feature. ⟶ c

EXTERNAL REBATE ⟶ p. 37-39
These windows are installed from the outside from a facade or erection scaffold. In this case, the window is fastened from the outside on to the basic building struc-

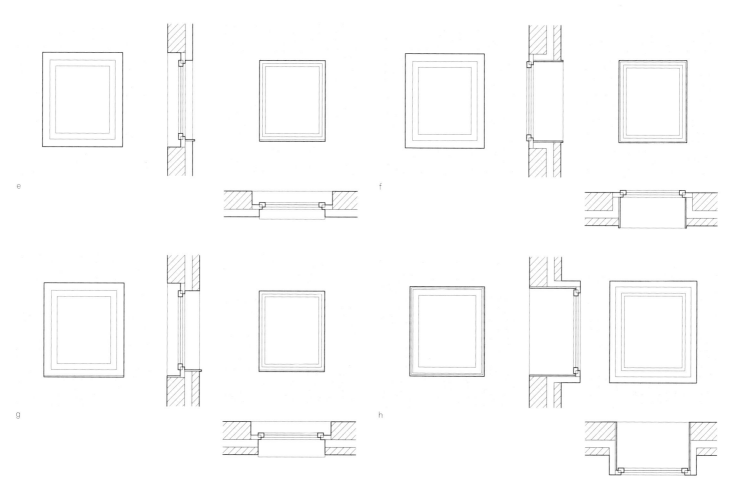

e

f

g

h

ture and lies within the insulation layer. A double frame ensures the line of the facade is maintained, which means that the window lies in the weathered zone. The resulting higher requirements for the joints between components and weatherproofing must be taken into account.
Possible construction details:
– The window is positioned flush with the outside edge of the monolithic wall construction. The width of frame visible from the outside is much greater than from the inside. ⮕ b
– The window is placed on the basic building structure. The insulation is thicker and hence is taken to the window profile, forming a flat reveal. ⮕ e
– The window forms design feature on the front of the facade. Subconstruction, insulation and seals must be taken to the window. The inner reveal is deep and can be functional or used by the room occupant. ⮕ h
– The window is placed on the basic building structure. the insulation is thicker and hence is taken with the external skin in front of the window profile, forming an external reveal. ⮕ g

NO REBATE

A window can be installed without a rebate in the masonry. This method is in common use today, as it simplifies the basic building structure and the actual window installation. However, the connections have to fulfill high requirements. Only the depth of the window profile is available for the detail to prevent the entry of wind, damp and rain and avoid creating a warm bridge. The window can be installed from inside or outside the building. The position of the window may be anywhere within the wall construction (central or flush with the inside or outside faces). However, care must be taken to take the insulation and seals to the window. The full height of the window frame profile is visible from inside and outside the building.

CONSTRUCTION AND FORM

The depictions of the various window typologies describe the design form, the architectural expression and the construction required for them. The wall construction and window forms are mutually dependent. Narrow, high opening forms are typical of masonry walls. Wide openings, on the other hand, require lintels and strengthening in the reveal areas. The method of constructing reinforced concrete walls means that they are able to accommodate large or small openings with relatively few problems. With cross-wall construction, the openings can be extended up to the limits imposed by the structural requirements of the loadbearing components of the walls and ceilings. A facade constructed as framing is made up of beams and columns, which span across supports, walls and floors and allow curtain wall construction to be used.

Punched windows are openings defined at the top by a lintel, at the bottom by a window sill and at the sides by reveals. The size of the opening has to be considerably smaller than the area of wall accommodating it.

Window strips are generally made up of window elements (punched windows) arranged horizontally and adjacent to one another on the same floor. They are normally used where window sill panels or are not required for aesthetic or structural reasons and they allow a more flexible division of space. Special connecting elements (tongue and groove principle) join the window frames at their sides. The frame sides can also be joined to other parts of the building, e.g. partition walls. Connections at the top and bottom are as with conventional punched windows.

A French window or window door is an opening element which starts at floor level and can also be used as a door.

A window wall is a room-high facade element made up of several window and/or door elements joined together. DIN 18056 defines it as a windowed area consisting of frames, mullions, rails and filling panels (glazing) at least 9.00 m long and with an edge length of at least 2.00 m on at least one side.

A curtain wall facade is an external wall construction which is usually used for framed buildings. The facade is placed in front of the building's walls, columns and floor slabs. A curtain wall facade either consists of storey-high elements or is a single loadbearing structure of vertical posts and horizontal rails. Filling such as solid panels, fixed glazing and opening glazing are inserted into this loadbearing construction.

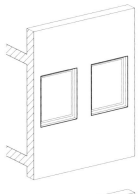

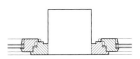

Punched window:
The serial arrangement of punched windows in a solid wall can be achieved by using intermediate wall pillars. Punched windows simply abutting a wall pillar.

Window strip, horizontal window, ribbon window:
The window elements are connected by connection pieces through their frames to create a ribbon window.

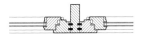

French window and window wall:
Window walls may consist of window elements with mullions or, in the case of very large openings, extra-strong mullions.

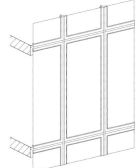

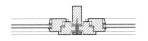

Curtain wall facade:
Curtain wall facade consisting of post and rail construction with inserted fixed and opening glazed elements.

DIN 1356 defines how windows should be represented in planning submission and construction drawings. The labeling and dimensioning of window heights, widths and sill heights are required at the planning submission stage. Construction drawings form the basis for the translation of a design into a building and must therefore contain additional information. The height and width of structural openings, external window frame dimensions, the unfinished and finished heights of window sills and lintels comprise the essential information.

CLG Height of ceiling above floor
FFL Finished floor level
SSL Structural slab level
SH Sill-to-head height
FSH Floor-to-sill height

Some of the requirements of local building regulations to be taken into account are listed below:
- All habitable rooms must be provided with adequate daylight and ventilated by vertical windows opening directly to the outside. (mandatory windows)
- Window openings that are also used as escape and rescue routes in the event of fire must have a clear opening of 0.90 m wide x 1.20 m high.
- Window sills must (except on the ground floor) be at least 1.00 m high. At fall heights of > 12.00 m they must be at least 1.10 m high.
- Windows must permit cleaning in safety. If this cannot be done from the ground or inside the building, then special means must be provided, e.g. cleaning balconies.

a Frame external dimension
b Frame internal dimension
c_1 Section thickness
c_2 Section width
d Sash external dimension
e Rebate dimension
f Sealing rebate dimension
g Glass dimension
h Glazing rebate dimension
i Handle height
j Glass clear width
k Sash external dimension (sash width)
l Frame external dimension (frame external width)
m Glass clear height
n Sash external dimension (sash height)
o Frame external dimension (frame external height)

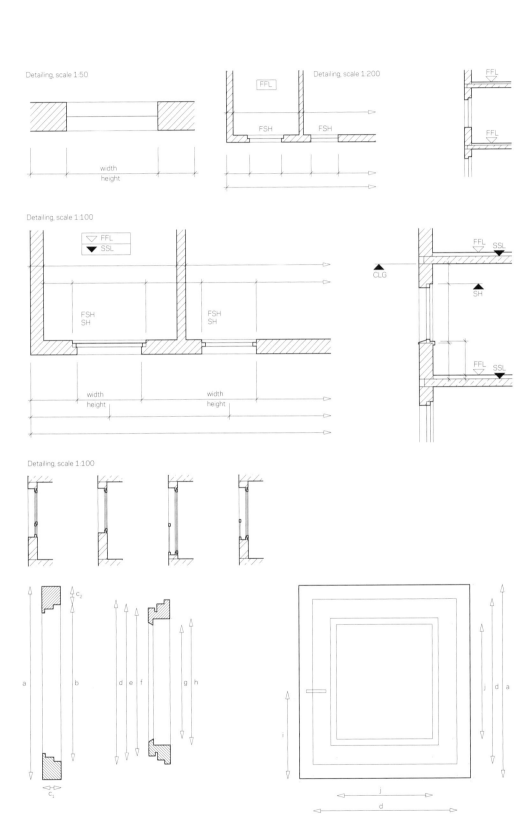

Detailing, scale 1:50

Detailing, scale 1:200

Detailing, scale 1:100

Detailing, scale 1:100

CONSTRUCTION TYPES AND FUNCTIONS

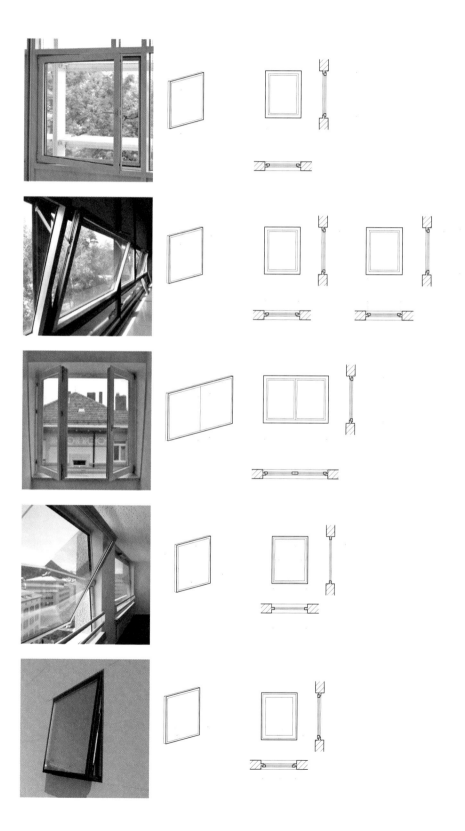

Side hung window
Whereas fixed sashes are fixed on both sides of the frame, a side hung sash opens about a vertical axis outwards or inwards. A window is described as left or right opening. (See DIN left DIN right).

Bottom hung window
The sash in a bottom hung window tilts inwards about its bottom horizontal axis. The tilt hardware limits the opening depth and prevents the sash from falling inwards.

Tilt and turn window
The tilt and turn window is the most common window type in use, combining the features of side and bottom hung windows. These windows normally open inwards. They are also described as left or right opening.

Double leaf window
The double leaf window has two window sashes. One is the active, the other the non-active leaf. The leaves come together to close without an additional vertical member in the window frame, the non-active leaf serving as the rebate and the seal for the active leaf. The joint in the seal in the area of the change of direction must be carefully detailed.

Horizontal pivot window
The horizontal pivot window turns about its central horizontal axis. The bottom part of the sash swings outwards and the top part inwards. The outside surface of the window swings inside for easy cleaning. The switchover of the seal position at the pivot bearing is complicated to fabricate. One half of the window opening must be kept clear as an emergency exit.

Top hung window
The sash on a top hung window is attached at the top and opens at the bottom inwards or outwards. An inwards opening sash does not provide adequate protection against rain. The outwards opening direction prevents rain entering when the window is open. It is important to ensure that the top joint between the sash and window frames does not allow driving rain to enter.

Vertical pivot hung window
A vertical pivot hung window operates in a similar way to a center hung window except that it turns about a central vertical axis. The technical problem with the seals is the same.

Parallel opening window
Parallel opening windows move outwards from the facade face by means of a telescopic or shear stay mechanism. Their ventilation performance is excellent, as the cold air flows in from the bottom while the warm air escapes from the top.

French window
French windows are combinations of windows and doors with various ways of opening. Usually both window and door elements tilt and turn. These elements are often used as balcony doors or as house entrance doors. Their great height makes them ideal for room ventilation.

Sliding window
Sliding windows have a sash which slides, usually horizontally, on the inside of a fixed element.

Lifting windows
The lifting sash in a lifting window usually slides vertically on the inside of the fixed element or, where there is no window sill, downwards into the floor to allow floor level exit.

Lift-sliding-tilting window
The fact that the sash lifts out of the seal before sliding makes this construction less susceptible to driving rain than conventional sliding windows are. Lift-sliding-tilting windows can also be tilted inwards about their bottom horizontal axis. These windows are designed to ensure ease of operation, but are mechanically complex and require considerably more space for the fittings.

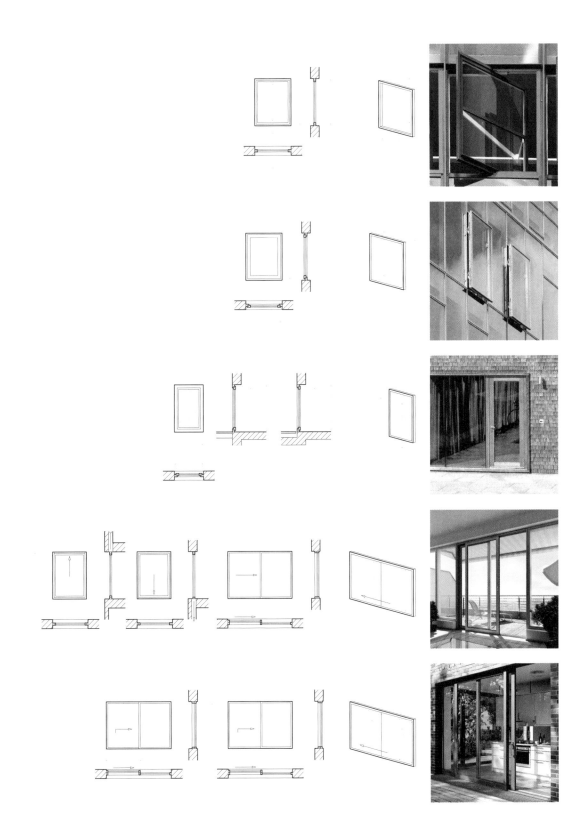

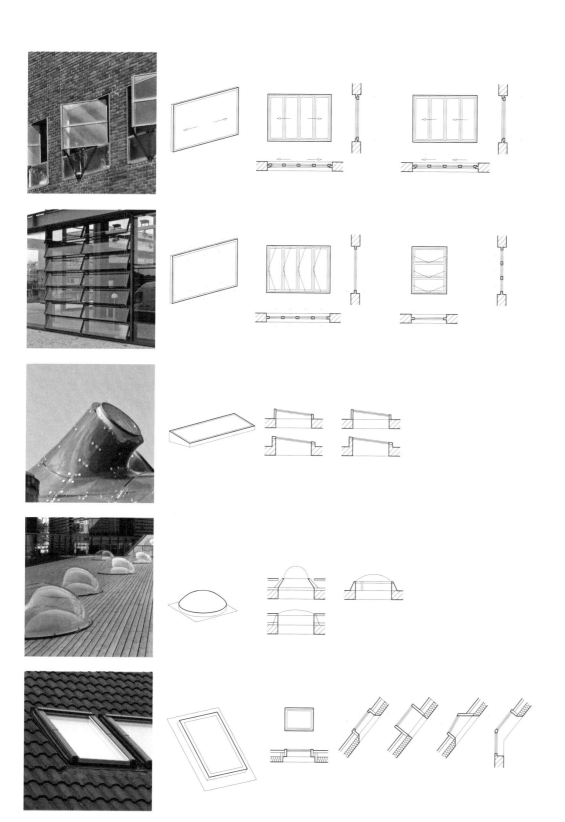

Folding sliding windows
Folding sliding windows consist of a series of sashes linked together by articulating joints, which slide in a track in the window frames. When opened, they fold up into a pack at the end of the frame. A bottom track is required in habitable rooms to prevent penetration by wind and driving rain. Brush strips may be used where there is no threshold.

Louver windows
A louver window is made up of a series of small side hung, vertically pivoted or center hung sashes. Each louver has its own frame and they close together like a double leaf window. The ratio of glazed area to frame area is relatively small and the arrangement has difficulty meeting the requirements for air infiltration.

Skylights
Skylights provide light from above and are available in various geometrical forms. Ribbon windows, raised roof windows, double-inclined skylights, single-inclined skylights, roof lanterns or shed roof windows are all forms of skylight. It should be noted that warm air can build up under skylights under sunlit conditions and that there should be some means of ventilating this space.

Domed rooflights
Domed rooflights are overhead point light sources. They may be almost any shape, including circular, rectangular or square, and are often used as a means of roof access or as smoke or heat vents.

Rooftop windows
Rooftop windows are fitted into sloping roofs. Roof coverings and waterproofing can be connected to rooftop windows, which generally consist of frames and sashes. Types of construction and ways of opening are many and include hinged, tilt-turn and roof balcony windows.

1 Window types:

a Window with single glazing, now only used for simple buildings, such as stables.
b Window with 2-pane insulating glazing unit. This form of construction complies with modern standards (section dimensions 56/78 mm).
c Window with 2-pane insulating glazing (section dimensions 56/78 mm).
d Window with 3-pane insulating glazing represents the present state of technical development (section dimensions 78/78 mm).
e 2-pane double-sash window
f 3-pane double-sash window
g Box frame window
h Box window

2 Proportion of aperture area of the whole system area for various window types.

3 Diagram showing incident light in relation to window type:

a 2-pane insulating glazing
b 3-pane insulating glazing
c Double-sash window
d Box window

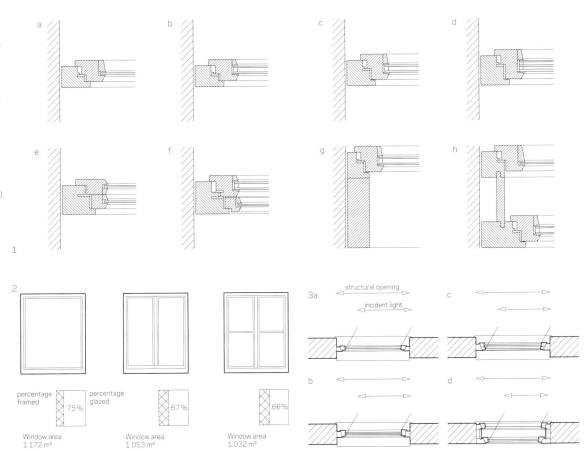

An adequate provision of daylight in a room is a physical and psychological necessity for well-being and productivity. Daily and seasonal changes in the angle of solar elevation can be experienced from the play of light and shadow and the changing tone of the light in the room. The size of an opening is determined by the architectural design. The building regulations contain series of minimum requirements which must be taken into account at an early stage in the design. Habitable rooms must have a window area at least equal to the usable floor area of the room. This minimum area correlates with the depth of the room. The areas further away from the outer wall receive less natural light from the windows. The window sill and lintel heights, its compass orientation, shading from the building's surroundings and the position of the opening in the building all have an influence on the daylight in a room. The daylight entering a room through vertical openings in the external wall is a factor of 5 less than for a horizontal opening of the same area in a flat roof. The size of the structural opening for a window in the wall is not the same size as the clear window area / glazed area. The latter is known as the 'aperture area' and is calculated from the size of the structural opening, less the frame and glazing bars. The amount of light passing through the opening is determined above all by the wall thickness and the type of window. The shading effect of the frame and window bars greatly increases with solar radiation striking the window at an angle. Therefore, a two-sash box window has a greater shading effect than a double-glazed frame window.

DOUBLE CASEMENT WINDOW WITH TOPLIGHT

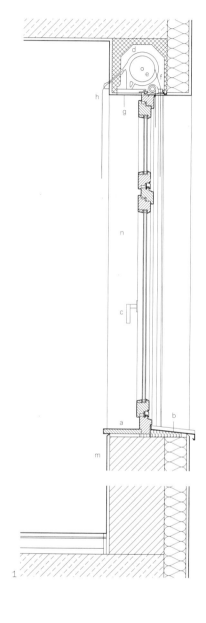

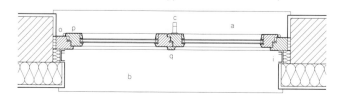

1   Double casement window with
mullion in wood with a bottom-
hung toplight and roller shutter box,
scale 1:20:

a   Window sill internal, wood
b   Window sill external, aluminum
c   Window handle
d   Roller shutter box
e   Roller shutter shaft
f   Insect screen shaft
g   Inspection opening
h   Roller shutter belt
i   Guide channel for roller shutter
    and insect screen
j   Sash / tilt-turn sash
k   Sash / side-hung sash
l   Toplight, bottom-hung
m Wall below sill
n   Reveal
o   Window frame profile
p   Opening sash profile
q   Window / frame cover plate

2   French window with a wooden
fixed side panel, scale 1:20:

a   Fixed side panel
b   French window with tilt-turn
    function
c   Window handle
d   Flush pull
e   Window sill external
f   Grating
g   Boards
h   Frame profile
i   Sash profile
j   Hinge
k   Mullion

FRENCH DOOR

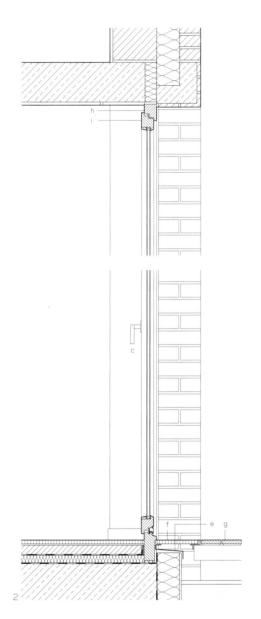

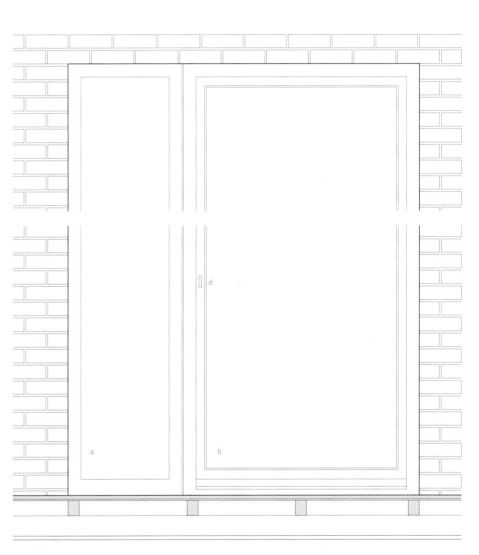

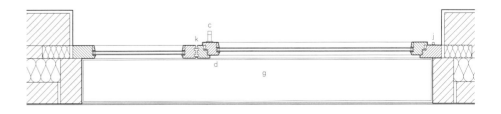

SLIDING WINDOW

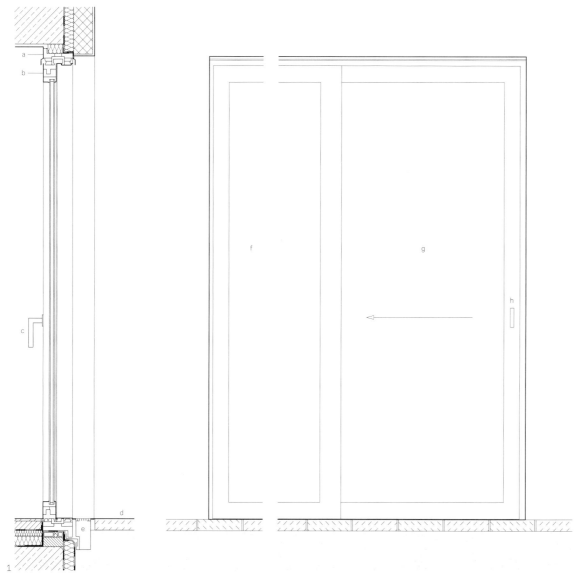

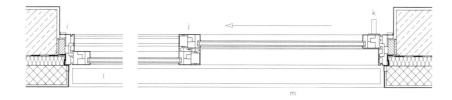

1   Aluminum sliding window,
scale 1:20:

a   Frame profile
b   Sash frame profile
c   Hand lever
d   Drainage layer
e   Drainage channel
f   Fixed side light
g   Sliding door
h   Handle
i   Fixed light profile
j   Sliding sash profile
k   Hand lever
l   Grating
m   Terrace surfacing/
    concrete paving

2   Skylight with a suspended plane
facing the interior space and sun
control, scale 1:20.

3   Skylight with a concrete upstand
visible from the inside, scale 1:20:

a   Gravel
b   Waterproofing
c   Insulation laid to falls
d   Vapor barrier
e   Reinforced concrete
f   Rooflight glazing
g   Steel section
h   Lighting
i   Light diffusing sheet, PVC
j   Steel angle
k   Concrete upstand
l   Laminated wood board
m   Suspended ceiling, wood-based
    board
n   Vegetation layer
o   Filter membrane, nonwoven
p   Drainage layer
q   Thermal insulation
r   Root barrier
s   Concrete laid to falls
t   Cover strip
u   Frame, aluminum
v   Flashing

SKYLIGHT

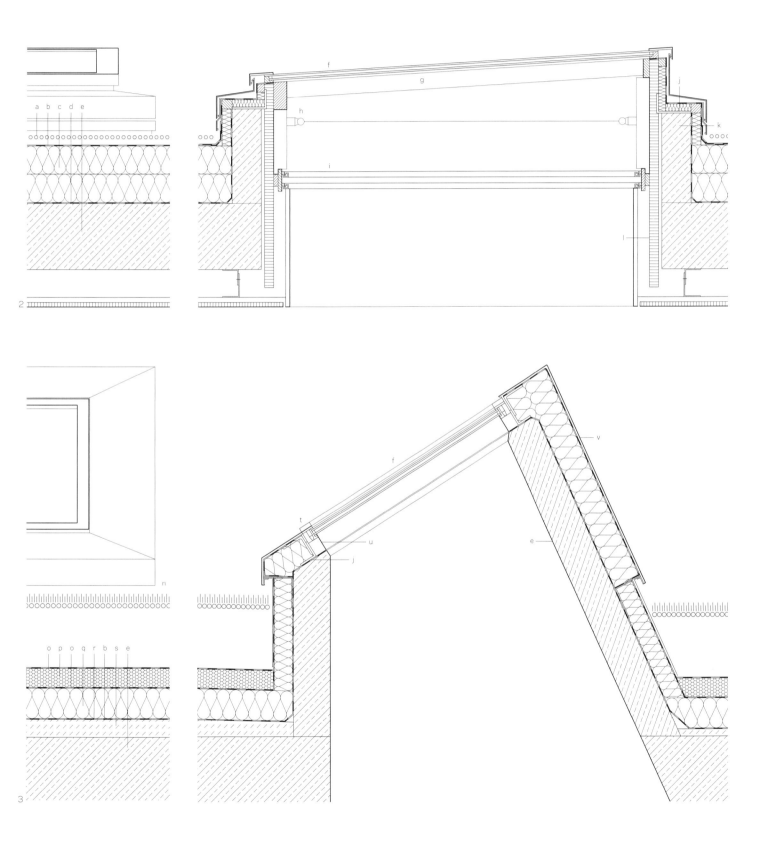

TECHNICAL CONSTRUCTION

THE WINDOW AS A SEMI-FINISHED PRODUCT

The development of window construction owes much to the evolution from the hand crafting of individual pieces to the mass production of system building components. For many centuries windows were designed according to traditional rules using sample or pattern books. These books are only available as reprints and are mostly used as the basis for windows in building restoration projects. The last 50 years have seen a fundamental revolution in window manufacture with the reduction to a few system profiles, the arrival of industrial materials and new production techniques. The window has become a standard product, now freely available to the masses, which stands at the end of a chain of production processes in the factories of raw material and semi-finished product suppliers. These suppliers provide window factories with a wide range of compatible products for system-specific and universal use. Newly gained scientific knowledge, standardization and quality certification have led to a significant increase in the quality and performance of modern manufactured windows, some of which have developed into high-tech products, such as sandwich elements like passive house windows.

In spite of the availability of high grade prefabricated window systems, today it continues to be very important for architects to be aware of the principles of window manufacture as they are developing and to understand the technical requirements. For only with this knowledge can they actively intervene in window manufacture and be able to influence the design to the best advantage of their project. It is normal for an architect to be offered a series of alternative systems from which he has to choose on the basis of his expertise.

When drawing a window profile in a large scale detail, it helps to know, for example, that most wooden window frame and sash members are routed from a square piece of wood approximately 8 x 8 cm in size. The router head machines all the grooves and rebates required for sealing the sash and frame in one operation.

Windows and external doors have to resist the effects of the outdoor climate in the forms of wind, rain, sleet, hail, snow, temperature fluctuations and solar radiation to a greater or lesser extent depending on the building's location, facade orientation and installed position. ↘ tab 1, 2-p. 158 The recommendations for windows in terms of wind load, watertightness and air permeability can be found in guideline FE-05/1, issued by the ift, which can be used to estimate the severity of the effects of the weather for a specified building location.

WIND LOADS

The wind load is normally the main load on the window and therefore determines the structural size of the frame, glass thickness and method of fixing into the building fabric. The loadings can be calculated using the provisions of DIN 1055, Part 4, taking into account the building height and location. ↘ tab 2-p. 158 This is verified by calculation or in exceptional cases by a testing institution. The structural design of profiles and glass and the changes in load capacity are determined using DIN 1055.

WATERTIGHTNESS

The new DIN EN 12208 specifies the requirements for watertightness and joint air permeability. While the old DIN 18055 referred to classes A–C and in special cases class D, there are now a total of ten classes, starting with class zero, which represents a window subjected to no load. Windows are tested by applying a load at a specified test pressure. The loading class of windows should be determined at an early stage in the design of a building. This also effects the choice of compressible filler in the joints between building components. A high level of watertightness is achieved by the correct design of the rebates and the seals, while the air permeability of the joints depends on the seals alone. The new standard has two test procedure classes:

Class A   for windows where there are no constructional measures to protect them from rain;

Class B   for sheltered windows, which may be in a reveal or below a roof overhang, for example.

BUILDING PHYSICS / PROTECTION FROM HEAT AND MOISTURE

Large temperature differentials in winter, with the cold outside and the heat inside, place high stresses on the window. The interior air is cooled at the cold window surface and sinks to the floor. Depending on the surface temperature and height of the window, this can give rise to air moving at speeds sufficient to cause discomfort for those near the window. The limits for the speed of these air movements are set out in DIN EN 13779. After cooling, the relative humidity of the air increases, which can lead to condensation on the glass surface. This does not reduce the thermal insulation and is not a defect. According to the provisions of DIN 4108-2, condensation is a temporary phenomenon, which is permissible in small quantities, as long as the moisture is not absorbed by the surface and adjacent components are not damaged. An exception to this rule is any condensation resulting from the temperature in the glazing cavity falling below dew point. Water forming in the cavity must be drained away. Condensation on the room-side face of the glass depends on the u-value of the glazing and on conditions in the room such as temperature, humidity and air circulation.

WINDOW TYPES

1   Window materials and their profile / construction compared, scale 1:2.

a   Wood has good thermal insulation properties; the conductivity of spruce J = 0.11 W/mK, compared with aluminum alloy at J = 209 W/mK

b   Aluminum profile. This material is softer than steel, and the sections for a given window frame size are thicker or are stabilized against buckling by additional cross-sectional stiffeners in the frame.

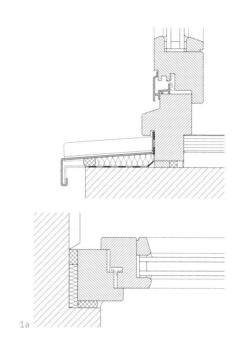

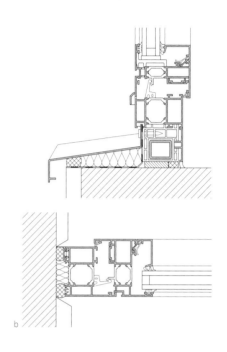

VENTILATION

As windows have become more airtight, so has the importance of designing the ventilation of buildings and rooms. All components of the building envelope should be mutually compatible. The traditional technique of pulse ventilation using opening sashes is user-dependent and not suitable for controlled continuous ventilation. The use of thermally optimized window constructions is recommended for very well insulated buildings such as passive houses. These buildings must have a system to provide controlled ventilation that is separate from the window. When existing windows are merely being replaced without any intention of improving the energy performance of the building envelope, then the use of traditional windows with only a centrally positioned seal is generally sufficient, subject to the particular conditions prevailing at the point of installation. ↘ tab 1, 2-p. 160

WINDOW TYPES / SYSTEM WINDOWS

The vast, almost inestimable number of different window forms and types can be best understood by classifying them according to their materials, frames and sash profiles. The most popular materials used to manufacture windows are wood, steel, aluminum and plastic. The frames and sash materials can be combined with one another even to the extent of forming complex composite constructions. The cross sectional dimensions for wood, aluminum or plastic frames generally match one another and are set out in various industry guidelines.

However, the influence of the material used results in differences in the design of profiles in window components, especially in construction of the cross section, such as thermal separation or break in frame profiles, or reduced visible profile thickness with stronger frames, as is the case with steel windows.

Windows are generally subject to very high loads. Fluctuations in temperature and moisture, and mechanical loads from opening and closing the windows demand a careful choice of materials. Wooden windows have the advantage of high thermal insulation properties. Spruce, for example, has a coefficient of thermal conductivity L = 0.11 W/mK. Metals, on the other hand, are efficient conductors of heat: Steel has 250 times the heat-conducting capacity of wood, for aluminum the figure is 62. Therefore metal profiles are always thermally separated. ↘ 1-p. 52 The dimensions of the frame are determined primarily from the maximum permissible deflection. Steel windows are structurally more efficient and therefore can provide the slenderest cross sections. Metals are the easiest materials on which to base window systems. There is a host of systems with anodized prefabricated parts available from system suppliers. The windows are manufactured and combined by metal fabricators.

WINDOW MATERIALS COMPARED

ECOLOGICAL EVALUATION OF WINDOWS

The ecological evaluation has been the subject of controversial discussions. What can be said is: No single type of window construction has overwhelming advantages or disadvantages in all environmental conditions.

As every building is unique, a consideration of material processing chains without reference to the construction process may not lead to the optimum conclusion.

Energy efficiency should be maximized, and is especially important for slender, lightweight window frames with low U-values. Consideration of the ecological credentials of typical frame materials shows that wood has a relatively good overall profile across a range of impact categories, given the appropriate care, quality and preparation.

Two of the strengths of wooden windows are their uncomplicated preparation and the sustainability of the raw material, in which forest management and short transport routes are highly relevant to the ecobalance.

Furthermore, wooden windows require neither complex manufacturing processes, nor complicated thermal breaks in the frame cross section.

However there are potential weaknesses, such as the paints and coatings applied to ensure protection from the weather. Burning contaminated wood (white lead paint) creates serious environmental pollution. The same applies during the manufacture of paint and the disposal of production waste. Comprehensive knowledge of coating materials and care in the choice of the products used are important. Wooden windows perform well in building fires. Dioxin poisoning is possible from the burning of just one PVC window. The release of dioxins and furanes from the fire can also render rooms or whole parts of buildings permanently unusable until they have been expensively decontaminated. Wooden windows can be used as part of a fire and smoke protection system. In a fire, wood chars on the surface only, retaining its strength and stability and giving off very little smoke.

Closed manufacturing and recycling cycles are necessary for aluminum and PVC windows to have an ecoprofile comparable with native softwoods.

The combination of different products and by-products from surface treatment often mean that this is not always achievable. The same applies to glazing.

Old window glass is recycled in the production of container glass or foamed glass. Float glass manufacture requires very pure raw materials and therefore recycled glass cannot be added to the melt.

Furthermore, window design should permit the recycling of individual window parts or components. Early component failure in particular is always ecologically disadvantageous. Therefore, windows should be designed to be easily repairable, allow parts such as dry seals (gaskets) to be replaced. The use of expanding foam and glueing frame components together should be avoided.

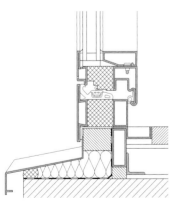

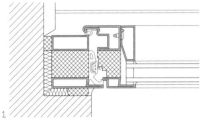

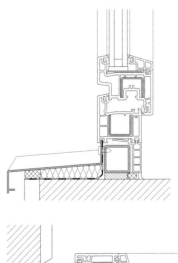

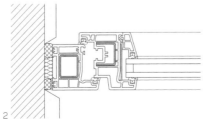

1   All profiles must be designed to ensure that water is quickly drained away, and that pockets of standing water or moisture are avoided. Capillary action should be interrupted by joints to prevent water from rising through surfaces bearing directly on the window sill. Profile edges should be rounded slightly on the side exposed to the weather.

2   Multicellular plastic profile with metal sections to increase rigidity. Positioning the metal sections well inside the profile eliminates the need for a thermal break. Drainage of condensation and vapor diffusion at the outside face is by outlets in the front cell. These caps are visible on the outside of the frame.

1

2

WOODEN WINDOWS

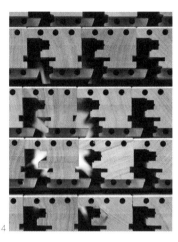

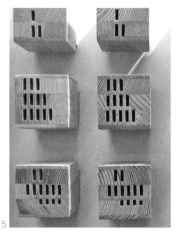

3   4   5   6

3 Simple window scantling high quality, glue-laminated, knot-free in radial / semi-radial cut in accordance with DIN EN 204 D4 in various types of wood. It is a semi-finished product and consists of layers of wood glued together, which improves the straightness and stability of window sashes and frames.

4 The squared timber is mounted, CNC machined and drilled. The profile is produced in one process.

5 Energy efficient wood scantling with air cells. It can achieve u-value of 0.79 W/m²K (with warm scantling and U_g = 0.5 W/m²K). This was developed to attain the limiting value specified for passive houses of 0.8 W/m²K. It is hoped that these values can be attained using window frame scantlings with air cells alone, i.e. without the other materials e.g. PU foam.

6 The wood used for making windows must have properties such as good dimensional stability, low shrinkage and good paintability, be easily worked and resistance to rot and insect attack.

WOODEN WINDOWS

Wood is the oldest window material and still commands a high proportion of the market today. Its popularity is due to its good thermal insulation properties, ease of working and availability.

Out of this tradition have grown numerous long-established finishing activities such as the manufacture of windows, external and internal doors, wall and ceiling claddings and joinery works.

The disadvantage of wooden windows is their comparatively poor weather resistance. Modern coating systems considerably diminish the earlier expense of normal maintenance.

A wood must have certain characteristics to be suitable for window frame construction. It must be adequately strong, resistant to weather and pests, have grown uniformly and have no tendency to warp. **tab 3-p. 159** These characteristics are present in woods such as pine, spruce, teak, afrormosia, agba, redwood, sipo, dark red meranti or pitch pine.

Various scientific studies have shown that the life expectancy of wooden windows can be higher than other materials because a wooden window can be repaired easily and without great expense. A case in point is windows in rooms which are occupied continuously by different people. The diverse range of user behavior demands a great deal from the hinges as the windows are set and reset to suit the needs of each occupant group.

Wood exhibits the lowest expansion of all window materials. Only the smallest tolerances are required of openings in the building's basic structure. It is able to absorb moisture in the air, store it and release it again. Wooden windows do not become electrostatically charged and therefore attract no dirt particles, which makes cleaning wooden windows easy.

PROTECTING WOOD

Wood must be protected from the effects of weather, whatever the species of wood. Wood can be protected by physical features of the building or the windows themselves. The position of a window in a building is determinant in this. **tab 1, 2-p. 160** Natural wood protection, which is defined for each wood in terms of five resistance classes in DIN EN 350-2, is another option, as well as physical and chemical protective measures.

Physical wood protection includes protective coatings such as varnishes, which allow the grain of the wood to remain visible, and opaque wood stains. Traditional linseed oil is still used for heritage buildings. Varnishes must have a minimum proportion of pigments so that the wood is protected from damaging UV radiation.

With all coatings, it should be borne in mind that darker paints cause the frame to heat up more in direct sunlight, which places stresses on the frame construction.

The selection of paint color and system depend on the type of wood and the climate in which it is to be used. Tables or the paint manufacturer's data sheets are helpful in making the choice. **tab 3, 4-p. 159** There are some primers which provide chemical protection on the surface against bluestain fungi discoloring the wood. Other chemical protection techniques include industrial pressure impregnation, in which the wood is saturated with a protective agent to prevent rot occurring as a result of the ingress of moisture.

PROFILE CONSTRUCTION

General requirements for the construction of profiles for timber windows and window doors are given in DIN 68121. While wood's ease of machining offers a wide range of options for building up a profile, the experience and knowledge of window construction and the typical damage and defects encountered in the past weigh against experiments in form. In the choice of details complying with standard, there is adequate scope for architectural variations in form. As the profile is intended to protect the wood by its shape, its design should consider the following points:

Water falling on the profile should drain away directly and in a controlled manner, avoiding the build-up of standing water. This can be aided by having a machined drip strip. Correct detailing can prevent water and pockets of moisture being trapped behind raised parts of the wood, e.g. on window sills.

Special care should be taken to avoid creating capillary joints where profiles abut; if necessary open up the joints. All edges of faces exposed to the weather must be slightly rounded off. Furthermore, the cross sections must be adequately dimensioned for the estimated wind load and the calculated longitudinal bending. The optimization of a window profile usually has consequential effects on the architectural appearance. Often the improvement in engineering terms of a window has a detrimental effect on its formal coherence as a part of building's overall appearance, both externally and internally. The task, when selecting a particular profile, is to check its wider relationship with reference to the overall appearance intended by the architect.

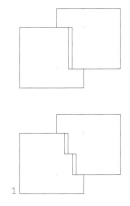

1 Typical arrangement of rebates in window construction, The principle of rebates. Squared timber approx. 8 x 8 cm.

2 Historic window, outward-opening:

a Straight rebate
b Folding rebate
c Clamp rebate
d Variation on folding rebate

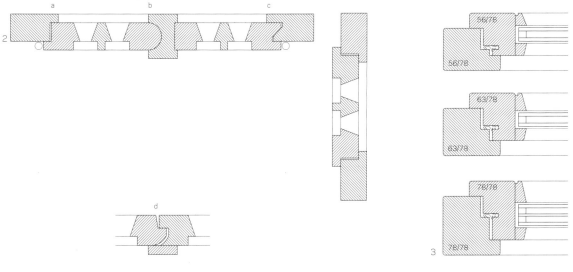

3 The frame dimensions always depend on the type of glazing, the choice of system-specific seals and the dimensions of the window area. The larger the area of glass, the more weight must be carried by the frame. The section must be adequately dimensioned.
The larger the window, the greater the area subjected to wind loads. The brief designation gives the depth and length of the profile in mm. A window frame of solid wood (e.g. 3-layer laminated) has a U_f-value of 1.0 m²K).

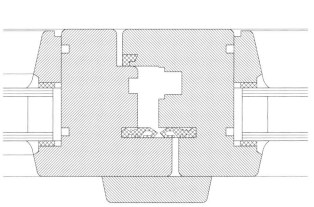

4 Shape of sections, scale 1:2.

Parts of the window. Section 1:2

a Window frame
Structure around the outside of a window fixed to the masonry. Depending on the wall rebate, the window may be described as opening outwards, inwards or installed without a rebate in the masonry.

b Sash frame
The sash frame consists of top and bottom rails and side styles. It fits against the rebates of the frame. The correct rebate pressure ensures that the joint between them is sealed.

c Glazing
Consists of at least one (usually more than one) pane of insulating glass which is fitted into the glazing rebate of a sash. The glass allows natural light in and protects against noise and weather (wind, rain, cold air etc.). The size of the panes and the prevailing wind pressure and building height are usually determinant in the design of the glass panes. This also influences the loading group of the window glazing. →tab 1-p. 164 Glazing types are single glazing, double glazing and multiple pane insulating glazing. Maximum window element sizes are determined by the weight of the glass and by the transport restrictions. Seals on windows are classed either as 'wet' or 'dry'.

d Glazing bead
This internal fastening profile holds the glazing unit in place in the sash and allows the glass to be replaced in the event of breakage.

e Metal weather bar
Fitted nowadays as an improvement on the traditional drip molding.

Window sill, exterior
Made of aluminum, artificial stone, formerly wood, and cover the external window parapet in the case of reveal windows. The water must drain in a way that avoids staining the facade. A fall of ≥ 5 % and a projection beyond the facade of ≥ 30 mm are required. Metal window sills must be fixed to the window frames with non-rusting fastenings.

Window board, interior
Fixed on top of the wall, inside, or attached firmly to brackets. May be wood, wood-based board, plastic, artificial or natural stone. The junction of the window assembly with the wall must be airtight at the internal window sill, too.

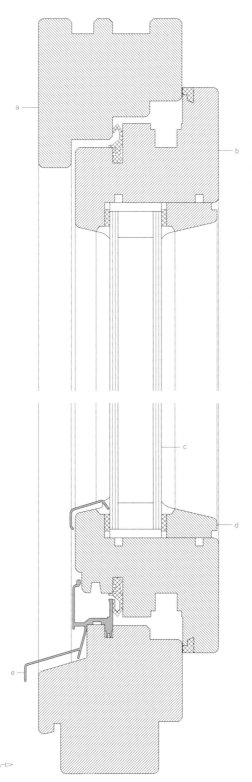

Wooden sections are now available in standardized sizes. Construction products and types that are not standardized and do not have a national technical approval nor a test certificate, but fall within the scope of construction legislation, require specific case approval by the highest national construction authorities.

DESIGNING A FRAME PROFILE
The fundamental principle of jointing a complete timber window profile is that two equally sized timber sections must engage with one another to ensure a wind- and rain-tight joint. The same jointing principle applies to all types of window, irrespective of materials. The profiles are shaped in such a way that multiple overlaps with rebate depths of approximately 8–10 mm are formed. A small intermediate space remains in the rebate, to accommodate deformations characteristic for each material and to allow further adjustment of the moving sash. Ever stricter requirements for the watertightness of joints has meant that the performance of traditional simple butt joints with a triple rebate, wood on wood, is no longer adequate. Additional seals are required. Against this background the bottom-opening window shows itself to be different to windows with other opening modes. Rainwater collects here and water may penetrate between the frame and the sash. To prevent this, the frame wood is given a different shape: A metal water bar with weatherstrips creates three lines of contact with the closing sash. This detail varies, depending on the manufacturer. However, they are all based on the relevant standards. The traditional drip molding is preferred in heritage buildings, consisting of a wooden bead screwed on to the weather board or a metal one fixed and anodized in the color of the sash.

STEEL AND STAINLESS STEEL WINDOWS

STEEL WINDOWS

Up to the middle of the twentieth century, wood was still the most popular material for window frames. Cast iron came on the scene in the nineteenth century with the beginning of industrialiszd window manufacture, followed later by steel, which made possible the slender frames so characteristic of Modernism.

Metal window sections can be made from mild steel, stainless steel, steel alloys or Cor-ten. Simple sections were made earlier from hot-rolled mild steel in the form of T-, Z-, I-, L-shaped cross sections. Today they are hollow sections, cold-rolled from strip steel. The high strength of the material allows large panel windows. Steel windows have a high torsional and bending stiffness and are much stronger than aluminum framed windows. As exposed steel corrodes, the windows must be given a protective coating. Steel windows are therefore supplied already primed and after installation are given further coats of paint. They can also be provided with a metal coating, for example galvanized. The uncoated or galvanized windows can be also be powder-coated at the factory. After this has been done, no further welding or machining should be done. If the windows are powder-coated they must also be protected after installation, as the traces of any remedial work which has to be done by hand on site, remain detectable.

The high thermal conductivity of steel causes water to condense on the profiles, which can be anticipated and the water collected in channels in the internal window sill. These simple hot-rolled steel profiles or hollow profiles can be used for single pane windows with no requirement for thermal or noise insulation.

Modern designs of steel windows with thermal breaks, high strength and low maintenance demands on their durable coatings are used to meet the higher requirements of public buildings. Very slim-line profiles, without a thermal break, have prominent fittings, ⟋1 and the proportion of frame in the window is considerably reduced. Therefore considering the frame in isolation makes little sense, in view of the immensely improved insulation of the insulation glazing with typical U-values of 1.1 W/m²K. For normally ventilated and heated rooms and windows with the appropriate detailing, dew point condensation is seldom a problem. Designing individual components with a view to saving energy would not be helpful here; it is far better in terms of EnEV compliance to refer to the annual primary energy demand of the whole building and not the U-value. These frames are insignificant when viewed against the overall energy performance with a correspondingly large proportion of glazing, and so they can be compensated for by general energy-saving measures.

However, one remaining disadvantage of these slim-line steel windows is the substandard protection against intrusion offered by their external, non-integral locking hardware.

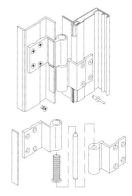

1 Screw-on hinge.

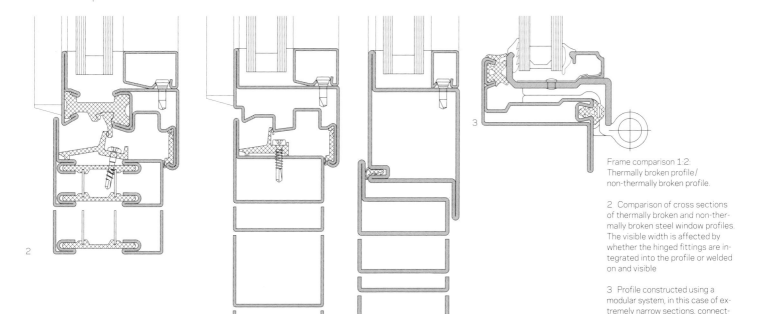

2

3

Frame comparison 1:2:
Thermally broken profile/
non-thermally broken profile.

2 Comparison of cross sections of thermally broken and non-thermally broken steel window profiles. The visible width is affected by whether the hinged fittings are integrated into the profile or welded on and visible

3 Profile constructed using a modular system, in this case of extremely narrow sections, connected by system-specific screw-on hinges and surface-mounted deadbolt locks.

ALUMINUM WINDOWS /
PLASTIC WINDOWS

4 Aluminum window system: construction depth 75 mm, extended insulation zone with foam-filled insulating bars, integrated slatted blind for sun protection.

5 Aluminum profile with a thermal break.

6 The majority of plastic windows are manufactured in white. The high coefficient of thermal expansion increases the risk of greater longitudinal expansion with dark colored frames when exposed to direct sunlight. Ultraviolet light can cause changes in deep colors.

ALUMINUM WINDOWS

Aluminum is well known for its high durability and ease of maintenance and care. Accurate manufacture of the aluminum sections results in tighter tolerances during fabrication due to the higher dimensional accuracy of the frames. Aluminum windows also weigh less than comparable steel products.

In contrast to timber windows, there has been no standardization of section dimensions. They differ greatly from manufacturer to manufacturer; not just in size but even more frequently in cross sectional shape. Hollow sections with thermal breaks are made up of extruded semifinished products. Aluminum, being relatively soft, is easy to machine. As it has a high thermal conductivity, the inner and outer skins must be thermally separated from one another, in this case by plastic strips or rigid foam. ⟶ 4, 5

In spite of higher initial costs due to the higher primary energy requirement for processing the raw material, aluminum windows are still economic compared to timber or plastic windows, because they last longer and are easier to maintain and clean. A further advantage is the combination of low weight and very high accuracy of construction. However, as aluminum expands more in response to temperature than wooden or steel windows, the movement joints at the connections to the building's structure must be able of accommodating movements of approximately 1–1.5 mm/m length.

The aluminum profiles are connected together to form complete frames by inserted, screwed and bolted joints. Unfinished aluminum oxidizes and therefore the surface must be treated. Methods include grinding, brushing, polishing or electrochemical processes such as anodizing. Stove-enamels or powder coatings are baked on to the surface in special ovens at temperatures of 180 °C.

PLASTIC WINDOWS

Plastic as a material offers good value for money and has as good thermal insulation properties as wood. Maintenance costs are very low. Plastic frames are normally manufactured as extruded hollow profiles out of rigid polyvinyl chloride. There are single or multi-chamber systems on the market; the latter having superior insulation properties. The current standard is the five air-chamber system. Stiffening steel or aluminum sections are incorporated into the plastic profile to strengthen it and increase the stability and load capacity of larger format windows. The steel stiffeners are screwed or riveted to the PVC profile. As steel reduces the thermal insulation effect, glass fiber reinforced plastic (GRP) is often used instead. GRP profiles raise the U_w value of the window by reducing the heat loss from the frame still further. This composite window can nowadays be recycled very efficiently. The disadvantage is a relatively thick frame in relation to the glazed area, which can detrimentally affect the amount of admitted light and the thermal gain from sunlight.

Plastic profiles can either be made of colored material or coated. However, they cannot be repainted later. The color of the frames has a great influence on changes in shape; dark colors heat up more. The quality of the PVC used also has a significant effect on the temperature stability. Windows made from lower quality material tend to deform under temperature fluctuations (e.g. due to solar radiation or fire), which can lead to leaks and difficulty in opening and closing. Plastic tends to creep under constant loads. This may lead to deformation of the sash as the steel stiffeners often do not continue into the corners. Plastic frames always have drainage outlets on the outside of the front chamber. They allow condensate to drain away and vapor pressure to equalize.

"SUPER WINDOWS"

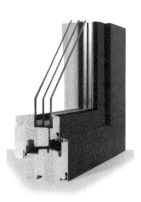

Frame material	U-value [W/m²K]	Internal surface temperature*
Wood	1.4–1.7	13–15 °C
Plastic		
PVC old (2 chambers)	2.8	ca. 9 °C
PVC new (7 chambers)	1.1	ca. 15 °C
PUR integral foam	1.7–2.1	11–14 °C
Aluminum		
Without insulation bar	ca. 5.8	ca. −2 °C
With insulation bar	2.8–3.5	6–9 °C
Thermally optimized profiles	ca. 1.5	ca. 14 °C
Highly insulating frames	ca. 0.8	ca. 17 °C
		* for −10 °C outside air temperature

WOOD / ALUMINUM FRAMES

Combining the materials wood and aluminum can create products that are an improvement on wooden windows. The loadbearing parts of the frame is wood, which is covered by a thin shell of aluminum on the outside. Weather protection is built into the design, avoiding the need for environmentally harmful coatings. The very high primary energy requirement for the production of aluminum can be reduced by the use of recycled aluminum. Another example of built-in wood protection is the sash with the glass glued to the outside face. ⌐ 1b-p. 62

FRAMES / THERMAL WEAK POINTS ON WINDOWS

Following the advances already made in window glazing, the thermal insulation properties of window frames have a greater role to play. The smaller the window, the more detrimental is the relative effect of the poor thermal insulation performance of the frame. A standard wood frame with double glazing with U_g = 1.3 W/m²K for a basic building opening of 0.36 m² to 7.2 m² would achieve U_w-values of 1.6–2.7 W/m²K. Similar values can be attained by conventional plastic frames, while metal frames with a frame component of 30 % achieve a considerably poorer U_w-value of 2.7 W/m²K. Normal frame designs are close to their achievable limits in terms of thermal insulation. To further improve the frame properties, there must be a move away from monolithic construction towards laminated and composite frames.

SUPERFRAMES / SPECIAL WINDOWS

As a result of the development of low energy and passive house technology, in recent years manufacturers have brought a wide range of different frame types on to the market, many with U_w-values of 0.5–0.8 W/m²K and therefore capable of complying with more stringent thermal insulation requirements. The new highly insulated superframes, such as wood frames with core insulation,

wood frames with integral air chambers or PVC multi-chamber frame profiles with internal steel reinforcement and PU foam filling, are manufacturer-specific. They must be designed to ensure that no condensate can collect behind vapor-impermeable outer skins.

The large profile thicknesses required for frames to meet the passive house standard, in particular if they are fitted with triple glazing for high thermal insulation, present a challenge to the designer. ⌐ p. 68ff.

SOUND INSULATING FRAMES

When compared with solid external walls, the window is a weak point for the transmission of airborne sound. The frame material has only an insignificant influence on the sound insulation properties of a window.

If better sound insulation is demanded by the building regulations, the necessary improvement in insulating performance can often be achieved by the appropriate choice of glass quality and thickness, the arrangement of the panes and careful design and construction of the joints with the building fabric. ⌐ tab 3-p. 160

GLAZING SYSTEMS

A glazing system consists of a combination of glazing, glazing rebate and sealing into the sash frame. As with any system, all the individual components must match each other exactly. Special glazing functions relating to heat, noise and fire influence the design of the system just as much as the method of supporting the glass or the design and choice of materials for the window seals. The number, type and arrangement of the glass layers are determined by the requirements for thermal and sound insulation, light transmission and, in some circumstances, the need for security. In addition to the material for and type of sash frame, the designer should also consider the thermal properties of the inserted glass and the limits on panel sizes imposed by production and transport consid-

1 Wooden frame construction designed in accordance with the Rosenheim window concept achieves a U_w-value of 0.9 W/m²K. The outer pane of the composite window is glued directly to the outer sash frame and completely covers the outside of the sash, protecting it from the weather. These glued-on glazing systems are not covered by the present standards.

2 Thermal insulation properties of window frames.

3 Isotherm plots in a wooden frame, with and without core insulation. The 10 degree isotherm for the water condensation point moves towards the outside and the frame becomes warmer inside the room. Condensed water on the frame and mould growth are avoided.

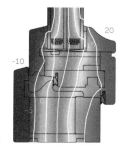

GLAZING SYSTEMS / GLASS TYPES

Comparison of insulation values of different glazing: New windows must be designed to allow energy and light in and let as little heat as possible out again. The g-value is the sum of the solar energy transmission and the heat dissipated into the room, the emission of long wave radiation and convection.

Windows should be selected to have a U_w-value of about 1.5 W/m²K. They represent the current state of the art in residential buildings.

A thermally insulating window reduces energy use by up to 75 % compared with single glazing.

inside	6 mm	float glass
middle	12 mm	glazing cavity
outside	6 mm	float glass

4 Comparison of insulation values of different glazing:
A reduction of the U_w-value of 0.1 W/m²K leads to a saving of 1.2 liters of heating oil per m² of window area and heating season.

5 Comparison of flat glass manufacturing methods:
95 % of flat glass, such as window glass, car windows and mirrors, is made using the float glass process. Therefore flat glass has become cheaper. The properties of float glass are:
Specific weight: 2,500 kg/m³,
Thermal conductivity:
0.8-1.0 W/mK,
U_w-value: < 5.8 W/m²K.

Single-pane glazing	←		U = 5.8 W/m²K 62 l oil/year·m²
2-pane insulating glazing	←		U = 2.9 W/m²K 30 l oil/year·m²
2-pane heat insulating glazing	←		U = 1.1 W/m²K 12 l oil/year·m²
3-pane heat insulating glazing	←		U = 0.7 W/m²K 8.5 l oil/year·m²
Without heat gain, joint losses or frame effect			

4

Process	Glass thickness	Surface	Air/material inclusions	
Cylinder blown sheet: Blown glass cylinder is slit after cooling, up to 1900		very wavy, very uneven, not plan-parallel	yes	some
Cast, rolled e.g. U-glass		strongly wavy	yes	none
Drawn (Fourcault process) 1904	from 0.8 mm	moderately wavy, drawing lines, uneven	little	none
Drawn Libbey-Owens process, Pittsburgh process 1904/1928	from 0.8 mm	slightly wavy, drawing lines, uneven	little	none
Float manufactured since 1959 Pilkington	1.5-25 mm	not wavy	very few	very few

5

erations. The results can be seen in the segmenting of larger window facades. Glass panels are manufactured with a wide range of properties and are selected to suit the project and situation.

Measures of the energy performance of a window include the heat transfer coefficient U_w in W/m²K, the energy gain through the glazing and the total solar heat transmittance g. The g-value of glazing is expressed in percent; the higher the value, the more energy enters the room.

GLAZING SYSTEMS / GLASS TYPES

Since 1950, 95 % of flat glass has been made using the float process. In this process, the molten liquid glass flows like a film of oil in a long bath of molten tin. The surface tension of both materials causes them to form very smooth surfaces. Production constraints limit float glass sheets to a maximum of 6-7 m long and 1.5-19 mm thick. The width of the glass sheet is determined by allowable transport dimensions, the turning circles of low-loaders and the effective widths of traffic lanes. The normal sheet width is approximately 3.20 m, depending on the manufacturer.

Float glass may be tinted. Its natural green color can be lessened or eliminated by reducing the amount of certain substances that are naturally present. Surface treatments such as etching, grinding or grit-blasting make transparent float glass translucent.

INSULATING GLAZING

The thermal properties of a single pane of flat glass can be improved upon by combining it with one or more glass panes and forming a single unit with airtight edges. The resulting gap between the panes, the glazing cavity, is at normal atmospheric pressure for structural reasons and is filled with dry air. A further improvement in thermal insulation can be achieved by filling the glazing cavity with a noble gas with a lower thermal conductivity than air. The gases normally used are argon, xenon or krypton. The inexpensive noble gas argon improves the U-value by about 0.3 W/m²K compared with an air-filled unit, while the more expensive noble gas krypton achieves 0.4 W/m²K in the same comparison. In some cases, even the noble gas xenon, which has the best properties but is very difficult to obtain, is used. The edge joint must remain permanently airtight, otherwise the improved insulation performance cannot be maintained. It is important to investigate the test criteria used.

The performance in the area of the edge joint can be improved by using stainless steel as the spacer instead of aluminum or mild steel, as it has a lower thermal conductivity. Glass fiber-reinforced plastic, which has a similar strength and temperature response, may also be used. This optimization of the glass edge zone is called a 'warm edge'. In normal room climates, water no longer condenses around the edges of insulating glass panels. The improvement of the U-value of the window is about 0.05 to 0.1 W/m²K, depending on the panel perimeter. The heat transfer coefficient for the spacer is indicated by the R si value and is given in W/mK. It varies, depending on the window frame material.

FUNCTIONAL GLASS

THERMAL INSULATING GLASS

Thermally insulating glazing comes in the form of a multi-pane glass window consisting of two or three panes with low emissivity coatings. These coatings of zinc oxide, silver or gold are applied to the outer face of the indoor pane. The objective is to reflect most of the thermal radiation back in to the room. The standard solution is an insulating glazing unit made up of 2 float glass panes each 4 mm thick, a glazing cavity of 16 mm, 90 % filled with argon, a U-value of 1.2 W/m²K in accordance with EN 673, a g-value of 63 % and a sound reduction index of R_w=32 dB.

In triple glazing there are three sheets of glass arranged one behind the other. The U-value of a triple glazing unit drops by approximately 1.2 to 0.7 W/m²K compared with the equivalent double glazed product. The U-value of insulating glazing depends on the emissivity of the coating, the type and density of the gas filling and the glazing cavity. In general, the thickness of the glass plays a secondary role in the calculation of the U-value, but it does have a strong influence on the g-value.

SOLAR CONTROL GLASS

Solar control glass reduces the amount of sunlight and accompanying thermal radiation passing through the glass into the room. The thermally functional layer is on the inside of the outer pane. The special coating reflects a proportion of the solar radiation. The layer can be neutral, greenish, silver gray or blue in color. This glass generally has a low g-value. Solar control glass delays but cannot prevent the effect of solar radiation and therefore is not a replacement for sunshades. The arrangement of the layers is reversed compared with heat insulating glazing.

SOUND REDUCTION GLASS

The sound insulating performance of a window is demonstrated by tests or comparison with common forms of construction. → **tab 3-p. 160** The required sound insulation is calculated from the outside noise level and the room use. Information on its determination can be found in DIN 4109 and the relevant VDI guidelines.

Thicker glass can be used to improve the sound reduction index R_w. Heavier pane weights reduce sound transmission, with the thicknesses of the inside and outside panes being different to avoid resonance. These two measures can increase the sound reduction index to > 39 dB, a value which is adequate in most cases and relatively inexpensive to achieve. The use of composite glass panels can further increase the sound reduction index. Composite glass consists of different panes of glass bonded together with an optimized edge seal. The requirement

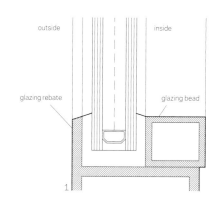

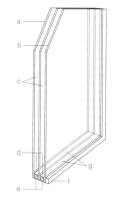

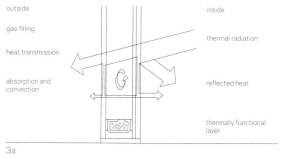

3a

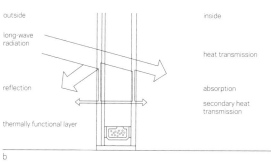

b

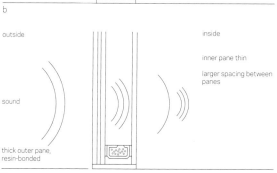

c

1 Glazing rebate dimensions in accordance with DIN 18545/1 The glass is fastened in place in accordance with the requirements of the loading group (1–5).
→ **tab 7-p. 161, tab 1-p. 162**

2 Triple glazing with two sealing levels:

a, b Functional layers, heat
c   Krypton filling
d   Desiccation agent
e   Primary seal (butyl)
f   Secondary seal (polysulphide)
g   Spacer

The date of manufacture is embossed on the inside face of the spacer. The black edge seal is always visible from the outside but is normally concealed by the glazing bead.

3 Operating principles of functional glazing:

a Thermal insulating glass
b Solar control glass
c Solar control glass

All double glazing must fulfill the following requirements:

- Translucency TL value
  TL value > 60 %
- Total energy transmittance:
  g > 55 %
- U_g-value < 1.8 W/m²K,
  neutral appearance from inside and outside

SPECIAL FUNCTIONS

4

5

6

7

4   3-pane heat insulating glazing

5   Functional glass has specific coatings or thicknesses, different tints and degrees of reflectivity. This must be taken into account in a building's facade and window concept. Modern glass has a different effect to historic window glass with its characteristic air inclusions.

6   Applications of laminated safety glass:
- Community buildings: Entire entrance area, sometimes mandatory for school and nursery buildings
- Sports facilities: In sports and leisure buildings, also in entrance areas. Recommended for indoor leisure pools
- Industrial and public buildings: Intrusion resistance, for increasing security and coupling with alarm wire systems
- Overhead glazing: Mandatory, toughened glass for the inside layer is inadequate
- Residential: Burglar resistance, for storey-high glazing and in parapets

The overall security concept must not be compromised by the design and construction of the windows. Every detail must comply with intrusion resistance requirements: Wall connections, materials and rebates, suitable hardware and appropriate glazing fixings.

7   Laminated safety glass is available with various wire interlayers.

for security should be taken into account in the choice of methods for achieving the desired sound insulation.

A further possible way of increasing sound insulation is to increase the width of the glazing cavity (20–44 mm). This approach soon comes up against geometric limits, as the glazing package has to fit into the window frame. → **4** Thermal insulation is also detrimentally affected if the glazing cavity is too large.

The airtightness of a window has a crucial influence on the sound reduction index. An open ventilation flap can halve the sound insulation effect. Therefore it is important to consider the installation situation as a whole, including the ventilation arrangements and roller shutters. The joints at the connection to the building fabric must be carefully designed and constructed.

FIRE RESISTANT GLASS

Fire resistant glass is classified according to DIN 4102 into fire resistance classes G, F and T. It can be in the form of special toughened or laminated safety glass, e.g. manufactured from chemically strengthened soda lime silicate glass. Normal window glass (float glass) is an incombustible material in fire resistance class A, but it can shatter when subjected to the high temperatures generated by a fire. G-glass prevents the passage of flame and gases for a period in accordance with its fire rating (e.g. G 30 = 30 minutes). It offers no resistance to heat, which may cause ignition of materials and components lying on the opposite side of the glass to the fire. G-glass is installed in the facades of high buildings to prevent flames from jumping between storeys. Propagation of the fire is delayed.

F-glass provides the additional protection in a fire of preventing the spread of heat. This is required to ensure that escape and rescue routes or stairwells in fire compartments are not endangered. Flashover is prevented in the

case where window openings are at intervals of less than the required minimum.

A gel filling inside the glazing cavity of multipane glazing foams in the event of fire to form a tough, solid mass or vaporizes (e.g. water glass). In Germany, F-glazing requires technical approval from the Institute for Building Technology in Berlin, which is given with reference to the component only. Fixed glazing can achieve a fire resistance up to class F 90. The glass must be considered together with the frame and above all with its method of fixing to the building fabric. The approval certificate specifies the number, type and position of the fixings to the building fabric. T-glass is used in doors as fire resistant glazing and works on the same principle as G-glass.

SAFETY GLASS

One or both panes in an insulating glazing unit are of safety glass. This may be of toughened safety glass, which has been hardened and when broken shatters into small cubes, or laminated safety glass, which consists of 2 or more panes laminated together with film interlayers. This allows the glass to support greater loads, and when broken, the glass shards remain bonded in place. Safety glass can also be resistant to burglars or bullets. Partially tempered glass is not as strong as toughened glass and breaks into larger fragments. It is used, for example, as anti-fall glazing and is described in EN 1863.

INTRUSION RESISTANCE

Intrusion resistant windows (security windows) are considered an integral component of a security concept. Windows for this purpose have to fulfill additional requirements in the form of a resistance class, categorized into classes WK 0–WK 6, and there is special glass for banks and post office counters. ENV 1627 prescribes combinations of hardware and glass for burglar-resistant

FITTING GLASS / SEALS

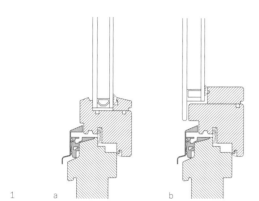

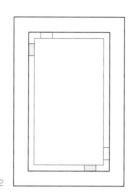

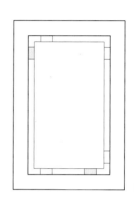

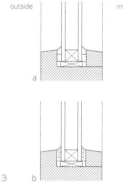

1   a   b

2   3

windows of resistance class WK 2 and above. The glass is classified according to its protective effect and duration in EN 356 Glass in building – Security glazing – Testing and classification of resistance against manual attack (formerly DIN 52 290). This cost-intensive certification is mainly offered by the large system manufacturers, in contrast to the in-house testing procedures and proofs of smaller manufacturers. This must be taken into account and clarified beforehand with reference to insurance policy conditions. All glazing can be combined with alarm wires and burglar alarm systems.

FITTING GLASS

Window sashes are stiffened by their connection to the glazing or filling panels. Support packers must be used between the panes and the frame to transfer the weight of the glass evenly. When the glass is inserted into the sash frame, no part of the pane must be in direct contact with the frame and the weight of the glass must be carried by the bottom sash hinge.

The support packers support the weight of the pane in the sash frame. They must be positioned so that the sash frame cannot deform. The spacer packers are a little thinner than the support packers and are intended to maintain an even distance between the glass and the frame. Support packers are made of hardwood or plastic (polypropylene). There are also flexible plastic spacer packers, which hold the glass in position without overstressing it. Packers are 80 to 100 mm long and should be about 2 mm wider than the glass. The packers must not be placed too near the corner of the pane but be kept at least 100 mm away on normally sized windows. The restraint-free support provided by the packers ensures that unavoidable movements of the components take place evenly and the glass remains properly in place in the frame, despite

changes in dimensions caused by heat or moisture. Condensation must be drained to the outside from the rebate and vapor pressures equalized. These openings must be independent of the window profile and be shielded from direct wind pressure. Equalizing vapor pressure to the inside of the room is not recommended as it can lead to an accumulation of condensation in the rebate.

A glazing bead screwed or nailed in place on the interior face of the window presses the glass against a rebate and holds the glass in the frame. Glazing beads fix the glazing and seal in place, pick up wind forces and transfer them to the loadbearing parts of the window frame. Their specification is governed by the loading group of the window glazing. ↘ chapter 6 An even contact pressure on the pane avoids the glass breaking.

WINDOW SEALS

The seal between the glazing and frame was previously achieved from outside with stiff putty (Fig.). Putty dries out and cracks, which creates ridges and hollows near glazing bars and sash frames, where water can collect and cause damage. Modern practice involves a combination of a glazing bead placed against a glazing strip with either a wet seal such as silicone, acrylate, polysulphide and polyurethane sealant or a dry seal system. Dry seal systems rely on prefabricated gaskets often made from synthetic rubber. The gaskets are extruded and have complex profiles. These gaskets can shrink over time, creating gaps at mitered joints and allowing water to penetrate.

REBATE SEALS

In contrast to a normal joint between building components, the joint between the sash and window frames is a functional joint. The number and shape of the rebates have

1   Methods of fixing glass into sash frames:

a   Glazing beads
b   Wood / glass bonding

With the bonded solution, the loads are transferred linearly into the glass, unlike the point loading from the packers. Slimmer window profiles, better weather protection are the possible advantages here. Material compatibility must be ensured. Sealant, material, profile coating, edge seal of the multipane glazing units and the glazing coatings must not react with one another. A higher UV resistance is required of the adhesive and the rebate base of the edge seal.

2   Typical arrangement of packers on a side-hung sash and a turn-tilt sash. There are two types: support packers and spacer packers:
support packers = dark
spacer packers = light

3   Joint seal between frame and glazing unit, two-sided and continuous around the edge:

a   Wet seal
b   Dry seal

WINDOW SEALS

4a

b

5

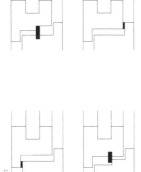

6

4 The sealing performance against driven rain of unsheltered inbuilt window elements is defined in classes 1A to 9A. The higher the class, the better the seal provided by the window against driven rain penetrating to the room side. The sealing performance against driven rain of partially sheltered inbuilt window elements is defined in classes 1B to 7B.

The window sill drains rain water away from the window. It should have a slope of less than 5° and the drip edge should project at least 30 mm. Window sills are either attached to the bottom of the window frame, the wall beneath it, or cladding.

5 Sash rebate gasket

6 Various installation positions for window seals:
High temperature differentials generate strains and hence place high stresses on the window. The fitting rebate is one of the coldest areas of a window. A seal on the room-side sash projection can be effective in limiting condensation and the build-up of mould in the inner fitting rebate.

7 Gaskets and cover profiles for a wooden window.

8 Isotherm curves for various installation positions:
a outside
b middle
c inside

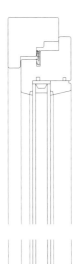

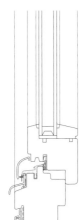

7

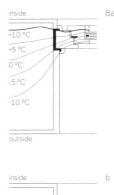

inside   8a
+10 °C
+5 °C
0 °C
-5 °C
-10 °C
outside

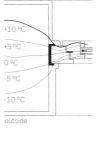

inside   b
+10 °C
+5 °C
0 °C
-5 °C
-10 °C
outside

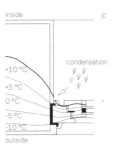

inside   c
condensation
+10 °C
+5 °C
0 °C
-5 °C
-10 °C
outside

very little influence on the effectiveness of the window seal. More important factors include the closing action of the hardware, contact pressure and the shape of sealing strips and gaskets. All windows must have flexible seals to ensure the joints fulfill the requirements for air- and water-tightness and are adequately proof against driving rain. Airtightness must be tested in accordance with EN 1026 and EN 12207. The classification relates both to the joint length and to the whole surface area. The main seal is the wind stop. It must have a one-piece, replaceable, continuous peripheral sealing strip that cannot be displaced. Most seals consist of PVC or rubber gaskets, with shapes that ensure they spring back into place, are highly flexible and resistant to ageing. Seals need to be cleaned and maintained. They must be installed in a way that allows them to be easily replaced. Types of seal include: Sash rebate seals, projecting seals, window frame seals and double rebate seals. The profiles vary in design for attachment to the different forms of rebates on each window type: wood, aluminum, plastic or metal. There are special seals available for renovation work. These seals are suitable for fitting into grooves cut in old frames and optimized for particular types of window construction. There are sealing strips that can be used in combination with lowering floor and door seals for particular functions such as sound insulation and smoke protection.

WEATHER BAR / WEATHER BOARD
A weather bar ⟶4a is used on wood, plastic and metal windows as a seal and to conduct water away. As specified in DIN 68121-1, it forms the lower collection chamber of the weathering zone, which is bounded and sealed on the inside by the sash rebate seal. Water penetrating into the weather bar must be able to flow to the outside, irrespective of pressure. Weather bars consist of

INSTALLATION OF WINDOWS

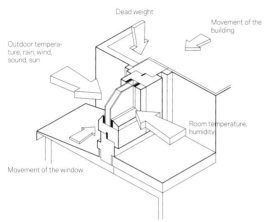

1

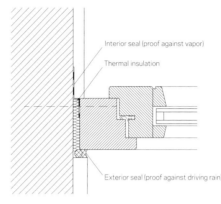

2

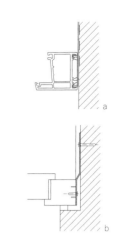

3

extruded aluminum profiles and are attached by screws, or in the case of wooden windows inserted into grooves cut in the wood. Weather boards are usually found on historic buildings. On old windows they are easily replaced. There must be an adequate drip groove on the underside. ↗ 4b-p. 63 The top surface must slope to shed rainwater.

WINDOW INSTALLATION

The fixing of the window into the wall opening determines the degree of thermal and acoustic insulation the window can provide. The type and form of the connection to the building depends on the wall and window materials, and the position in the depth of the wall. Window openings generally either have an internal rebate, an external rebate, or no rebate in the reveal. The window frame must be fixed to the main structure at 80 cm intervals. The connection may be rigidly fixed or may allow movement. A secondary frame or window case allows windows to be replaced easily later. The fixings hold the window in place and transfer the forces on the window safely

into the building fabric. Construction tolerances must be taken into account in the installation. Forces in the plane of the window are transferred by compression on the support packers, while dowels, straps, fishtails, angles and anchors carry horizontal forces only. With this arrangement, deformations and imposed strains are avoided, which otherwise could have a detrimental effect on the functioning of the window. Screws and other installation fittings must be made from non-corroding materials.

REBATE SEALS

Irrespective of the window position in the reveal, the joint between the window and the building must be carefully formed. The joint is filled with a flexible sealant designed to allow movement. Two seals, one on the room side and one on the outside, seal the joint. The sealing system must be more effective inside than it is on the outside: Inside, in the warmth, it must be bonded continuously for its full length and be proof against water vapor. Outside, the sealant has to protect the joint against the effects of weathering, wind and moisture penetration. The require-

1 The surrounding loadbearing construction transfers loads arising from shrinkage and creep, thermal expansion and deflections in the lintel zone to the window. Added to this are loads caused by opening and closing, the general use of the window, dead weight and wind pressures. These forces must be borne by the fixings.

2 Principles for sealing a joint with the building: A sealant layer installed on the room side must act as an effective vapor barrier/stop.

3 Fixings:
a Wall anchor for plastic windows
b Claw brackets for wooden windows

4 Methods of fixing window frames:
a Frame dowels
b Sheet metal straps, claws or fishtails
c Frames/cases
d Loadbearing straps made from metal profiles
e Brackets
f Adjustable fixing systems
g Guide angles

5 Examples of specific installations. Seal at the joint between window and external wall in accordance with DIN 4108-7.

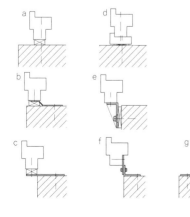

4

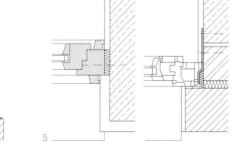
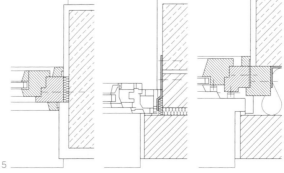

5

Examples of joint sealing in window installation:

6   Joint seal tape for the joint between the window and the building component.

7   Internal masking, vapor diffusion-proof.

8   External masking around the outside of the window element.

9   Joint insulation between the window and the building component using in situ foam.

ments for sound insulation must be carefully considered in the design of the joint.

Usually in situ foam is used to provide insulation in the joint. It automatically adjusts to fill between uneven connection surfaces, such as brickwork. It is an inexpensive and technically good form of insulation, but it is not a sealant. Foams are not governed by DIN quality criteria and their use as installation foam in traditional German brick-paneled timber post-and-beam buildings and listed buildings is not permitted. Installation foam must never be assumed to carry load.

WINDOW INSTALLATION WITH CASES

A mounting case is an auxiliary construction that separates the formation of the window joint from the main processes of building and permits easy removal of the window when it requires replacement. It serves to fix the window and transfer the load from it, and acts as a stop or template for works in the reveal area (plaster, thermal insulation and bonding systems). The cases are installed in the basic fabric of the building. The delivery and installation of the windows can then take place during the finishings phase of the building. Cases have to

be precisely installed, in line, plumb and to the correct dimensions. They must be constructed and installed to ensure that the sealing requirements of the joint with the building and between the window frame and the case are met. Cases even out the movement in the joint with the building arising from floor deflections and thermal expansion of the window frame, and are especially beneficial with large windows. The case construction must not be allowed to reduce the effectiveness of the thermal separation of the window frame. Many windows are replaced as part of a building refurbishment project. Normally, these windows are built into the external wall and replacement is complex and costly, with plaster to be renewed inside and out. Therefore, a special system for older buildings has been developed, which entails leaving the old window frame in place in the external wall to act as a case. Damage to the interior and exterior plaster is then so little that the windows can be replaced without significant loss of functionality. In the post-war period in Germany, this was often done with a metal case known as a 'Monzazarge'. The advantage of the case lies in the simplification of the building process, time savings and ease of replacement.

WINDOW HARDWARE

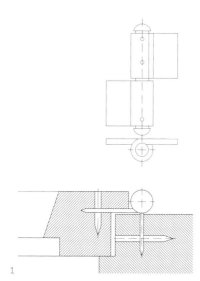

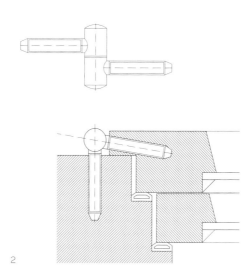

1

2

Window hardware is a term used to describe all the parts of a window with which it is opened, closed, moved, locked or held together. Hardware items are generally made of metal or plastic.

HINGED FITTINGS

Hinges form the moving connection between the sash and window frames. There are different types with different installation methods. Usually they are two-part hinges, often described as drill-in hinges, in contrast to a surface hinge, which is screwed or nailed in place, or a mortise hinge (butt hinge) or lift-off hinge, which is notched in.

Mortise hinges have plates that are mortised into the frame. Slots or notches are formed with a routing machine or manually with a mortising chisel in the wood of the sash or the door leaf and frame. A mortise hinge plate is then placed in each slot or notch. Then metal pins are driven through the frame and predrilled holes in the hinge to fix the hinge in place. Alternatively, screws can be used. This practice was common at the start of the 1960s. Mortise hinges are only used with rebated windows. They can be lifted off and consist of two plates; the bottom one with the pintle on the window frame and the top one with the gudgeon on the sash. There are different types, depending on the length and shape of their knuckles, including the olive and bullet knuckle hinges.

Drill-in hinges are fixed in place with drill-in studs. They are drilled into the window frames using jigs or templates. Surface mounted butt hinges have leaves which are usually attached by screws to the frames.

Pivot hinges allow you to design hidden openings. Angle hinges and corner angle hinges are used to attach a sash at a corner and give it extra strength.

Strap and snake hinges and their variations rely on the same principle as angle corner hinges. They are shaped like an S or a rounded shovel.

The choice of hinges is usually governed by the weight of the frame and glass they have to carry. Drill-in hinges may be two- or three-part, depending on the estimated load, which increases with the sash size.

Hinged fittings are made of steel or aluminum. The design and choice of fastenings is determined by the frame material. In wood they are drilled, mortised or routed; in plastic they are drilled or screwed, while hardware for aluminum frames is screwed, clamped or welded in place.

The surface finish of the hinges is particularly important, as the hinge knuckles are normally visible and contribute to the look of the window. The range of surface finishes include matt-nickel plated, chromium plated, stainless steel and standard color plastic coatings. The quality of the surface finish is important, not just on aesthetic grounds. It also has to provide the hinges with appropriately durable corrosion protection. If possible, stainless steel hinges should be used in damp rooms or in locations exposed to extreme weather conditions. Anodized aluminum provides very good protection against corrosion.

1   Lift-off hinge

2   Drill-in hinge

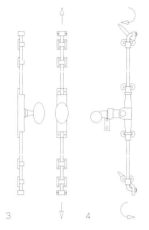

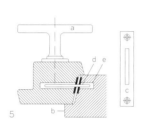

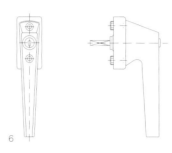

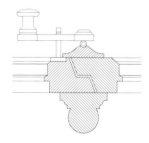

3 Surface-mounted window mechanism with lever bolt (bascule, cremone) and handle, still in common use in France. The bolts lock top and bottom.

4 The turning bolts, espagnolette, consist of an iron rod with attached hooks. Turning the rods causes them to engage in the window frame and lock the window.

5 Sash fastener:
a Handle
b Window frame
c Strike plate
d Tongue
e Machined slot

6 Lever handle, lockable

FUNCTIONAL HARDWARE

If movements beyond simple edge pivoting of the sash are required, then functional hardware must be used. Functional hardware includes: Rooflight fittings, tilt-turn, horizontally pivoting, sliding window, vertically pivoting and intrusion resistant fittings (mushroom-head locking points).

The tilt-turn window is typically found in German post-war buildings. About 85 % of all windows installed in Germany since the war have sashes which can be set to tilt or turn. DIN 68121 was introduced in Germany in 1968 and covers the design and construction of wooden tilt-turn windows.

Tilt-turn fittings are designed for one-handed operation. They allow window and window-door sashes to be operated by a hand lever (handle) and brought into a pivoted position or by means of a scissor mechanism into a tilted setting. When set for gap ventilation, the window is opened only a limited amount and the sash is normally tilted. This is a simple way to ventilate a room without having to open the window fully. Gap ventilation achieves only a certain rate of air change, which generally depends on the size of the gap. Over a long period, gap ventilation is as effective as purge or cross ventilation. With a simple side-hung casement window, the sash is held open by a stay with a special hook and eye fitting.

WINDOW LOCKS/CLOSURE FITTINGS

The most common form of window hardware is the turning handle. Various functions are performed just by turning it: Opening, closing, tilting. In Germany, a window handle

7

was earlier referred to as an olive. The name came about because of the noticeable thickening around the middle of the short, two-armed lever where the handle was connected to the spindle. When viewed from inside the room, these handles looked like olives. Since then they have been replaced by single armed levers. The single armed lever allows the user to exert a greater force when moving the inner mechanism and gives a clear visual indication of whether the sash is locked.

Simple locking fittings include the bolt, which can be drawn or slid into position, the quarter-turn sash fastener, either single or double armed, which clamps by friction on to a wire stirrup (either to the top or side). Other locking fittings include wing hooks, pivoting bolts, drop latches, turning bolts or espagnolettes, and lever bolts (bascule bolt, cremone).

SYSTEM WINDOWS

DESIGNING WITH WINDOW TYPES

The more complex the functions performed by the hardware are, the more precisely the fittings must be installed and matched with the rest of the window components. This complexity of function is only possible with manufacturer-specific window types and systems. Simple window factories are no longer able to manufacture such complicated windows. The architect therefore is tasked with searching out compatible window systems and combining them in accordance with their stated parameters, which are generally dictated by the system.

The desire for narrow, slender frames requires accurately designed window construction. The development of profiles over recent years, as well as the increasing importance of energy conservation, has resulted in a movement away from wide, high performance frames to narrow frames. ⟶ p. 58 The structural engineering requirements of the frame material can be satisfied equally well in a wide, hollow profile as they can in a flat, narrow profile, such as is used in post and rail facades.

Often the answers lie in the transformation of the principles behind traditional regional window designs. This approach creates new scope for design in conjunction with advances in hardware technology, reduction in functions, more accurate analyses and the optimization of technical requirements. The principle of narrow but deep frame profiles can be found in the Berlin-style window, a historic, inward-opening wooden window type. The general lack of light in the typically congested Berlin block development districts and high room ceilings could have led to the development of this type of window.

A further field of profile development is the simplification of the hardware technology and the reduction of tilt-turn functions to simple turn, tilt outwards, pivot or slide mechanism. Manufacturers are working closely with architects on this. The exchange of specialist knowledge of the requirements of window construction from one side, and the architectural design requirements from the other, sets off an evolutionary process out of which come innovative solutions.

OUTWARD-OPENING WINDOWS / SLIDING WINDOWS

These window types can only be slid, or turned or pivoted outwards to open; only in this way can the outwardly slender framed appearance be achieved, because in this case the hardware mechanics determine the design of the profile. The individual window elements can be combined with one another and placed in series to form a window wall. There are limits to the maximum height, width and weight of the individual elements. How to clean the window must also be taken into account. The methods

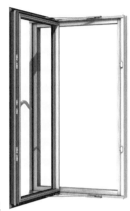

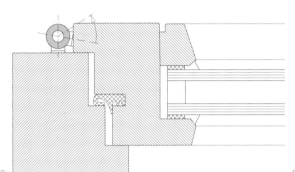
2a

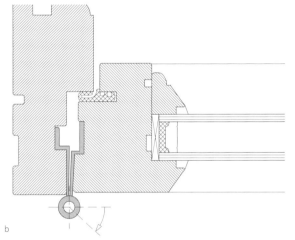
b

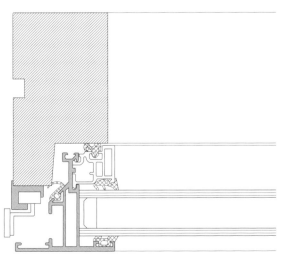
c

1   Sidehung projecting window

2   Profile comparisons from high to deep profiles, scale 1:2:

a   Simple standard wooden profile

b   The traditional Hamburg-style wooden window has been rediscovered, which opens outwards like its Danish and Swedish forerunners, with very simple hardware. The outward opening sashes are particularly wind- and weathertight. The sashes can be opened without obstruction even with a full window sill; a simple and easy way to provide healthy, energy-saving pulse ventilation. They can be recognized by the apparent narrowness of the sash profile and mullion. In the upper storeys they cannot be cleaned from the inside.

c   Wood / aluminum window with very narrow frame and sash widths. There is no apparent offset between opening and fixed glazing. U_w-values up to 0.9 W/m²K are possible. This example shows: Air permeability in accordance with EN 12207 up to class 4, driving rain resistance in accordance with EN 12208 up to class 9A, intrusion resistance in accordance with ENV 1627: 1999 up to class WK3.

3, 4 Room-high glazing can be designed with slender profiles with a cross sectional depth of 137 to 157 mm and a visible width of 68 mm.
With sash sizes up to 15 m², the frame members can be installed flush with the surfaces at the floor, lintel and reveal.
The sliding sash is on the outside in the front of the frame. Rollers allow the sliding sashes to move without the need for brush seals.

3

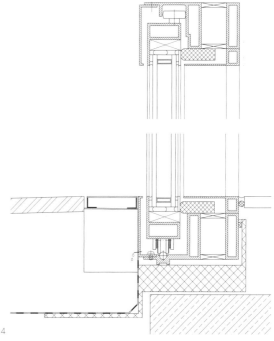

4

Requirements of the bottom connections DIN 18195 ff.

of cleaning, maintenance and care of a window should be considered at the time of design. This is simple with windows that are accessible from the outside from terraces or balconies. Fixed glazing, sliding windows or windows that only open outwards should be accessible from the outside. Otherwise they have to be cleaned using an aerial platform or cradle.

Sliding/pivoting windows can be used for multi-storey buildings if they are to be cleaned from the inside. The combination of sliding and pivoting avoids difficult situations, for instance with 3-sash windows. Also cleanable from the inside are vertically pivoting windows, which can be turned on a central pivot. Turning them round completely brings the outer pane to the inside for cleaning.

The quality of sliding windows depends on the material, system and manufacturer. The seal and the ease of cleaning of sliding windows becomes a problem above the first floor and needs special connection details. It should be borne in mind when designing multistorey buildings that at least one window component of sliding or outside-opening windows will have to be cleaned from the outside. Ground-level openings with no threshold can be achieved by using lifting-sliding door mechanisms, inlaid rain channels and lowering brush seals. Vertical sliding—gap ventilation solutions offer better resistance to intrusion. They offer ventilation comfort through the louver grill module integrated into the handle side of the case. Continuous ventilation is therefore available without having to open the sliding door.

Connection to a building plinth:
The wetting of the connection from surface, spray or seepage water requires a 150 mm seal taken up the wall above the damp-proof membrane, the surface of the paving or the drainage layer.
It must be secured against slipping and kept in place by an intact, impermeable, smooth, load-bearing backing layer.

Arrangement of the seals at a door threshold:
1 The required height of seal cannot usually be achieved at entrances for the disabled, terrace doors, balconies or roof terraces.
2 Clamping strips can produce a watertight junction
3 Shallow threshold connections or those with no upstand can be protected from the worst effects of water by features such as canopies, facade projections and/or drainage channels with grates.

Connections at doors:
1 Connection height 150 mm above top of paving or gravel fill
2 The connection height may be reduced if water can be completely drained away in the area of the door by shaping the terrace or by a drainage channel. The connection height should be a minimum of 50 mm from the top of the seal/connection plate under the weatherbar/plinth profile.
3 Barrier-free thresholds have to be specially designed.

MAINTENANCE / REFURBISHMENT OF OLD WINDOWS

1   2   3

Windows must receive regular maintenance. Good accessibility makes it easier to carry out regular maintenance and repairs, which results in lower maintenance costs. The seal and the associated energy loss depend on regular adjustment of the fittings and care or renewal of the seal. In earlier times, the local carpenter came along once a year shortly before the onset of winter and adjusted all the old windows so that the optimum contact pressure was maintained. As this does not take place any more, it is not surprising that old windows do not work as they should. Although new windows are always easier to clean than older ones, regular maintenance of the parts more exposed to the weather is still necessary. If they are in good condition, the windows will last longer and be more effective. All seals, hardware, glass interfaces and surfaces should be regularly checked. It is recommended that when you buy a new window you also enter into a maintenance contract with the supplier and specify the scope and level of service. Correctly designed and installed seals, either retrofitted into old windows or as replacements for old seals in modern windows, can raise the temperature in a room by 1–3 degrees without increased expenditure on heating. A gap 1 millimeter wide and 1 meter long can reduce the insulation value of a window by 65%.

REFURBISHING WINDOWS

The normal life of solid, well-maintained wooden windows can be 100 years or more. Therefore, original baroque windows are only found in listed buildings today. This indicative value for service life can only be applied to wooden windows, because no other window material has been in use for such a long period.

Intact windows offering examples of 19th century carpentry are still present in some of our buildings, but they are rapidly disappearing under the drive for buildings to have energy passports. In 1980, the annual demand for windows in Germany was approximately 10 million units, with half of these being installed in single and multiple household dwellings. 10 to 20% of these units were required for refurbishing older properties. In 1995, 26 million windows were produced, over 60% of them in plastic. Building renewal programs from the time of German reunification produced a rapid and sustained transformation over wide areas of the historic window landscape in Germany. The greater weight of insulating glazing requires thicker profiles and threatens proven traditional solutions. The window as a standardized mass-produced product has exerted pressure on manually crafted windows since 1960. This must be considered carefully and sensible solutions found. Nowadays, when the thermal and noise insulation performance of a window needs to be improved, the whole window is usually quickly replaced. Many old windows are discarded out of ignorance. There are historic components, often a whole system made of frame profiles typical of the region, forged hinge and closing fittings or custom-made filtering and shading elements and sometimes even complete, cased carpentry works. Its value in terms of craftsmanship and as an example of the history of building technology is quickly overlooked and the window considered as merely a functional and locking component of the building. It is frequently forgotten that the desired functions would be fully available again after repair, improvement or augmentation. From a historic and architectural point of view, the window must be viewed in its close relationship with the facade and the appearance of the building, both inside and out. The aspect of building physics is important, too; the repair or replacement of a window should be viewed at in the context of the general standard of the building. The replacement of windows can have effects on the whole fabric of the building.

Defect record:
Condition survey of an existing window in an old building before drawing up detailed measures:
1 Window before refurbishment
2 Defect record of the whole system; items noted include damaged metal angles, wooden components or joints to be replaced.
3 Window after refurbishment

Repair:
Window repair must be considered in relation to the design of the window and the whole building. This applies equally to the replacement of wearing parts and glass. In particular, the following should be taken into consideration when deciding on the dimensions of glass panes:
– Dimensions of the glass sheets produced by the glassworks
– Transport limits on the streets and turning circles
– How the glass will be moved around the building; the options available may become restricted or disappear during construction as the interior works are competed. Therefore the designer should look in particular at: Clearances at door openings, staircases and passageways, lifts, access to the windows

Window or glazing putty acts as an additional seal on the glass. It can replace the glazing bead and give the glass extra support. Traditional putty is a mixture of chalk and linseed oil. The glazing cavity in insulating glazing must not be completely sealed or condensation water will build up. The sash frame has a glazing rebate ventilation hole to allow the moist air to diffuse outwards.

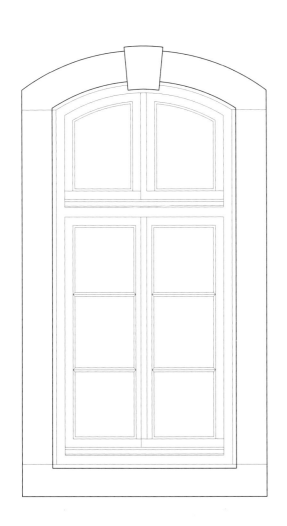

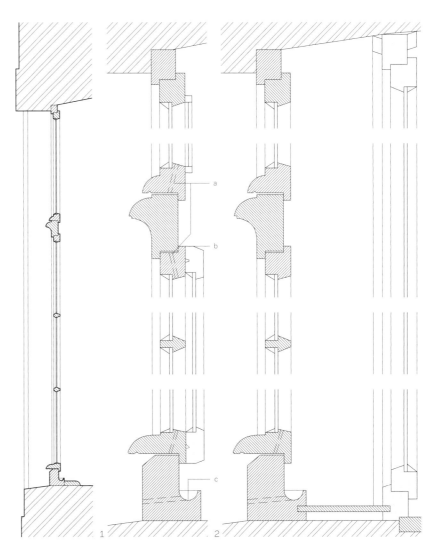

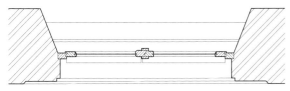

Planning condensation drainage for the space between the panes during the repair of a historical window:

1 Principle: compound double window:
a Retrofitted ventilation/ de-aeration
b Retrofitted sealing
c Internal gutter for condensation in winter
2 Principle: box window

UPGRADING OPTIONS

The most airtight window is not always the best. In older buildings with inadequately insulated external walls, windows being too airtight can lead to damage such as rot and mould. Wooden windows ensure air changes take place; this was essential in the days of open fires and stoves, which depended on air from the room. Wood has the advantage that it shrinks in summer and allows more ventilation. In the winter it swells and becomes more airtight. The predominant material for historic windows was wood: mainly softwoods such as pine and spruce, but also resistant hardwoods, such as oak. Building conservation bodies place an emphasis on the preservation and repair of historic windows (retention of listed building classification). In Europe, whole towns and districts can be protected as conservation areas. If a building is listed, the conservation authorities must be consulted in every case.

Historic windows can be upgraded by various means. There is the simple option of having the windows repaired or restored by a craftsman, who would renew wear parts such as weather bars or parts of the window frame or opening sash. Renewal of the putty is often necessary, which was made to an old recipe from a mixture of chalk and linseed oil.
Another possibility is to improve the thermal and sound insulation properties of a window by adding a secondary glazing element, e.g. making it into a composite, double or box window. Non-airtight windows can have new seals added in grooves cut into the frames. If this is done, the possibility of condensation must be taken into consideration, which will largely depend on the window construction and the characteristics of the particular building. Incorrectly attached seals can cause damage to historical windows. The appearance of the hardware can become unattractive as a result of room moisture load-

ings and wood rot. The coating used when repainting windows must be compatible with the background and should generally be permeable to water vapor. Historical records should be consulted. Good results can be obtained with resin-free linseed oil paints. Maintenance intervals should be specified contractually. The latest developments in refurbishment techniques and the use of suitable woods and materials have to be incorporated into the guidance documents.

RETROFITTING OF INSULATING GLAZING

A window does not just consist of the frame material and its construction: there is often historic glass typical of particular epochs present, such as cylinder glass, crown glass and hexagonal glazing. The associated specific fastening techniques such as lead bars, grooves, winders and putty are also characteristics of historical value. The glass surface has a great influence on the appearance of a facade and on the internal appearance, especially on the impression given to the observer. This applies both to tinted and clear glass. A window with slightly wavy glass gives different reflections and views out compared to a window with float glass panes. Glass manufacturers offer special restoration glass for use when replacing broken panes or installing double glazing to maintain the compatibility between glass and frame.
This restoration glass is manufactured by the Fourcault process and recreates the characteristics of the various epochs. Glass with the ability to filter out UV radiation and short-wavelength light is produced for use in museums and galleries to prevent damaging valuable cultural objects by the bleaching of dyes and pigments.
Special insulating glazing units with reduced thickness are now available. ➔ 2 These units can be retrofitted if the hinges, frame profiles and sash bars are strong enough to carry the increased weight of glass without

1 View out of Goethe's birthplace, a house in Frankfurt am Main. A colorless glass with the characteristic irregular surface of old window glass.

2 The slimmer installed thickness of the special insulating glazing units maintains the original appearance of existing windows with traditional putty seals.
Here shown in comparison with current glazing techniques incorporating glazing beads and weather bars.

3 Upgrading a historic profile: Renewal of weather board, driving rain diverted.

4 Special insulating glass preserves the original appearance of the existing window and traditional putty seal in this listed building. The dimensions of the frame must be checked to see if it can accommodate the glass or requires to be machined. Thermal insulation of the glazing in accordance with DIN 4108.

2

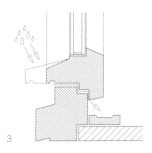

3

Thickness	Sound insulation	U_w-value [W/m² K]
10 mm	34 dB	1.8
11 mm	34 dB	1.8
12 mm	34 dB	1.4
13 mm	34 dB	1.4

4

5, 6 Improvement of thermal performance by the use of low-emissivity double glazing (Low-E glass).

7 Historic sash bars with putty.

8 Dimensions of real sash bars for insulating glass by comparison: Small-format insulating glass units resembling glazing with actual sash bars are designed for higher physical loadings. Sash bars in the glazing cavity are not real sash bars but create a more refined appearance:

a–d glazing bars, thermally decoupled, single panes:
a wooden glazing bars
b plastic glazing bars with aluminum bar
c light metal glazing bars
d wooden glazing bars, light metal bar
e–f imitation glazing bars:
e Viennese sash bars: Glued spacers in the glazing cavity do not divide the glazed area, sash bar profiles are attached to the outer surfaces. The system carries no loads.
f Swiss cross: Powder-coated aluminum sash bars are built into the glazing cavity.

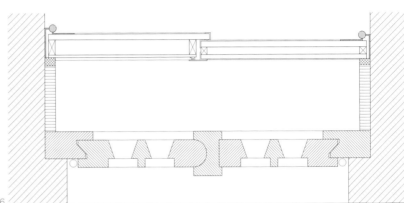

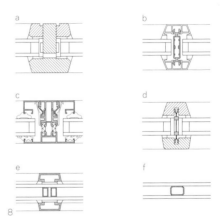

damage. This is possible with smaller window elements. The additional weight of this glass can be about 2.5 kg for a 40 cm x 35 cm pane. Nevertheless, this can amount to as much as 15 kg with 6 panes in the frame and a total sash size of 1.20 m x 1.00 m.

The amount of light entering the room is reduced when insulating glass is fitted. In spite of the good thermal insulation properties of insulating glazing units, it should not be forgotten that single-paned glazing has a better g-value. Given a favorable orientation, the solar energy admitted to a room through a single-glazed window can be higher under certain circumstances and there may be no overall energy saving effect from the installation of a new window with insulating glass. In a careful cost comparison of window replacement or repair, it must always

be appreciated that only new windows with the required U-values will be able to completely fulfill the thermal insulation requirements.

The weight and construction of the glazing demands larger dimensions for frames and sash bars, which frequently are glued on to both sides. The solution no longer follows the principle of the original. If insulating glazing cannot be avoided, concealed metal profiles can be used to reduce the dimensions of the glazing bars dividing the glazed area. In the case of listed buildings, the complete retention of windows may be imposed as a condition. Application to the authorities for confirmation of an exemption from the Energy Conservation Act is recommended in this case.

WINDOW REPLACEMENT IN A HISTORICAL CONTEXT

If it is not possible to retain a part or the whole of a historic hinge, or a suitable hinge of the right constructional type or design cannot be found for the listed building or ensemble, then the use of a new window, appropriate for the location, should be contemplated.

This window should be appropriate in the choice of materials, function and form and of a construction that accords with the design of the historical window in the listed building. The style of the windows here must be expressed but given a new yet appropriate interpretation. As a rule, wood is the most suitable material, but metal profile solutions are also available.

New windows in a listed building or ensemble are not a replacement for the loss of historic building fabric and therefore do not have to be faithful to the original down to the last detail. However, a form of construction should be chosen that if necessary has slender wooden cross sections, divides the glazed surface appropriately and allows the use of standard profiles.

Developing special profiles for windows in a historic context is always more expensive than the use of standard windows and is encountered less often in practice.

This independent route is only possible with the knowledge contained in the previous sections. But it offers a quite different quality that is hardly ever attained with standardized window manufacturing systems. Detailed drawings down to a scale of 1:1 should be produced as part of the meticulous process of designing a new window and the manufacture of a sample window is worthwhile. In many cases this is possible when designing box or composite windows.

It is important to pay attention to details such as the type and number of opening sashes and the shape of the weather bars, sills, flashing of the external window sills and depth of the window frames. Wooden weather bars are in accord with the appearance of historic windows. Likewise the designer should choose traditional hardware, which is still manufactured by specialist companies. Standardization since 1960 and the applicable regulations can be only a guide here. The detailing of the metal drainage profiles required today leads to a conflict of objectives.

1

2

Example of a reinterpretation by architects Philippe Vander Maren and Mireille Weerts with the extension to the former presbytery in Leuven, where details such as the reduction to a horizontal window bar and the choice of an internal glazing bead made from a delicate steel angle profile were used. The choice of internal sunshading in the form of traditional internal shutters leaves the external facade completely untouched. The intervention exhibits subtlety in the use of characteristic red and white striped internal shutters, which are divided into two parts. From the inside, they set the color theme, from the outside they make an interesting sight from the road, varied by the numerous options for folding them.

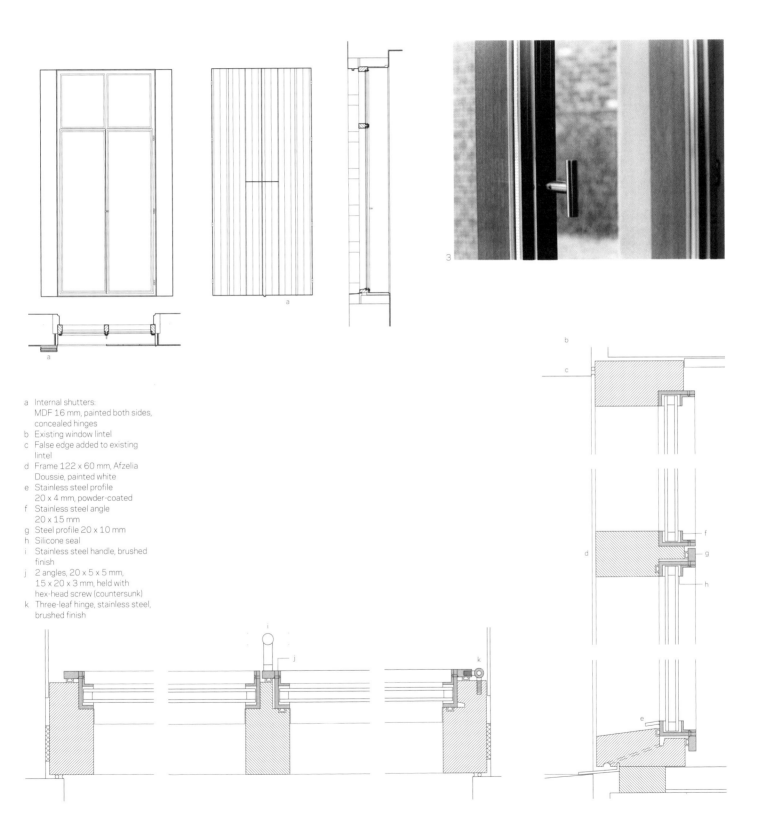

a Internal shutters:
  MDF 16 mm, painted both sides,
  concealed hinges
b Existing window lintel
c False edge added to existing
  lintel
d Frame 122 x 60 mm, Afzelia
  Doussie, painted white
e Stainless steel profile
  20 x 4 mm, powder-coated
f Stainless steel angle
  20 x 15 mm
g Steel profile 20 x 10 mm
h Silicone seal
i Stainless steel handle, brushed
  finish
j 2 angles, 20 x 5 x 5 mm,
  15 x 20 x 3 mm, held with
  hex-head screw (countersunk)
k Three-leaf hinge, stainless steel,
  brushed finish

SPECIFICATION OF WOODEN WINDOWS
ADVICE ON SPECIFICATION

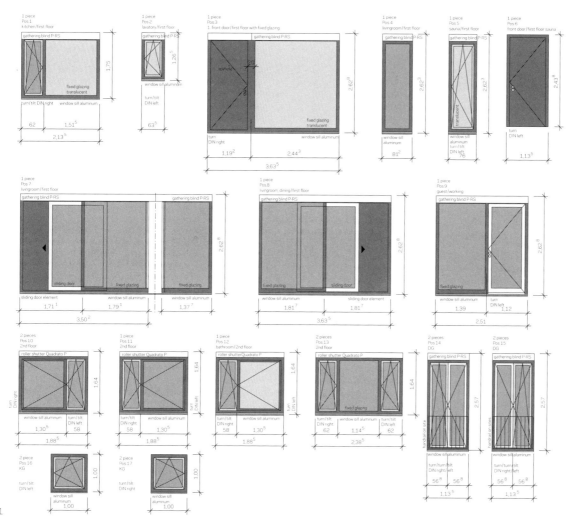

1   Example window schedule for a wooden window tender:

Location: Building class 1 Section 2 Cl. 3 Hesse Building Regulations, ±10.45 m AOD, building height. External facade

Frames: Wood type Niangon; alternative native Douglas fir 3x glued, color as specified

Sash: Wood type Niangon oiled

Glazing: Thermal insulating glass U_g = 1.0 W/m²K,
Float glass panes 4/10/4, g = 60 %,
U-value: Window U_w = 1.3 W/m²K incl. frames

Hardware: Siegenia Favorit or equivalent hinges, e.g. drill-in hinge, matt nickel-plated steel

Handles: FSB Type, stainless steel

Rain protection: Ev 1 anodized Channels

Window sills: Outside Ev 1 anodized, inside Niangon oiled

Sunshading: Inbuilt module system Outside suitable plaster for external blinds incl. guide channels

Operation: Hand crank from indoors, inspection from below regular

As required care and cleaning, regular inspection. Inspection interval for damage, dirt, corrosion acc. weather conditions.

Maintenance: Lubricate and check the hardware once per year. Wood surfaces should be reoiled at regular intervals.

All high quality construction begins with a technically correct specification. This is an important precondition to receiving a quote or bid for products that fulfill the desired and legal requirements and to ensuring a defect- and damage-free execution. The goods and services must be clearly and unambiguously described, so that the prices returned by the various suppliers (or tenderers in the case of a tender) can be properly compared.

Specifications often use clauses from official sources such as the German library of specification texts for standard construction works (StLB) written by the joint committee for information technology in building and construction (GAEB). All content is checked and if necessary edited and updated every six months. The standard library covers the full range of building and construction but addresses the specific particularities of windows and external doors only to a limited extent. Tenders issued by public bodies (including national, regional, city and district authorities) are modified with their own special regulations and requirements.

Specifications may also be written in terms of a description of functions in which, apart from the dimensions, sash division and color, only functions such as thermal and sound insulation are given, and the choice of construction is left to the tenderer.

Preparing tender documents with a full specification in which all the important details are given requires a great deal of specialist knowledge. The author will need to find, read and understand the content of relevant DIN standards, edit it to suit the project and incorporate it into his own text. Keeping the text up to date and checking the validity of the standards and guidance documents is very time consuming. Normally, a numbered window schedule or list ↘1 giving the window sizes, sash division and

Since 02/2007 product standard EN 14351-1 applies to windows and external doors. It sets out the performance characteristics for windows and external doors with no requirements for resistance to fire or the spread of smoke. This allows the application of the CE mark to windows and outside doors.
The European Construction Products Directive is implemented with EN 14351-1.

The CE mark indicates conformity (compliance) of the product with the relevant European directives and allows the product to be traded within Europe.
But the process of tendering is not made simpler as a result of the new product standard.
Tendering resource can be used at the website of the German window research institute ift in Rosenheim to create technically competent and standards-compliant tender documents for windows and external doors. In addition, the specifier is offered practical information in the form of explanations and detailed drawings for drawing up technically correct tender documents.

opening type for each item in the bill of quantities is prepared. Important points that cannot be described in this simple form should be included on the drawings. This information often includes the method of attaching the window frame to the building fabric.

TECHNICAL PREAMBLE

The preamble contains all the basic information applicable to all the goods and services in the tender. In addition to all the tender information that is the same for all projects, it also highlights special information relevant to particular items. The information is generally split up into the requirements for the design, materials, construction and installation of windows.

GENERAL NOTES

The general notes contain a list of contract conditions, the applicable DIN standards, the construction contract procedures (VOB in Germany) and the general conditions of contract used. It is recommended that the drawings of the principal details of the window construction and methods of attachment to the building fabric are independently checked before the window manufacturer starts production.

DESIGN REQUIREMENTS

EN 14351-1 is the product standard for windows and external doors not required to resist fire or prevent the spread of smoke. The product standard applies across Europe and determines most of the properties and performance classes of windows and external doors, irrespective of the material. Designers, users and manufacturers rely on the product standard to provide the basis for the assessment of windows and doors in general and in specific usage situations. The designer can determine the performance requirements from this product standard taking into account the relevant national regulations. The normative requirements from the standard are: Resistance to wind loads, snow and permanent loads. Basic performance characteristics such as resistance to driving rain, air permeability, heat transfer coefficient, sound insulation, durability, long-term tests and intrusion resistance are also covered. In addition, there are separate selection criteria such as installation height, wind loading zone and terrain categories.

Technical and constructional requirements include:
Connections to the building fabric at the side masonry rebates and at the lintel, frame section geometries, rebate shapes, weather bars and window materials, loadbearing requirements of the window construction and the connections. Here it should be checked by calculation that all the design forces on the window can be borne and transferred

into the building structure. Wind loads are taken from DIN 1055-4. Vertical forces such as forces on the sides from opened sashes are assessed in accordance with DIN 1055-3. Profiles between two supported points may only deflect a maximum of 1/300 x length, and a maximum of 8 mm between the pane corners in the case of multipane insulating glazing. Window wall anchorages are governed by DIN 18056, with fixing points every 0.80 m.
In principle, a tender document should cover four important aspects required for a technically competent specification of the goods and services provided in the contract:
1. Location and basic information: The basic information for achieving a technically competent specification for the project includes, for example, the conditions of use (new build, building restoration, window refurbishment, new wall opening, etc.).
2. Requirements in accordance with EN 14351-1: The parameters given in EN 14351-1 are considered and listed for selection. The user can specify the standard classes or include his own information.
3. Material-specific requirements and characteristics: This section contains information about different frame materials, in particular wood, wood-metal, metal and plastic.
4. Connections and installation: The specifications for all aspects of the installation and connection to the building fabric are given here.

Checklist for a specification
- Number of units, position in the building
- Outside dimensions of the window frames
- Division, opening type (if necessary referring to notes on window schedule)
- Frame cross sections or information for calculation, or manufacturer's system
- Frame material
- Construction of spandrel or sill panels, or the necessary information
- Fixing and sealing of connection to building fabric, preferably with drawings and information about classification
- Hardware and opening type, locks, operating controls (window handle) and surface finish / color
- Safety class / noise reduction class
- Weather bars
- Sealing strips between sash and window frame, rebate type in terms of either outside rebate seal, middle seal, or room-side seal
- Air permeability / driving rain resistance
- Glazing type / thickness, glazing cavity / thickness and arrangement of panes (consider wind loads). In the case of functional glazing, precise information, e.g. sound, solar and thermal insulation, gas filling to glazing cavity / glass coatings
- Glass seals with information about the loading group, glazing type (wet or dry), information about glazing beads, gaskets, or putty
- Color of surface treatment
- Wood preservatives
- Paint system details (exposure group)
- Departures from general specification
- Instructions on care, necessary inspection intervals / maintenance measures

OPEN | CLOSE
FILTERS

INTRODUCTION / TYPES OF FILTERS

Openings mediate between interiors and exteriors. The filling element at the junction between the two varies. Constructed in different ways and from different materials, the facade may be open or transparent, permeable or translucent, multi-layered or homogenous: a facade is a filter. There are many possible constructions and arrangements for a filter system: folding, panel and sliding shutters, sun blinds, roller shutters, slatted or gathering blinds are only some of the many different systems on offer. Fundamentally, they can be divided into fixed, moveable and integrated systems. All of these regulate climatic and weather influences on the opening and on the interior space in a targeted way. They either allow moderated daylight and direct sunlight into rooms or exclude them entirely. They also provide effective privacy, noise reduction and intrusion prevention, in the night-time as well as during the day. The filter, as well as the opening itself, is an important functional element that also changes the face of a room. For instance: for a sliding / folding shutter, should the leaves be arranged to slide away symmetrically to either side, or only to one side? What are the material properties and transparency of the leaves? Is the guide rail for the leaves mounted visibly on the facade, or is it concealed? The construction and function of different filter systems require a specific geometrical space to be available in the wall or on the wall's surface—something which has to be considered in the first stages of planning. Owing to the complexity of the situation and all the different requirements, it is essential to plan filter systems carefully.

FIXED FILTERS

Fixed elements cannot be adjusted for changes in direct sunlight levels and in the course of the sun throughout the day or year. This must be taken into account when constructing them. Examples include projecting components such as porches, balconies, cornices, horizontal and vertical shades, brise soleils, loggias and fixed louvers. Depending on the construction method and the filter layer's depth, they may create an interesting in-between space that can be used for other purposes.

FLEXIBLE FILTERS

Flexible filter elements can be adjusted to the time of day or desired amount of sunlight. Light management systems adjust the daylight yield to the function of the room. As filters work in different ways, the sun control and light management systems must be tailored to the specific space.

INTEGRATED FILTERS

Integrated filter systems are filter systems that are part of the glazing. Certain glazed surface structures and special electro-optical or temperature-sensitive layers reflect or absorb incident light. Other options include glazing with integrated slats or expanded metal inserts and special structures that direct sunlight and ensure a mainly diffuse daylight yield.

1 Alten- und Pflegeheim, Steinfeld, 2005, by Dietger Wissounig: flexible wooden filters create a familar atmosphere similar to those in local barns.

2 Villa Shodhan, Ahmedabad, 1951–1956, Le Corbusier: brise soleil, mood of the light in the living room.

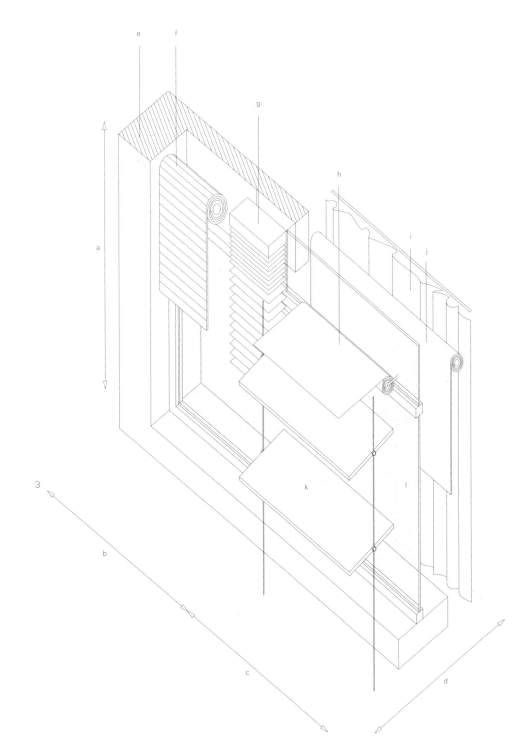

3 Axonometric view of sun control systems, including fixed shading, roller shutters, external gathered blinds, sun blinds, internal roller blinds and curtains, showing their position in relation to the wall construction.

a perforated facade
b homogeneous
c multilayer
d filter system depth
e roller shutter shaft with belt

Flexible filters:
f roller shutter
g external gathered blinds
h sunblind
i curtain
j inner roller blind

Fixed filters:
k external slats (fixed)

Integrated filters:
l glass with functional layer

SUN AND GLARE CONTROL SYSTEMS

Sun and glare control systems play an important role in energy conservation in residential and commercial buildings, as well as the well-being of users. Apart from integrated sun control systems, such as special-purpose glass or insulating glass with sun control inserts (horizontal slats) in the space between the panes, flexible external sun control systems can be installed. Depending on the way these are fixed and operated, they are described as panel, folding or sliding shutters, sun blinds, roller shutters, slatted blinds or gathered blinds. External installations make sense in energy terms, as they can respond flexibly to sunlight levels, interior conditions and the functions of rooms, as well as achieving a low solar energy transmittance by allowing moderate amounts of light, air and heat to enter. Another advantage of externally mounted devices is that they can remain in operation while allowing sliding windows and inward-opening casements to be opened. Such moveable, exposed components, however, are vulnerable to the wind and storms. This aspect is regulated by EN 13659, which classifies wind resistance. Germany is divided into four wind load zones, with terrain categories and installation heights also taken into account. ↘ tab 1, 2-p. 158

The European directive DIN EN 13659 is one of a series of directives on enclosing building elements as defined in EN 12216. In particular, these are products such as external slatted blinds, roller shutters, swing shutters, folding shutters with no tracks, folding shutters with tracks (flat-closing), folding shutters with tracks (accordion) or sliding shutters, with or without a tilting mechanism.

Internal and external filter systems for doors or windows that are designated as escape routes must also be hung in a way that leaves the route clear during emergencies. Emergency mechanisms for gathering blinds may be located, for instance, in the upper rail of the blind unit. They pull the hanging upwards without requiring electricity.

POSITION OF THE FILTERS

The higher the degree of reflection and the lower the g-value (the overall degree of solar energy transmittance), the more efficient a sun control system is. As a sun control system positioned in front of the glazing reflects most of the sunlight and prevents the room from overheating, external filter systems provide optimal sun control. The effectiveness of a sun control system can be estimated approximately using the solar heat gain coefficient. External systems are often difficult to implement in high-rise buildings, owing to wind exposure. Internal shade systems can be used instead—these are also easier to clean and to maintain.

The disadvantage of internal sun control systems is that any warmth generated remains within the room. As sunlight strikes the internal sun control, part of the radiation is converted to infrared radiation. As this long-wave radiation cannot pass out again through the window pane, it contributes to the heating of the room (a heat trap). In spite of this, internal filter systems are commonly used. External sun control devices are often not permitted on listed buildings and cannot be combined with certain facade designs.

SOLAR HEAT GAIN COEFFICIENT S

The solar heat gain coefficient is calculated by taking the sum of the heat gain through the glazing in relation to the floor area of the space within. The effective g-value (obtained from the g-value of the glazing reduced by a factor for the sun control system) is crucial. Reduction factors for sun control systems are specified by DIN 4108. However, it is a good idea to check the manufacturer's information for each individual product, as this often gives a better value. ↘ 2

$$S = \sum_j \frac{(A_{w,j} \cdot g_{total,j})}{A_G}$$

$A_{w,j}$	=	window surface areas, based on structural shell measurements [m²]
$g_{total,j}$	=	total energy transmittance of glazing, including sun control elements
g_{total}	=	$g \cdot F_C$
F_C	=	reduction factor of sun control devices
g	=	total energy transmittance
A_G	=	net floor area of the room or part of the room [m²]

1

1 Formula for calculating the solar gain value S.

2 Classification of sun control systems according to their position, from inside to outside. The reduction factors of each system are referred to in order to calculate the solar gain coefficient.

3 Functioning of internal and external sun control:
a outer
b inner

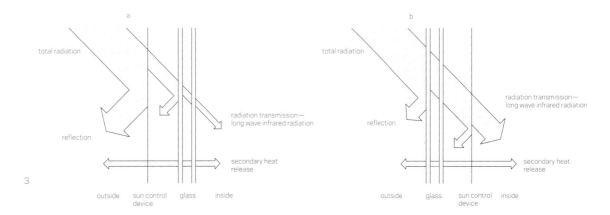

system	absent	on the pane	inner		between the panes	outer				
description		film	inner roller blind	inner slatted blind	roller blind between the panes	shading, canopy, loggia, balcony	external slatted blind	external roller blind	roller shutters, panel-sliding shutters	sun blind
reduction factor	1.0	0.3–0.5	0.6–0.7 0.4–0.5	0.5	0.5–0.6 0.3–0.4	0.3	0.25	0.4–0.5	0.3	0.4 0.5

2

a

total radiation

radiation transmission— long wave infrared radiation

reflection

secondary heat release

outside   sun control device   glass   inside

b

total radiation

radiation transmission— long wave infrared radiation

reflection

secondary heat release

outside   glass   sun control device   inside

3

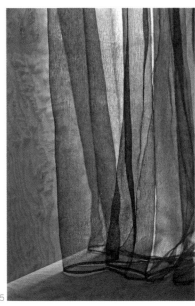

4 Apartment building in Carabanchel, 2007, by Foreign Office Architects: folding sliding shutters made from bamboo canes filter the direct sunlight and create an atmospheric play of light that changes throughout the day.

5 Studio in Haldenstein, 2004–2006, by Peter Zumthor: the airy curtain immerses the interior in atmospheric light.

4

5

ORIENTATION AND ALIGNMENT

A suitable filter is chosen based on a knowledge of the building's location, the climatic and weather conditions and the position of the opening in terms of orientation and altitude. Sun control, glare control, intrusion prevention, maintenance and ease of use are further important criteria.

The impact of sunlight on the facade depends on its orientation and the position of the sun at different times of the day or year. The position of the sun is given by the angle of solar elevation α and the azimuth angle β, which, in a two-dimensional projection, describes the deviation from true south. ➘2 In winter, the azimuth angle is very small, meaning that facades facing east or west receive little sunlight. Neighboring buildings or vegetation will also shade individual facades to varying degrees. The shade situation may furthermore be different for each storey or room.

SHADE SYSTEMS

Slatted structures can be adjusted to the changing position of the sun by adjusting their position. There are two different fundamental construction principles for slat structures. Horizontally arranged slats can exclude steeply inclined summer sunlight, or reflect it deep into the interior to improve interior lighting. Ideally, these systems are installed on the south side of a building. Vertical slat systems block incoming shallow sunlight, and are therefore suitable for east or west-facing facades.

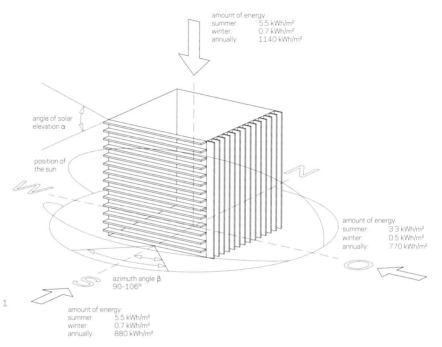

amount of energy:
summer: 5.5 kWh/m²
winter: 0.7 kWh/m²
annually: 1140 kWh/m²

angle of solar
elevation α

position of
the sun

amount of energy:
summer: 3.3 kWh/m²
winter: 0.5 kWh/m²
annually: 770 kWh/m²

azimuth angle β
90-106°

amount of energy:
summer: 5.5 kWh/m²
winter: 0.7 kWh/m²
annually: 880 kWh/m²

1 Diagram of the path of the sun in relation to a reference volume, showing the amount of energy incident on different surfaces of the building envelope, with separate values for a summer day, a winter day and the total annual insolation.

2 Specimen solar radiation values for different surfaces of the envelope of a building located in Stuttgart.

Surface	Summer day	Winter day
Horizontal		
Azimuth angle	55-305°	130-230°
Horizontal angle	0-63°	0-17°
Sun exposure duration	16 h	8 h
East/west		
Azimuth angle	55-180°/ 180-305°	130-180°/ 180-230°
Horizontal angle	0-63°	0-17°
Sun exposure duration	7.5 h	3.5 h
South		
Azimuth angle	90-270°	130-230°
Horizontal angle	33-63°	0-17°
Sun exposure duration	9 h	8 h

2

SUN CONTROL, GLARE CONTROL, LIGHT MANAGEMENT

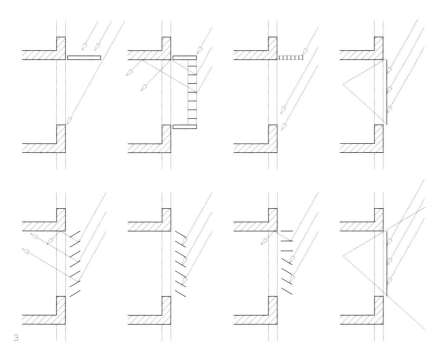

3

3   Principles of sun control systems and how they work.

4   Functioning of light-deflecting gathered blinds with two hanging zones:
a   computer screen work when the sun is shining. Light deflection/glare control
b   heat control
c   overcast day
d   computer screen work (in a deep room)

5   Functioning of perforated slats in winter and summer.

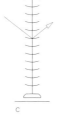

4   a   b   c   d

Requirements for computer workspaces according to workplace directives and DIN 5035 Part 2

Glare prevention:
max. luminance L < 400 Cd/m² acc. DIN 5035 and DIN 66234
Summer heat control:
solar gain values S < S_perm acc. DIN 4108-2
Brightness:
illuminance E > 300 Lux acc. DIN 5035 and DIN 5034
View of the outside:
required under workplace directive §7
Adjustability:
required under workplace directive §7

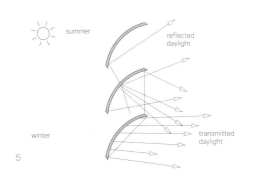

5

GLARE CONTROL

Glare can result from the direct or indirect incidence of sunlight or artificial light and by surface reflection. It can occur on the inside or outside of a building. The importance of avoiding glare depends on what rooms are used for—it is particularly important for office spaces with computer workspaces.

An internally installed anti-glare element can be used together with an external sun control element, thereby allowing desirable solar gain during the winter period. This moderates and redirects incoming daylight without actually reducing the daylight yield. At the same time, the view of the outside space should be retained as far as possible.

The curtains, sliding screens, roller blinds or slatted blinds used for internal glare control have implications for the interior, affecting its design both in their closed and in their open state. The way they function, the size of their individual elements and their materials and colors can structure the outer wall or create a particular lighting mood for the interior. If the anti-glare systems run in front of the wall, then the relevant sections of wall should be accessible.

Vertical slatted blinds can be adjusted on their vertical axis. They control the room's light level and can black it out completely if given the right coating. If the slats are in the right position, it is still possible to see out of the window. Blackout fabrics are specially classified fabrics that are generally coated with an artificial material on the side facing the light source.

LIGHT-DEFLECTING BLINDS

Light-deflecting blinds are vertical anti-glare systems. The individual slats, moved horizontally on cords, can be rotated around their lengthwise axis. In a process controlled by the slats' type and cross-section, light is redirected into the deeper parts of the room, creating uniform lighting with no glare.

Such light management systems are most commonly included in the planning of computer workspaces. Gathered blinds with two separately adjustable hanging sections are ideal for satisfying the requirements of workspace directives. The lower part of this kind of blind can be closed to provide glare control while allowing daylight into the deep part of the room through the slats in the upper section.

Perforated gathering blind slats are a technological refinement of conventional coated aluminum slats. Their transmittance is between 25% and 60% depending on hole diameter. They also restrict the view out.

CONSTRUCTION TYPES AND FUNCTION

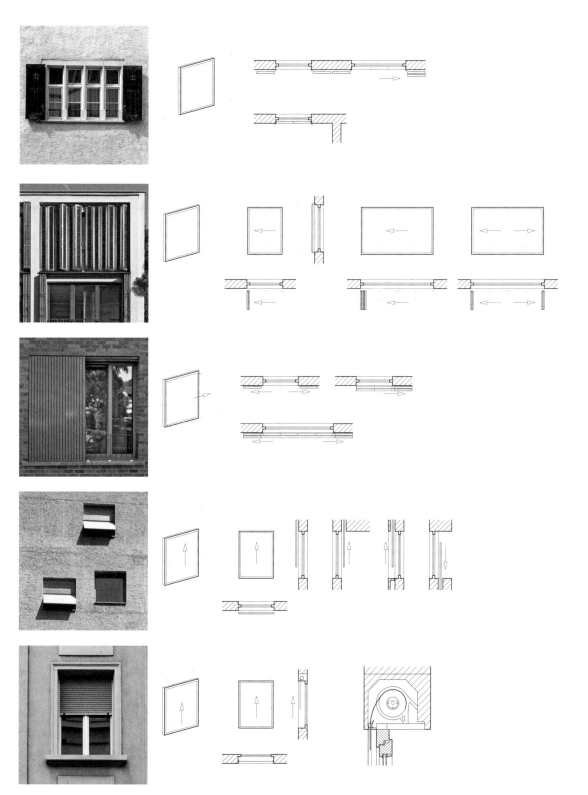

Panel shutters
Panel shutters are the archetypal flexible sun control. They are fixed at the side of the opening, either to the masonry or to the window frame, by hinges and pintles. A panel shutter is opened by turning it on the vertical axis; either to rest against the window reveal or further round against the facade.

Folding/sliding shutters
A folding/sliding shutter consists of connected vertical elements. Each of these moves along a guide rail at its fulcrum. The elements can be parked in the window reveals or in front of the facade. Folding and stacking the blinds reduces the area of facade needed, but creates a bulky package.

Sliding shutters
Sliding shutters move horizontally along guide rails, parallel to the facade. The shutters can be slid in one, two or more planes, as the depth of the construction increases. The size of the opening determines the shutters' dimensions. How the shutters lie when open should be taken into account when designing the facade.

Falling or pull shutters
Falling or pull shutters slide vertically. The shutter is integrated into the wall construction above or below the opening. It is slid along rails at the sides. Space has to be provided for the necessary counterweight as well as for the shutters.

Roller shutter systems
Roller shutters consist of linked, non-adjustable slats; they run in side-mounted U-channels. To open it, the roller shutter is pulled upward and coiled around a rotating shaft. The roller shutter has a weatherproof box, which can be mounted externally on the facade or integrated into the wall construction. The way the roller shutter is hung and the height of the opening determine the height and breadth of the shutter box.

Gathering blinds

Slatted or gathering blind systems move vertically. They are made from profiled slats restrained by guide rails or cords in the reveals at the sides of the window. The slats can be rotated on their longitudinal axis to regulate light influx. At rest, the slats form a compressed horizontal package in the blind box on the opening's upper edge. The height and breadth of the blind box depends on the opening's height and the nature of the hanging.

Sun blinds

A sun blind is a vertical sun control system. It consists of a textile sheet moved along rails or cords mounted at both sides. When not in use, the hanging is rolled up inside a blind box. Its light transmission and reflection level depend on the qualities of the textiles.

Awnings

The awning is a variation on the sunblind. An additional deflection roller and an extension arm allow for a partial view.

Drop-arm awnings

Two so-called drop arms are connected together at the ends by a tube. The fabric covering is rolled down over the facade at a fixed angle by means of gravity.

Jointed arm awning

Jointed arm or folding arm awnings allow the rolled textile covering to be extended at different angles and to different depths. An additional joint controls the awning's angle. Jointed or folding arm awnings are used as sun control for balconies and loggias or to shade display windows, as they can be extended some distance.

Folding sun sails

Folding sun sails can be used inside or outside. The textile covering moves along cables in sections of approx. 1 m or 2 m max. breadth and up to 10 m in length. An outdoor folding sun sail should be inclined to allow rainwater to run off rather than pooling. Depending on the intervals of the cable suspension elements in the covering, the drawn-in sun sail will form a package of about 25–50 cm thick.

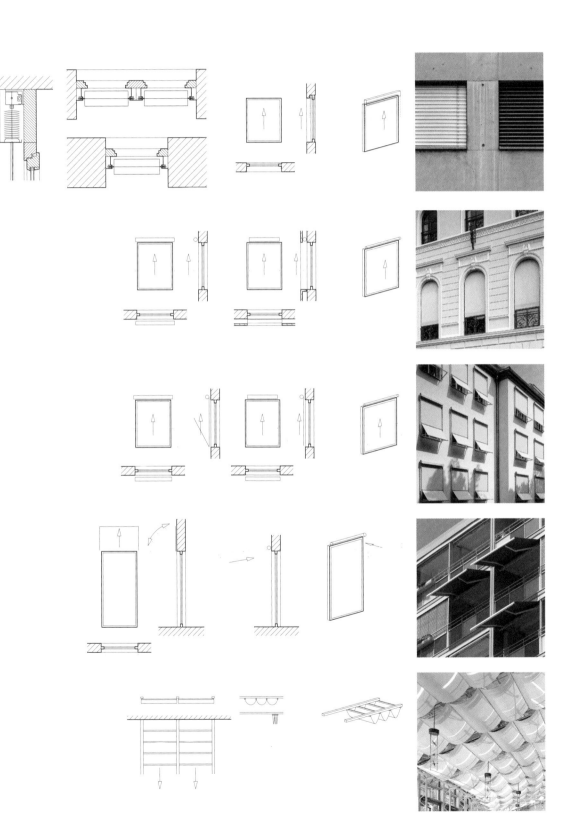

PANEL SHUTTERS / SWING SHUTTERS

WINDOW SHUTTERS

Simple board shutters developed over time into the large number of moveable elements mentioned above. Basic weather protection was gradually combined with a need for sun control and privacy. The French carpenter Cachot is considered the inventor of the first adjustable louvers, paving the way for all modern shade systems. External panel, sliding and folding shutters can be used to seal openings of almost full room height. Their size depends on the materials used and their strength and construction (type of fixing). They may be bolted on the inside to prevent intrusion. The heat transmission resistance of a panel shutter and the layer of air between the shutter and the window increase overall thermal insulation. It would be possible to classify this according to DIN V ENV 1627, but this has not yet been done. A fitting detail with a frame and a shutter having a solid, insulated construction and a sealing strip are ideal.

MATERIAL

Window shutters are traditionally made of wood—usually coniferous woods such as pine or fir. Hardwoods like oak and, today, occasionally tropical woods such as Meranti are used for parts of the construction requiring greater durability. Window shutters are exposed to the weather, and must retain their fit. They must therefore be well-protected. For wooden shutters, the usual rules for protecting wood constructions apply. A coat of paint or a thick-layer of varnish with a sufficient level of pigment provide good protection. Technical regulations do not permit simple impregnating varnishes or colorless coatings. Regular maintenance and repairs are also essential. For this reason, shutters are now also made from PVC or aluminum, extruded and powder-coated or partially roll-formed and coil-coated. PVC is not sufficiently light-resistant without additional surface treatment, especially when its color is dark, and furthermore it needs metal reinforcement.

FRAME

The frame is the loadbearing element that accommodates the panel elements and anchors the hanging components. It must be stable enough. The usual measurements for a wooden construction are: frame thickness 31 mm, breadth approx. 85 mm. For other materials, the proportions are similar. Where the frame is very tall, it will need to be braced horizontally by transom rails or rails, which can also be used as design elements.

PANELS

It is possible to use many different kinds of panel to fill in the frames:
– Non-projecting slats:
  Standard construction, angled arrangement, measurements for a wooden construction approx. 32 x 11 mm
– Projecting slats:
  angled arrangement, measurements for a wooden construction approx. 72 x 11 mm
– Bar panel:
  molded bars fitted into a groove (e.g. roller shutter laths) partially with slanted light slits
– Solid panel:
  tiles, panels or similar fitted into a groove.

The slats may also be adjustable. ➔1 Different types of panel can be combined within the frame, with a rail as a separator. A solid panel shutter can improve noise reduction.

PANELS

The simplest type of shutters are swing shutters. The leaves are turned on a vertical axis, a pivot set in close to the window reveals, swinging round to cover the opening. This may involve a single individual leaf or several connected (or coupled) individual leaves. The type of fitting used for swing shutters varies from region to region:
a Flush with the reveal
   reveal depth at least 40 mm
b Lying on the wall
   a wide gap between the shutter and the reveal when the shutter is open
c With rebate
   wooden panel shutters only
d In rebate
   standard construction for wooden casings
e On the window frame
   disadvantage: deeper reveals require longer pintles and hinges, less space for fastenings

There must be enough space for the opened leaves on each side of the window. For two-leaved shutters, half of the window's breadth plus 100 mm is taken as a rough benchmark. Where there is insufficient space, the leaves must be divided into halves which are then coupled. If there is not enough space between two windows, then the shutter leaves can overlap, although this means that they will have to be opened and closed in sequence. When planning a new building, care should therefore be taken that the windows are not too large and that there is enough space for the opened shutters. This should also be factored in when planning a dormer.

External wooden panel shutters are used as weather protection. Indoors, they were used in the past to shade rooms containing light-sensitive textiles, furniture or wooden surfaces.

1 Tilt shutter panel.

2 This kind of fitting did not remain widespread in the long term because it was hard to operate. For rows of windows with no space for swing shutters to be folded back, modern fittings provide folding and sliding solutions. It is also now possible to operate the shutters from the inside by means of a crank, without having to open the window. Where this is the case, hand cranks or motorized electric systems should be planned in.

The leaves of swing shutters are constructed to provide sun control and allow enough light to enter the interior (with the exception of insulating shutters). Special features, such as adjustable slats in the panels and catches that allow the shutter to be partially closed, can be used to regulate the shade level, with the slats adjusted by means of a coupling rod and a flexible attachment to the frame. ➔right

Tilt shutter panels are installed in a subframe that can be tilted outwards. This subframe is not as stable as the actual frame, and can easily become distorted. Different panel types can also be combined within the frame, with a transom rail to separate them.
Simple solid board shutters are leaves without a frame, often made of glue-laminated spruce boards reinforced with inserted horizontal rails or diagonal braces. They barely allow any light into the room.

3 Swing shutter
outline, cross-section and top view,
1:10:

a Pintles:
Fixed pivots for the shutter are secured to the wall or to the window
frame. Depending on the wall's construction type, lug mounts (mortared in) or strap mounts (screwed
into wood, metal and other smooth,
solid surfaces) are used. Screw-
in threaded pintles are used with
wooden beams, dowel types are
used with solid masonry or concrete, and types with a metric
thread are used with nuts (e.g. adjustable pintles for external thermal insulation.) A durable attachment is very important. The pintles
should not move (or, in the case of
external thermal insulation, should
only move slightly). Where intrusion
protection is required, it should
not be possible to unscrew them.

b Hinges:
connect the leaves and pintles;
many different types. They should
be sufficiently strong.

c Fastenings/locks:
fasten shutters closed (double claw
fastening) or fix them half-open by
means of gate hooks. Construction
varies widely from region to region.
Fasteners should be stable and impossible to open from the outside.

d Shutter tie backs:
These hold the shutter open. There
are several different types, sometimes with a stop to limit how far
the shutter can open. The simplest
form is the shutter dog, a revolving
wrought metal lug. The contact surfaces of the leaf with the tie back
should be protected against damage by screwed-on brackets, slide
contact wires or similar components.

e Shutter corners:
Regardless of the frame's stability,
manufacturers recommend shutter
brackets or shutter caps.

f Impact bar:
This covers the chink between the
individual leaves.

g Rake

2

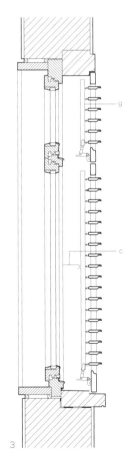

3

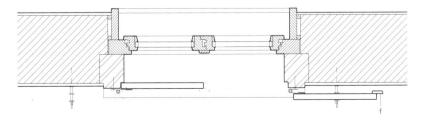

SLIDING SHUTTERS

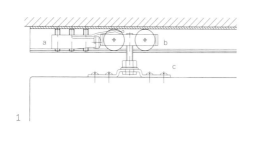

1

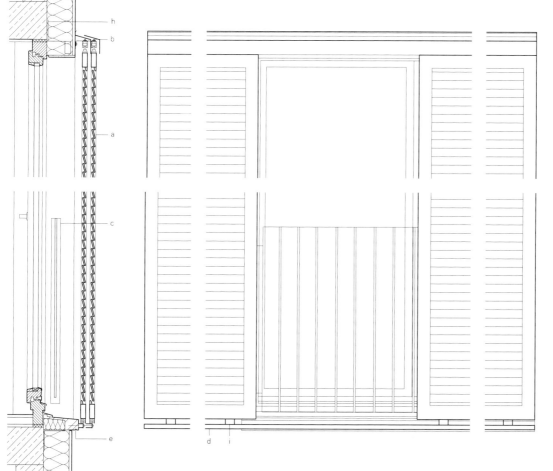

2

1 Detail of carriage with rollers and stopper:
a Stopper
b Carriage with rollers
c Mounting

The mounting of the shutter leaves can be visible, or hidden by a metal fascia. Due to their surface exposure to wind, sliding shutters must have a bottom guide rail for safety purposes.

2 Sliding shutter with clasp elements, carriage and mounting 1:20:

a Leaves:
Sliding shutters are either slid laterally across the facade, in front of the balcony or into cavities in the facade. As elsewhere the main construction elements are the frame, various panels and possible crossbars and centerpieces, or solid timber elements.

b Runner rail:
Shutters sliding behind each other with a telescopic action plus their rails, set on two or more planes, increase the thickness of the overall package. The rails' dimensions depend on the weight of the leaves.

Motor:
Involves a special track with a motor at one end and a deflection roller at the other end. A control panel with a power feed must be included in the interior.

Construction sizes:
Window shutters are manufactured in a limited range of sizes. Height is restricted to approximately 1.00 to 1.50 m where no rails or braces are used. Breadth is particularly subject to restrictions:
Wood: approx. 60 cm. Beyond this, vertical dividing strips should be used.
Aluminum: restrictions apply above 60 cm, depending on the panel type.

c Railings
d Guide rails
e Prefabricated window ledge
f Thermal insulation composite system
g Reinforced concrete
h Steel angle bracket
i Slider

SLIDING FOLDING SHUTTERS

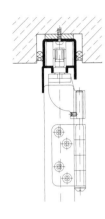

3

3 Pivot and hanger of a folding/
sliding shutter:

4 Folding/sliding shutter 1:10:
Where wide-area, storey-high view
and sun control is needed, flexible
folding/sliding shutters are more
unified than roller shutters or conventional panel shutters. The smaller and therefore lighter leaves coupled to pivots can close very large
openings without taking up the
same wall space as open swing or
sliding shutters.
The space needed for the package
of folded elements at the side must
be planned for. Leaf breadth is restricted to 650 mm, with a maximum of eight leaves per package.
The shutters can fold either outwards or inwards, with a top track
and hanger. The bottom guide rails
allow the shutters to be folded together and slid laterally onto the
window front at 90°. The track and
guide rails must be continuous.

Folding shutters without upper
and lower rails to restrain them are
correspondingly more delicate.
They are often used as inner shutters mounted in the inner window
reveals. They are widely used in
France, and consist of very small
leaves (up to approx. 20 cm in
breadth). They are usually made
from squared-off sheet metal or
aluminum.

a Angle bracket
b Film
c Ventilator block
d Precast concrete part
e Window
f Sliding/folding shutter
g Sheet metal
h Mounting bracket
i Joint seal tape
j Reinforced concrete

4

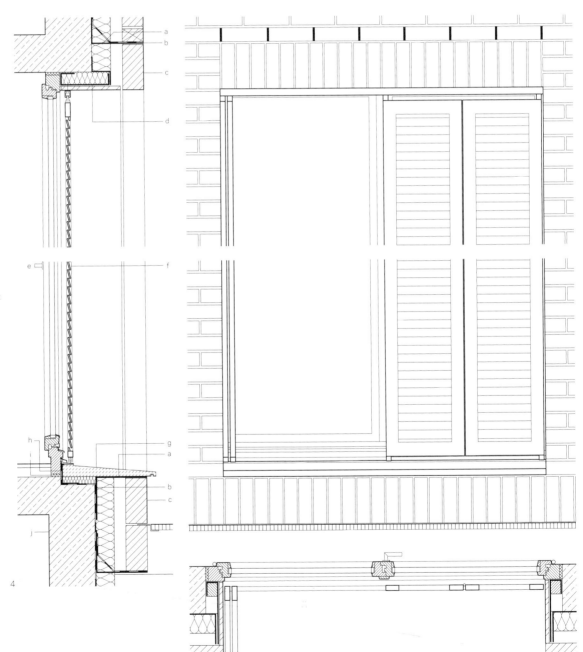

ROLLER SHUTTER SYSTEMS

The roller shutter box lies above or in front of the window. It is secured to the window together with the roller shutter as a single unit, and is usually installed with it. The box makes the opening in the structural shell smaller, meaning that room-high openings are not possible with a roller shutter. The box's measurements are based on the size of the shutter laths when rolled up. It is located in the roller shutter lintel, which both supports the masonry above the window and forms the upper window rebate. The greater the clear height of the window opening, the thicker the coil and the larger the size of the box (approx. 20–30 cm) can be, meaning that the lintel box has a geometrical relationship with the external wall. Where prefabricated roller shutter boxes are used, the installation also depends on whether the external wall is planned to be statically loadbearing, self-supporting or non-loadbearing. All this means that roller shutter installation has to be considered early on, during the planning of the building's shell, ⌐1 taking into account the breadth of the roller shutter, the position of the U-section guide rails in the reveals and the way the join between the upper window frame and the lower edge of the box will be constructed. The space for the coil must not allow water vapor into the interior, and must be well insulated. If the shutter box casing is to be

tendered for in the fit-out works, the junctions with the wall and the reveal must be taken into account.
A manual belt pull is the standard operating method for roller shutters. DIN 18073 requires the pulley and the belt feed-through (which should have no sharp edges) to be in line, the belt to be at least 13 mm in breadth and the tensile force on the belt to be not more than 150 N. If the maximum tensile force is exceeded, a belt transmission must be used. The belt winder is either swivel-mounted on the reveal or integrated into the wall surface. ⌐7a, b, c This has implications for the building shell and must be assessed at an early stage. How and where a belt or crank emerges from the box affects the form of the whole opening. There must also be enough space to operate the crank. The opening must have enough clearance on the side where the belt emerges from the box, to allow for the pulley. As linear systems, the profile of roller shutters and slat blinds is determined by their span. Restrictions on maximum breadth (to prevent deflection due to wind load) depend on the materials used and on the manufacturer. The thicker the individual laths of a roller shutter are, the longer they can be (approx. 2.50 m for high-stability aluminum and approx. 1.70–2.20 m for plastic roller blind laths). For larger openings, two rollers

1 Mounting:
a below the window lintel
b below the ceiling
lintel suspender beam
c lintel within ceiling depth, formed by reinforcement.

Effect on structural design: integrated top box with inner inspection opening behind or underneath and a front box. DIN EN 13569 covers roller shutter elements, including front elements.

2 Top box with broad inspection opening: can be equipped with roller shutters or gathering blinds and integrated into the wall without a visible front box.

3 Detail with belt winder and plaster subcoat: in the wall surface, the surface where the belt emerges on the underside of the box. The following measurements are approximate: depth 170 mm, breadth 55 mm, height 200 mm.

4 Roller shutter laths. Aluminum, double-skin, roll-formed:
a with foam (intrusion prevention)
b the broad lath is more stable (opening breadths approx. 3-4 m)
c extruded hollow section plastic lath (max. breadth 2.00 m). These laths are lighter than the previously used wooden ones.

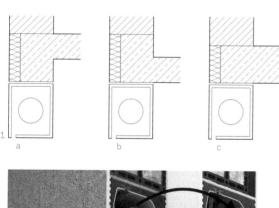

1

2

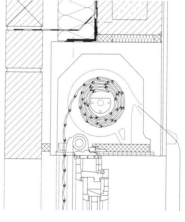

3

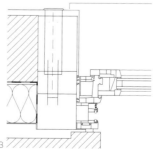

a

b

c

4

SLATTED BLINDS / GATHERED BLINDS / SUN BLINDS

5 Staggered stacking of crimped slats: space-saving nipple heads minimize the slat package's size. The slimline under-rail decreases the package's volume. The unit moves via side U-channels. The shade and the level of light it provides can be smoothly regulated using a pull cord. Warm air rising in front of the facade does not build up significantly thanks to the open slat structure.

6 Awnings:
Continuous blind box with projecting extruded aluminum rails, color-anodized. Awning arms move on roller-sliders. The drop arm is extended so that the awning is vertical until it reaches the deflection roller, which can be positioned as desired. The fabric is tensioned by means of a cloth roller tube with a groove to secure the hanging. Sagging is kept to a minimum.

7 Operating systems for roller shutters:
a integrated belt winder
b pivoted visible belt winder
c crank, manual

5

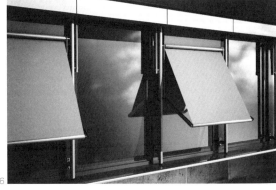

6

7a

b

c

are available. This, however, means an additional section in the middle of the opening. Roller shutters can only be tilted outward given a wind resistance class of 0. Roller shutters are of limited use as glare control—for computer workspaces, for instance—as they do not preserve a view of the outside.

SLATTED BLINDS / GATHERING BLINDS

Unlike the interlocking laths of a roller shutter, which are fixed in relation to each other, the angle of blind slats can be changed—this allowing graduated control and steering of incoming light, providing transparency or sun or glare control as required. Again, the height of the package inside the blind box should be taken into account during planning: the higher the opening to be covered, the taller the box needs to be. The aluminum slats travel along channels or steel cables at the sides.

Wind stability depends on the construction of the slats, which are available flat or in crimped, extra-stable forms. Slats of 60–80 mm in a secure mounting ensure a long service life. They are controlled by wind sensors. Slat blinds or roller blinds installed between two layers of glazing are used with double-glazing and box windows.

SUN BLINDS

A sunblind is a hanging, fixed in place or made to be rolled up or folded, that protects an opening from sunlight. Facade sun blinds are used for larger surfaces. They have guides at the sides and are available in various different forms and sizes and as multi-part constructions (with up to three sections). They can also be constructed in angled shapes. The winding shaft and the cover plate are often secured to the guide rails. These elements affect the form of the facade, and are mounted using spacers. 6

Heat can build up behind sun blinds. This can be minimized by choosing a suitable fabric or by attaching the sun blind at a sufficient distance from the building's structure. The load on the cantilever arm (wind drag) means that to be folded outwards awnings need a solid anchorage.

Sunblind fabrics are used both indoors and outdoors as sun control. Manufactured in a similar way to tricot fabric, these fabrics regulate the climate by maintaining air circulation and channeling buildups of warmth. They control light transmission, daylight yield, degree of reflection and, by means of their color, the room's light level and mood. Pale materials can scatter light very widely, which can produce glare in interiors. They are also more prone to getting dirty. Sunblind fabrics are often given a Teflon coating to make them water-resistant and rot-proof. Acrylic fabrics, which are worked vertically for hanging breadths of more than 120 cm, are also used, as are fabric screens or PVC fabrics, which are given cross-seams according to the size of the hanging.

Sun blinds roll up into blind boxes. The size of these also depends on the opening, and their position must be taken into account during planning of the structural shell and the facade. The fabric's unit weight (300–450 g/m²) and the widths of fabric rolls available depend on the type of fabric used. If the sunblind elements are over 2 m in breadth, several lengths of fabric are seamed together crosswise. DIN 4102 gives the fire ratings of various fabrics and specifies that construction material classes A2/B1 be used for public buildings. It is important to agree on the fire rating of the fabric to be used, so as not to increase fire risks unnecessarily. EN 13561 deals with sun blinds and with their performance and safety requirements. The light-fastness of all textiles is governed by DIN 54004. Color-fastness when exposed to daylight is evaluated on a scale of 1 (worst) to 8 (best).

Fully transparent screen fabrics can deflect up to 96% of the sun's energy. There are now two types of screen fabric on the market: glass fiber PVC and polyester screens with the same optical properties. DIN 4102-B1 is the target that must be reached. The openness factor for screen fabrics corresponds to the percentage of the surface that consists of openings (the spaces in the mesh).

CURTAINS / SLAT CURTAINS / SCREENS

1 Gathered curtain system.

2 Internal roller blind: may be up to 6 m in width, with a surface area of 36 m².

3 Push-back curtain system.

Sun blinds can either be manually operated, with or without a compensating spring, or electrically powered and operated by remote control or by means of sun and wind sensors. The space needed for the coiling rollers in the box and for the operating mechanisms (belt or cord ducts and outlets, possibly with electric cable connections) must be considered at an early stage. The maximum breadth for single-section facade sun blinds is 2.5 to 4 m. Several hangings can, however, be coupled together, permitting maximum breadths of between 20 and 25 m.

INTERNAL SYSTEMS

In principle, external shade systems provide the most effective sun control. An internal shade system is less effective because the heat it stops is already inside the room, where it builds up. For these systems, the g-value is only about 0.30. This means that internal blinds, curtains, screens or internal sun blinds are only effective in providing glare control to counteract pronounced differences in light density, not for sun control. They allow solar gain to be exploited in the winter months and can be used regardless of the weather. The cost of buying and maintaining them is also significantly lower than for external systems. Effective internal sun control systems need to include a highly reflective layer. This can be provided by mother-of-pearl-coated or aluminum vapor-coated fabrics. Internal aluminum slats also have a sufficiently high degree of reflection and, by redirecting the light, create optimal room lighting. They are preferred in clinics and nursing institutions and anywhere there are stringent requirements for hygiene and resistance to damp, mold and rot. It should always be remembered that in the case of windows and doors designated as escape routes, the hangings must always leave the route clear in an emergency.

PUSH-BACK CURTAIN SYSTEMS
The gathered fabric naturally creates vertical folds. Simple to operate manually. The curtain falls in regular waves. Enough space should be left for the waves of fabric to project. ↘ 3

CORD PULL / CABLE PULL CURTAIN SYSTEMS
These are opened and closed by pulling on the control cord. This is a sturdy operation system for light to medium-weight fabrics. Manufacturer's load tables show the dimensions of guide rails and whether rollers or sliders are required. Calculations are based on the maximum curtain weight (fabric used, size of elements—breadth/length).

ELECTRIC HOIST SYSTEM
A simple way of operating tall or heavy curtains. The new systems are compact and almost noiseless. Almost all are horizontally flexible. They can be operated via a switch or a remote control or integrated into the existing building management systems (bus control).

ROUND TUBE SYSTEMS
Also used for flexible room partitions and mounting in front of walls.

GATHERING CURTAIN SYSTEMS
The gathered fabric naturally creates horizontal folds. Often used with decorative drapes or panel curtains. ↘ 1

ROLLER BLIND SYSTEMS
Possible measurements almost unlimited up to 6 m in breadth and a surface area of up to 36 m². ↘ 2

BOX ROLLER BLIND SYSTEM
Used to provide total darkness, equipped with suitable blackout fabrics. Guide rails must be mounted with no gaps.

4 Vertical blinds, wavelike laser cut polyester.

5 Four track aluminum curtain rail for a panel curtain.

CURTAINS

Choosing the right fabric, as well as the right technology, is very important. Translucency classes give information about a fabric's light transmission in a space. Translucent fabrics are preferred for north-facing facades, or in combination with external sun control. Semi-translucent fabrics are used to regulate bright direct sunlight to an ergonomic and comfortable level. Black-out or dim-out fabrics and heavy multi-purpose fabrics create a dimming effect in a space. There are three grades: slight dimming, moderate dimming and total darkening (for photographic laboratories, for instance). Easy-to-operate vertical slatted blinds with black-out materials have become increasingly popular for conference rooms. Depending on what they are being used for, the fabrics can fulfill very different requirements with regard to acoustics, fire rating classes and solar values. These properties, which should be tested and certified, are particularly important for public spaces. Specially designated moisture-proof hangings should be used in damp areas (bathing facilities). Swimming pool buildings, where the air contains chlorine, should be evaluated separately.

SLIDING CURTAINS / PANEL CURTAINS

The sliding curtain or panel curtain is Japanese in origin. It is used to decorate windows and rooms, as a sliding door, a background or a partition between rooms. With a large uninterrupted area, it can display broad expanses of decorative fabric to best advantage. Lengths of fabric are secured to a so-called panel carrier mounted on rollers or sliders using Velcro tape. If CAD laser cutting technology is used, special kinds of fabric are necessary. ➘ 4

NET CURTAINS / SLATTED BLIND CURTAINS

The slatted blind curtain is also known as a strip curtain or a vertical blind. It is both a blind and a curtain. It is unlike a horizontal blind in that its slats do not sag, turn or bend. Common materials include vinyl-coated textiles, natural fibers, plastic-coated glass fibers, PVC plastics and aluminum, in different material variations and colors depending on the manufacturer and the relevant color chart. Measurements for the slat breadths are approx. 89 mm and 127 mm.

They are operated via a pull cord, chain or crank, by hand or electrically. The slats can be turned on their vertical axis to adjust the view or the amount of incoming sunlight. They are either free-hanging (weighted and connected by spacing chains) or mounted between an upper and a lower guide rails. They are also available for slanting window formats and roof lights.

4

CURTAIN RAILS

Curtain rail systems are available with anything from one to five tracks. They can be built directly into gypsum board, set into the ceiling slab or installed as normal surface-mounted rails. They can also be installed on finished surfaces as panel curtain rails. These rails are available as standard in white (RAL 9016) and gray (RAL 9006), integrating perfectly with exposed concrete ceilings. ➘ 5

CURTAIN RODS

Curtain rods of all kinds can be mounted visibly on the wall using spacers, as a decorative element.

5

OPEN | CLOSE
DOORS AND GATES

INTRODUCTION

Doors and gates create a transition between inside and outside, or between spaces within a building. They are the prelude to entering a house or space, and their visual and tactile properties are very significant. Surface, door handle type and operation, the effort needed to open the door, and the sound it makes as it opens all go to make up a door's character and our expectations of what lies behind it. These qualities should all be considered and planned for.

Many different door types and constructions have developed in response to function and design requirements. There are three basic groups: gates, exterior doors and interior doors. The function of any given door determines the position, size and shape, materials, finish and construction of the door leaf, as well as the type of door frame and fittings used. Doors and gates are subject to a variety of criteria and regulations, described in the following chapters.

EXTERIOR AND INTERIOR DOORS

Exterior doors, together with windows, are crucial to a building's external appearance and must therefore be well designed and satisfy structural and performance requirements. A building's entrance also says something about the building's role and significance: a door's position, size, role and decoration are intimately connected with its character, which may be grand or humble, public or private. ⤳ **chapter 1** Doors at the entrance to a building or apartment, balcony doors, window doors (vent windows) and gates may all be subject to the technical requirements relating to exterior doors, involving weather loads, mechanical strength, stability and warping resistance, sound insulation, thermal insulation and intrusion pre-

vention. Within a building, doors' construction, shape and materials depend on the function, present use and needs of rooms.

SPECIAL DOORS

Used for interiors and for exteriors, special doors fulfill unusual requirements. Fire resistance, smoke containment, radiation protection and resistance to weapons fire require special door leaf constructions and special-purpose fittings. ⤳ **p. 111**

GATES

A gate closes an opening big enough for both pedestrians and vehicles. It is defined as having a horizontal clearance of > 2.50 m, a surface area of > 6.25 m² or a weight of > 160 kg per leaf.

Doors impact on our use of the various functional structures within a building and should therefore always be planned with their environment in mind. The main planning parameters are doors' opening mechanisms and the direction they open in. Hinged doors, sliding doors or folding sliding doors have their own operational and space requirements, which must be considered early on in the planning process.

Important planning criteria are:
- The purpose of the spaces connected by the door.
- The door's position, size and arrangement, taking into account other openings, lines of sight and routes, as well as light sources.
- The impact of the closed door leaf on lines of sight and light influx. In this respect, the door can be supplemented with a transom light or by transparent or translucent elements at the sides.

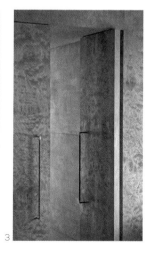

1, 2   Entrance, Gelbes Haus, Flims, 1999, by Valerio Olgiati.

3   Interior door, Zumthor's studio, 2004-2006, Haldenstein, by Peter Zumthor.

1

2

3

TERMINOLOGY AND PLANNING GUIDELINES

4 Approach areas of doors designed to be barrier-free.

5 Different door arrangements and opening directions.

6 The representation and drawing of doors and gates is regulated by DIN EN 12519, which contains standards for the dimensioning of ground plans and sections. They are shown very differently in drawings (1:100) and working drawings (1:50).

CLG Height of ceiling above floor
FFL Finished floor level
SSL Structural slab level
SH   Sill-to-head height

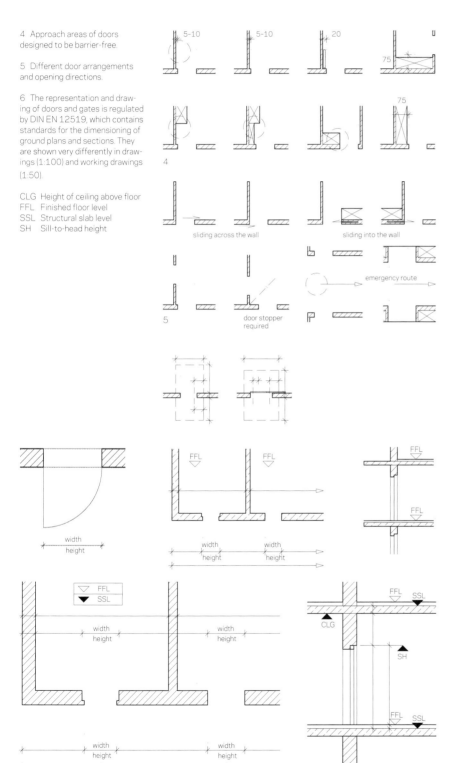

sliding across the wall   sliding into the wall

emergency route

door stopper required

width
height

width
height

width
height

width
height

width
height

width
height

width
height

6

– Access width and access height in relation to user requirements.
– Minimize disruption of the room's atmosphere and use from the open door leaf.
– The door's opening direction and movement area, and how these affect the future furnishing plan.
– The width and alignment of escape routes.
– The required 100° opening angle.
– The way the door unit fits into the wall
– The construction of the door leaf and door frame: their materials, their color scheme and choice of fittings, as well as the overall effect on the space.

BARRIER-FREE DOORS AND GATES

According to DIN 18225 1 + 2, public buildings, workplaces and residential apartments must have a barrier-free design. Barrier-free planning allows disabled people, wheelchair users, the blind and deaf, the elderly and children to access and use a building with as much independence as possible. All doors must have a clearance width of 90 cm (i.e. structural shell dimensions of approx. 1.01 m), and should have a clearance height of 210 cm. The doors of sanitary rooms, toilets and shower rooms should be constructed to open outwards. Thresholds and differences in floor level greater than the 2 cm permissible should be avoided as far as possible.

Movement and approach areas should be provided on both sides of doors, so that the door can be opened by a wheelchair user. The force needed to operate the handle and to close and open the door should not exceed the compressive force of 2.5 kg specified in EN 12217-2 25 N. Where this value is exceeded, a powered opening mechanism and delayed closing system can be added.

CONSTRUCTION TYPES AND FUNCTION

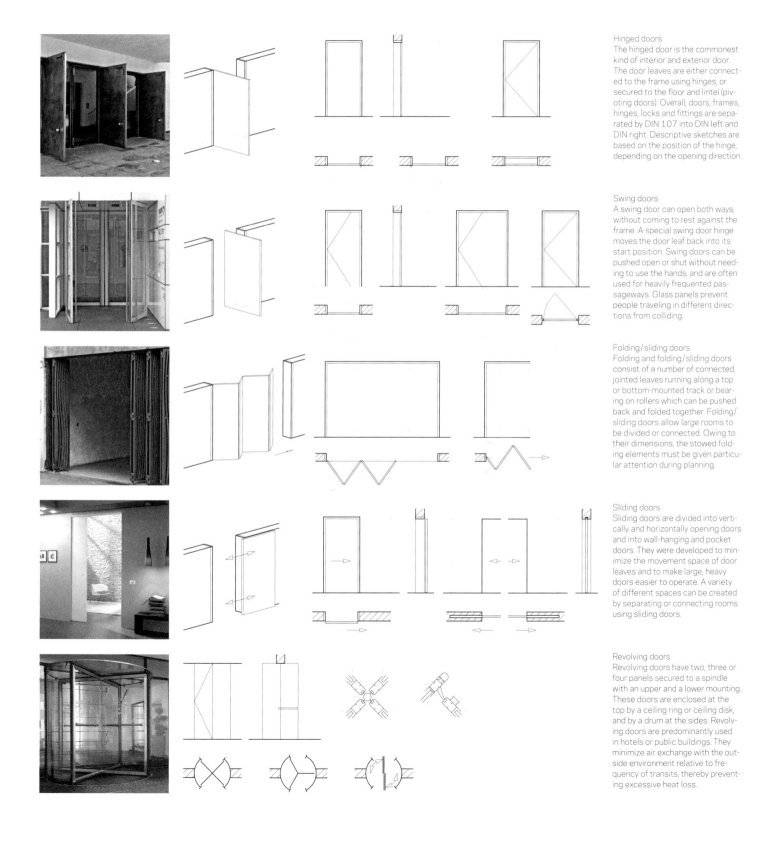

Hinged doors
The hinged door is the commonest kind of interior and exterior door. The door leaves are either connected to the frame using hinges, or secured to the floor and lintel (pivoting doors). Overall, doors, frames, hinges, locks and fittings are separated by DIN 107 into DIN left and DIN right. Descriptive sketches are based on the position of the hinge, depending on the opening direction.

Swing doors
A swing door can open both ways, without coming to rest against the frame. A special swing door hinge moves the door leaf back into its start position. Swing doors can be pushed open or shut without needing to use the hands, and are often used for heavily frequented passageways. Glass panels prevent people traveling in different directions from colliding.

Folding/sliding doors
Folding and folding/sliding doors consist of a number of connected, jointed leaves running along a top or bottom-mounted track or bearing on rollers which can be pushed back and folded together. Folding/sliding doors allow large rooms to be divided or connected. Owing to their dimensions, the stowed folding elements must be given particular attention during planning.

Sliding doors
Sliding doors are divided into vertically and horizontally opening doors and into wall-hanging and pocket doors. They were developed to minimize the movement space of door leaves and to make large, heavy doors easier to operate. A variety of different spaces can be created by separating or connecting rooms using sliding doors.

Revolving doors
Revolving doors have two, three or four panels secured to a spindle with an upper and a lower mounting. These doors are enclosed at the top by a ceiling ring or ceiling disk, and by a drum at the sides. Revolving doors are predominantly used in hotels or public buildings. They minimize air exchange with the outside environment relative to frequency of transits, thereby preventing excessive heat loss.

Hinged gates
The hinged gate has one or two opening leaves, each secured at the side. Large gates with a wide opening radius and consequent difficulty in operation can be problematic. A folding jointed gate with two or more connected and jointed leaves has a smaller opening radius. These are guided or braced at the top or at floor level.

Sliding gates
Depending on size and weight, sliding gate leaves are guided by an upper or lower guide rail or mounted on carriages, or trolleys. Sliding gates can further be divided into single or double, telescopic, sliding/hinged, sliding/folding or surrounding sliding doors. One important factor when choosing a construction type is the desired width of the opening in relation to the width of the opened door leaf.

Lifting or lowering gates
For a lifting or lowering gate, the whole gate is pulled upwards or lowered into the ground. The design should allow space for parking the gate when open. Ease of passing through the gate and safety provisions also important.

Overhead (up-and-over) doors
Overhead doors consist of a tracked single leaf that rests horizontally at the upper edge of the opening when parked. The opening curve may be insignificant or project out a considerable way. When planning, the area required by the opening curve should be taken into account, as the door can only be opened when this is free.

Roller doors
Roller doors open vertically and upwards. They consist of connected jointed laths (an interlocking roller shutter) and a shaft with a drive. The door moves along guide rails at the sides.

Sectional doors
Sectional doors are divided into individual, connected rectangular segments. The door is opened vertically, upward. The loading area extends right up to the door.

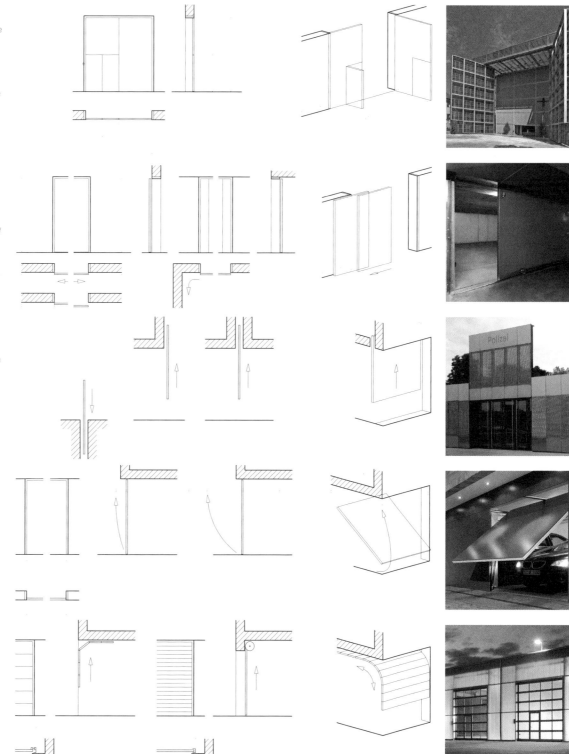

FITTING AND DOOR FRAMES

The various technical and formal requirements for doors have led to different types of rebate. Essentially, rebates are either formed in solid construction components or in the door frame. A door can have upper, lower and side rebates.

Door frames and casings are made of materials that retain their fit, such as wood, metals or plastic. These can absorb the tolerances of the structural opening. They also provide anchorage for door fittings. The frame's construction depends on the demands placed on the door: e.g. watertight and wind-tight properties, thermal and sound insulation, and the required level of security and barrier-free design.

The method of fitting influences our visual impression of a door. If a door leaf is fitted flush with the wall and painted the same color as the wall, it makes the opening inconspicuous. Fitting the door against a recessed block frame is a simple way of creating a niche with the depth of the wall reveal that invites anyone standing outside to enter. Ornamenting an entrance with lining or an architrave emphasizes the opening, as does a raised threshold.

Doors connect or separate interior and exterior spaces. The construction of the junction with the floor plays a significant role in this. At one time it was common to use raised thresholds, which covered the junction between two different floors, to reduce draughts and noise. More recently, however, there has been a switch to continuous flooring without breaks (for formal and functional reasons). Where a door is combined with a change in flooring or there are sound and thermal insulation requirements, floor rails or floor seals are used. Various floor joint seal systems have developed in response to the different requirements of interior and exterior doors. These are principally divided into contact seals, drop-down seals, magnetic seals, acoustic seals and threshold seals. ➜ p. 120

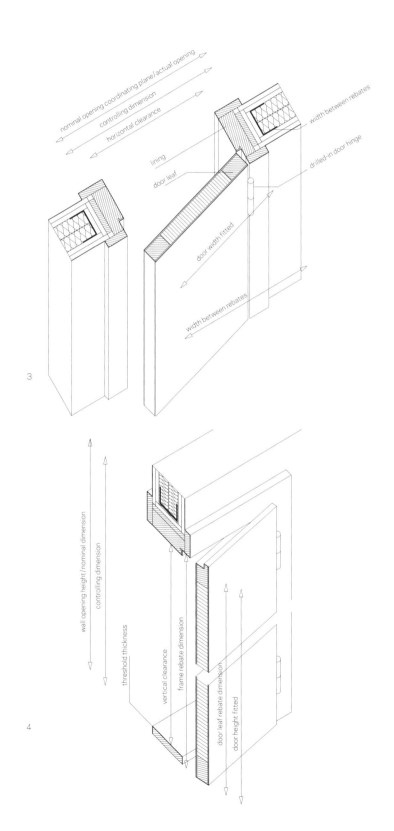

3, 4   Specified dimensions and relevant technical terms for door openings, with wooden frames with lining and architrave, and a rebated door leaf. The relationships between the dimensions of the frame and door leaf and the door hinges and door lock are governed by DIN 18101.

Basic dimensions + 10 mm = nominal wall opening width
Basic dimensions + 5 mm = nominal wall opening height

5   Wooden doorframes:
a   frameless door leaf, with rebate, closing jamb in wall depth
b   frameless door leaf, without rebate, closing jamb on wall surface
c   superimposed surround, door leaf with rebate
d   door leaf on casing frame, door leaf with rebate
e   door leaf on lining and surround, door leaf with rebate
f   door leaf on frame, door leaf without rebate

6   Steel doorframes, horizontal section:
a   steel corner frame for rebated door leaf
b   steel corner frame for flush-edged door leaf
c   steel wraparound frame for rebated door leaf
d   steel wraparound frame for flush-edged door leaf
e   expansion joint frame, door leaf with rebate
f   expansion joint frame, door leaf without rebate

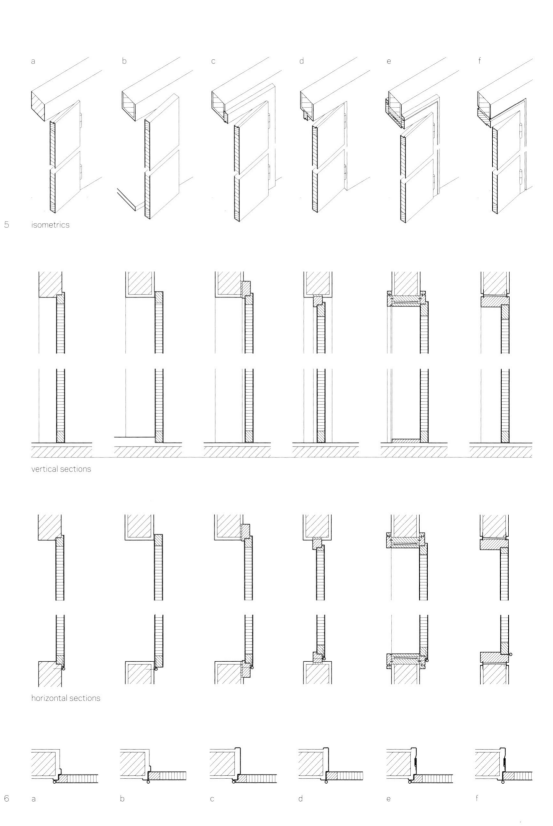

a   b   c   d   e   f

5   isometrics

vertical sections

horizontal sections

6   a   b   c   d   e   f

EXTERIOR DOOR

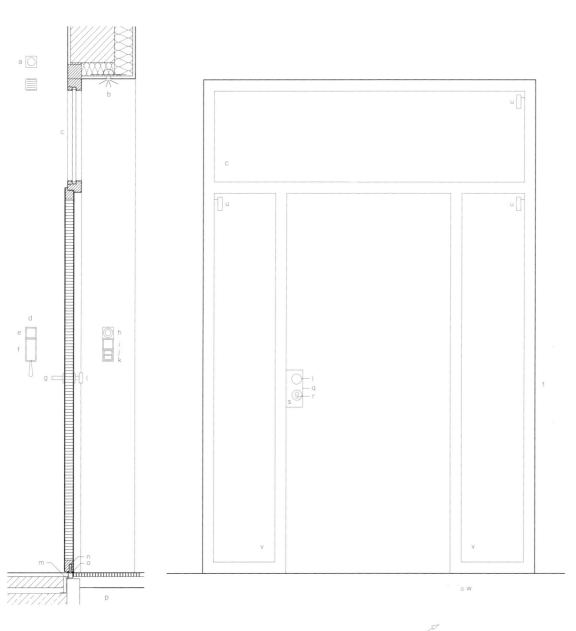

Wooden building entrance door with glazed side panels, scale 1:20:

a   Doorbell
b   Lighting
c   Transom panel
d   Intercom
e   Screen
f   Receiver
g   Door handle
h   Camera
i   Speaker
j   Bell-push
k   Light
l   Doorknob
m   Metal angle
n   Drop-down floor seal
o   Contact seal
p   Gravel
q   Door rosette
r   Hole for profiled cylinder
s   Mortised lock
t   Camera/intercom
u   Alarm sensor
v   Side panel
w   Door stop
x   Door hinge
y   Grid/dirt-trapping mat

SPECIAL-PURPOSE DOOR

Glazed hinged door with aluminum frame for use as an emergency exit door, scale 1:20:

a   Overhead door closer with folding arm actuator
b   Door handle
c   Drop-down floor door seal
d   Contact rail
e   Panic bar
f   Push button
g   Electric door opener
h   Bolt switch contact
i   Fixed side panel
j   Fire alarm
k   Central emergency electricity supply
l   Control device
m   Fire protection glass
n   T30 fire-rated door constructed using thermally broken, self-supporting aluminum sections
o   Door handle
p   Tiled plasterboard strips (isolators) glued to the inner side

T30 doors must block the passage of fire for 30 minutes and restrict the passage of smoke and increased temperature to the area on the side where no fire is present. They are self-closing, with hydraulic dampening function on the door closers. The door, the door frame and the necessary special function fittings are tested as a single functional unit. The manufacturer must provide installation and maintenance information for every fire-rated or smoke-stop door. For glazed doors, special fire protection glass is used. The cavity of the metal section is filled in with fire protection materials such as plasterboard or ceramic fire protection compound. This compound connects stably with the steel section and must not be affected by the fitting of the door or by the recess for the lock.

Where fire-rated doors are used to secure emergency routes, being designated as such with signs, they are usually connected to surveillance and alarm devices. For this reason, they are supplied with a channel for wiring. This allows electrical connections to be retrofitted easily.

The door seals must have a low-flammability construction. Specialist lowering seals are used for the threshold area to exclude smoke. The component join between the wall and the door frame must be constructed according to requirements. For smoke-stop doors, certification in line with DIN 18095 must be submitted during acceptance of construction work.

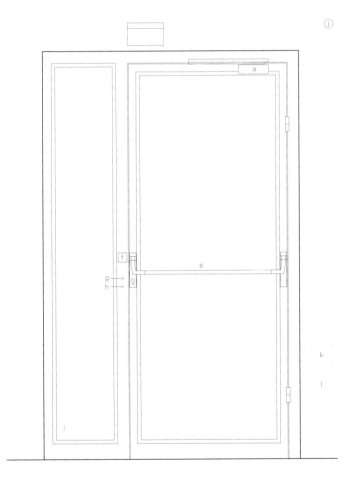

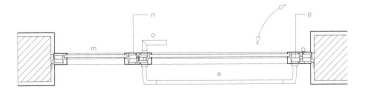

HINGED DOOR (INTERIOR)

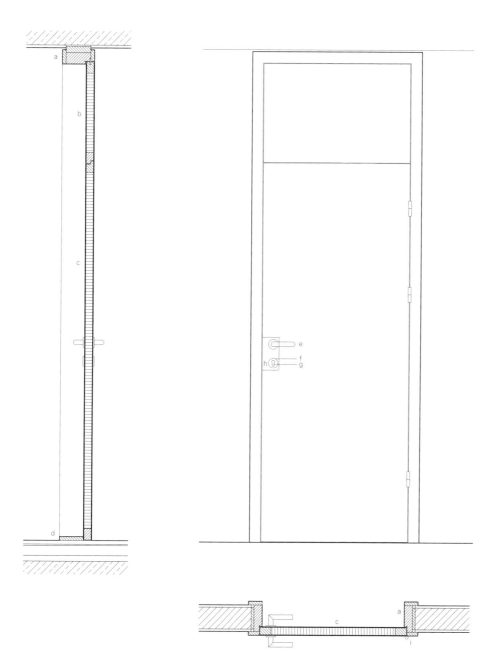

Wooden hinged door with a continuous door frame, scale 1:20:

a Frame
b Upper casing
c Door leaf
d Threshold
e Door handle
f Door rosette
g Hole for profiled cylinder
h Mortise lock
i Drilled-in hinge
j Door stop

SLIDING DOOR (INTERIOR)

Wooden sliding door with concealed guide rails, scale 1:20:

a   Steel U-section
b   Track rail
c   Sliding door leaf
d   U-shaped running groove
e   Grip element
f   Wall channel
g   Guide pin
h   Metal stud wall

Door hand grips:
Single-leaf and double-leaf sliding
doors can be fitted with a hook-
shaped catch or a curved bolt. The
door grip may be a simple recess
or a fold-out ring.

Floor guidance:
The floor-mounted guide rail fits in
a channel set into the door leaf. It
lies directly next to the door opening at the starting point of the
wall cavity. There are two different
types: T- section and pin section.

Fittings:
The fittings for a single-leaf sliding
door consist of a track attached
to the ceiling and the lintel. Within the wall cavity, a buffer stop and
a holding spring are attached to
the rail. The door leaf is secured
by a two-way hanger and the running gear has rollers that rest on
the track.

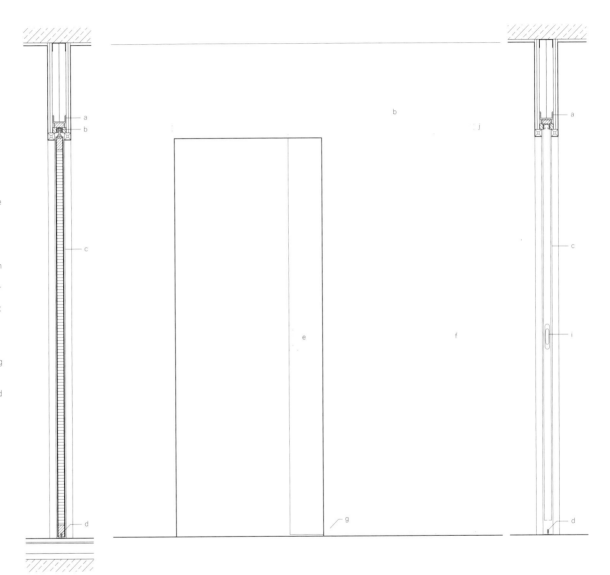

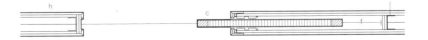

REVOLVING DOOR

MERCEDES-BENZ MUSEUM IN STUTTGART, GERMANY
UNSTUDIO, AMSTERDAM

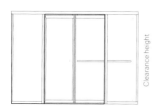

Clearance height

2a

Breadth of emergency exit

Pivoting leaf opened

c

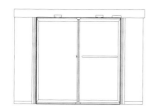

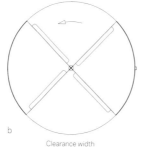

b

Clearance width
Outer diameter = Structural opening width − 80
Width of structural opening

Bracing

d

1   Entrance / foyer of the museum.

2   Revolving door types:
a   Revolving door with 3 panels
b   Revolving door with 4 panels
c   Revolving door with 3 panels and
    emergency exit lock
d   Revolving door with 3 panels and
    night lock

Revolving doors can be operated
automatically, servo-powered, or
manually. If operated automatically,
safty sensors ensur the doors stop
immediately in case of an emergency.

ENTRANCE DOOR WITH DRAUGHT LOBBY

MUSEUM FÜR UR- UND FRÜHGESCHICHTE IN HAGEN, GERMANY
ZAMEL KRUG ARCHITEKTEN, HAGEN

1 Entrance, scale 1:20:

a Rectangular hollow section
   40/40/4 mm
b Bracket
c Safty glazing 10 mm
d Dirt-trapping mat
e Sandstone slab 25 mm
f Screed
g Thermal insulation,
   compression-proof
h Steel angle 40/40/4 mm,
   galvanized
i Floor spring door closer,
   stainless steel
j Edge fitting
k Push bar
l Frame profile, steel, coated
m Weld-on hinge, stainless steel,
   coated
n Door leaf, sheet aluminum 3 mm,
   coated
o Insulating glazing (laminated
   safty glass) 26 mm, UV-proof
   sealing
p U-section
q Inside the glazing joint bracing,
   tension rod, dia. = 8 mm, stainless steel
r Masonry (existing)

2 Exterior view.

3 Interior view.

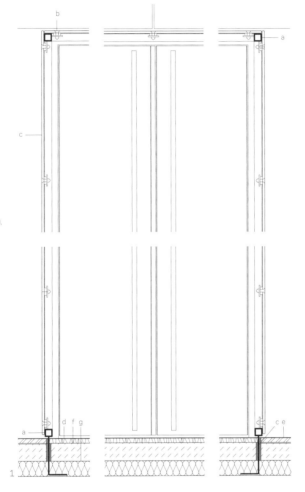

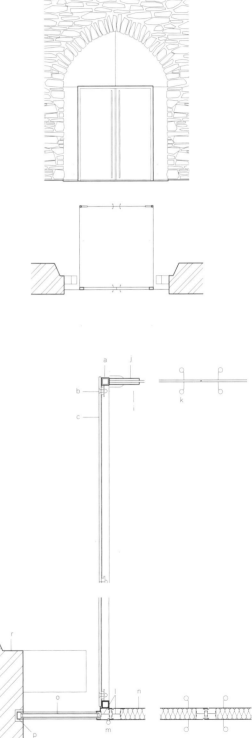

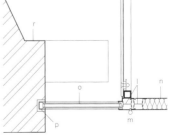

DOOR LEAF CONSTRUCTIONS

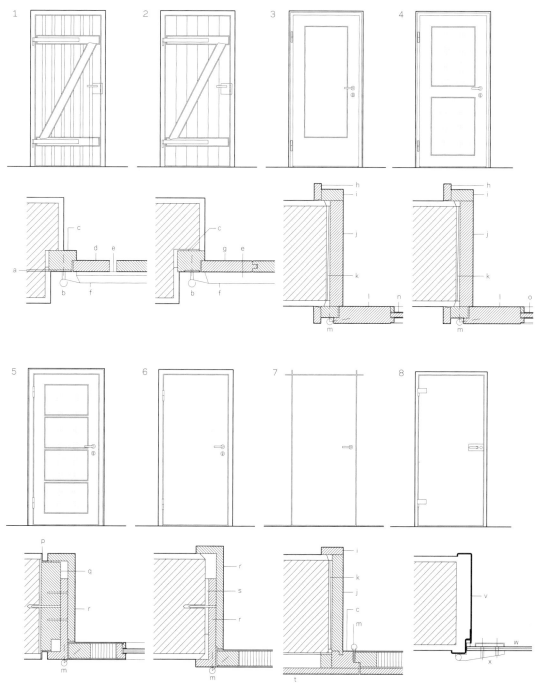

1   Batten door with doorpost in wall rebate, side rabbetted, hinge side.

2   Plank door with ledges and bracing bar, doorpost in wall rebate, side rabbetted, hinge side.

3   Frame doors
Mitered doors with a paneled wood or metal frame. The panels may be of plywood, glass or other material. In this example, a plywood insert with veneer on both faces was used. Panels (one or several) fit into grooves in the frame which has either mortice-and-tenon or dowelled joints. The frame door is a traditional construction. Inserted or screwed-on fittings and hinges are used. Integrated special-purpose fittings are not possible, owing to the thinness of the door leaf.

4, 5   Frame door with glass paneling and glazing bars.

6   Flush doors
Flush door leaves generally consist of a frame, the core material, facing and a finish layer for both sides. They are called flush doors on the basis of their construction, and are regulated by DIN 68706.

7   Concealed door.

8   Fully-glazed doors
Standard fully-glazed doors are available with many different glass types, structures and fittings. The frameless door leaves consist of 8 mm to 10 mm thick laminated safety glass. The glazing should be installed in such a way as not to be subjected to serious tension. A separating strip (e.g. neoprene) must always be installed between glass and clamping frame and around the fittings, the joint with the wall etc. Glass edges can be treated in a variety of ways (coating, grinding, polishing etc.). All measurements and necessary gaps must be established before the door unit is completed, as it is not possible to alter anything on site.

a Bracket	g Boards	m Door hinge	s Inside lining
b Hinge	h Decorative strip	n Door panel, chipboard	t Wood cladding
c Door post	i Head strip	o Door panel, glass	u Door leaf cladding
d Battens	j Lining	p Plaster angle	v Steel lining
e Cross rail, brace	k V-strips	q Mounting block	w Fully glazed door
f Strap hinge	l Door frame	r Casing/frame	x Clamped-on pivot hinges

FLUSH DOORS

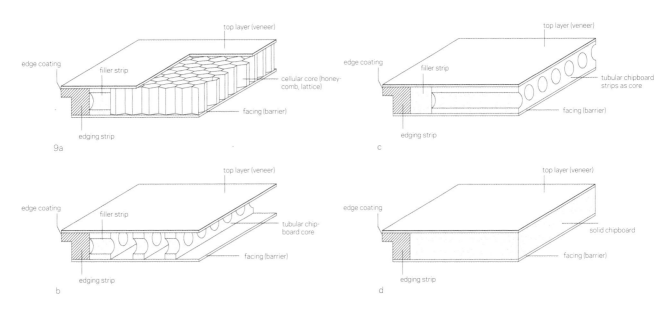

9a

c

b

d

9 Inner construction of flush door leaves for normal requirements: from the simplest, lightest construction to deluxe, heavier constructions. Sound insulation increases with mass, and hinges must be appropriate to the door's weight. The simplest construction is shown here: a cellular core (honeycomb)

a   cellular core (honeycomb)
b   semi-solid core
     (tubular chipboard strips)
c   tubular chipboard core
d   solid chipboard core

General requirements for interior doors and doors for residential buildings are specified in DIN 18101.

Different structures for frame and panel doors and solid wood doors. The simplest construction consists of non-laminated solid wood, which is worked as a whole. A groove absorbs swelling and shrinkage in the panel. Cracks or warping can develop over time. The laminated blockboard frame door, another kind of solid wood door, was developed to minimize this. The structure of the blockboard panel is concealed behind cladding (e.g. veneer). If glass paneling is chosen, one of the retaining strips for the wood paneling will be a flexible glass retaining strip.

THE DOOR LEAF
The door leaf is the moveable part of the door unit. Put simply, there are two basic types: unframed doors ↘ 6, 7 and frame doors. ↘ 3-5 Historically, door leaf construction methods have ranged from the early simple board doors made from wood battens or wood planks to the mortise-and-tenon solid wood frame door with coffered or glass infill and the flush door leaf. The leaf has an inner wood or metal frame and an outer layer or veneer, possibly with a double construction. Numerous special requirements have led to special modern high-performance sandwich construction door leaves. The fully-glazed door is a modern development.

Most doors are now made as mass-produced factory products, rather than in workshops, and are fitted by carpenters. This has led to the standardization of doors—regulation, prefabrication and classification. A door that looks identical to others from the outside may have a different inner construction.

FLUSH DOOR LEAVES
The flush door is the most commonly used door construction today. A flush door leaf is a plain door leaf with a covered frame ↘ 6 plus core material, facing and a finish layer. The visible layer consists either of wood veneer, laminate sheets or foil. Alternatively, the surfaces of the facing can be varnished or painted. A single-piece wooden construction frame approximately 45–60 mm wide and 30–34 mm thick (alternatively made from metal or plastic) is covered on both sides (faced) with plywood board, or plastic or metal sheeting. A standard door leaf is approx. 40 mm thick. The cavity is filled with different core materials according to the intended purpose and physical requirements, depending on whether it belongs to an interior, exterior or soundproof door. Specialized doors with particular smoke containment, fire protection or sound insulation requirements will have different door leaf constructions corresponding to their function.

INTERIOR DOOR LEAVES
Interior doors are mainly manufactured with frames and panels and with either plain, varnished, wood-veneered or plastic-coated surfaces. Solid wood interior doors are barely used today due to their higher price and failure to meet modern fitting requirements. Door units in a historical context ↘ 1, 2 are an exception. The middle layers of interior flush doors can be made from tubular chipboard, rigid foam, cork, solid chipboard, honeycomb or lattice sandwich material or tubular chipboard inlay, ↘ 9 with the construction depending on the relevant stress group and climate class. A lattice sandwich construction is used for cheap interior doors, while full chipboard is used for more expensive models. Plain interior flush door leaves made from wood or wood derivatives are governed by DIN 68706.

EXTERIOR DOOR LEAVES
Exterior doors are available as simple, plain flush door leaves, as double-construction doors (with vertical / horizontal facing on both sides) or as frame doors with molded panels and dividing elements (intermediate rails and muntins). Exterior doors with cladding may be batten doors, board doors or plank doors. Exterior door systems may have one or two leaves, with or without a transom light or side lights. Apart from normal exterior doors, there are swing, hinged and sliding door systems, with

DOOR SURFACES

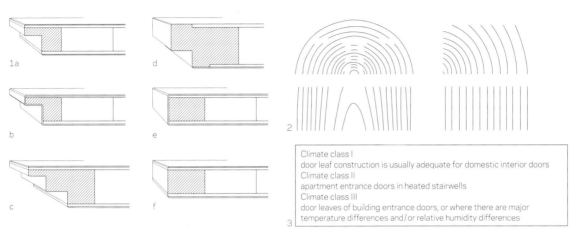

1a
b
c
d
e
f

2

Climate class I
door leaf construction is usually adequate for domestic interior doors
Climate class II
apartment entrance doors in heated stairwells
Climate class III
door leaves of building entrance doors, or where there are major
temperature differences and/or relative humidity differences

3

1 Edge geometry and edge construction for flush door leaves:
a with rebate (F), standard rebate,
inset edge band
b with rebate, plastic, veneer edge
depending on surface
c double rebate (D), inset edge
band
d with rebate, non-concealed
wood edging (solid construction)
e flush-edged (S), veneer edge
f flush-edged (S), inset edge band
concealed

This is an example of an exposed
inset wooden edge band with a
coated edge. This contrasts with
the concealed non-inset wood edging, which could also be exposed.
Depending on the manufacturer,
edges may be sharp, rounded or
polyurethane-treated.

2 Manufacture of veneers, depending on the grain of the wood.
Flowery veneer (dosse: flat cut or
crown cut) is often used for door
leaves, while plainer veneer (applied
on carrier paper) is used for wooden
frames.

3 Climate classes for doors:
A climate class defines the temperature range within which a component can and may be used. General
requirements such as the climate
class and stress groups of doors
are governed by RAL-RG 426-T1.
This is a product directive issued
by the quality association for interior doors made from wood and
wood derivatives. It lists various
quality and testing criteria, allowing door manufacturers to institute
neutral quality checks. This is maintained by the quality association
through independent assessments.

or without automation, which are particularly common in official buildings, hospitals and schools. Sometimes they act as escape routes, and are subject to special requirements. Before doors can be planned or tendered for, these special requirements must be clarified. The operating license depends on certification and on choosing the right door system, among other things.

SURFACES
The coating used on the leaf and frame changes a door's appearance. Coatings have technical as well as aesthetic applications. Solid wood generally has to be protected against weather in the case of exterior doors and against dirt gathering in open pores during daily use in the case of interior doors. Plain door surfaces are easier to maintain and more durable in an outdoor environment.
Paint or colored varnish is used for opaque coatings, and glazes for non-opaque coatings, as well as wood veneer, various laminates or special coatings.
Protective oil-based finishes (varnishes) are applied as wax, glaze, matt coating or polish. Wood stains only color the wood, changing the natural tone but leaving the grain visible. Unlike glazes, they are not a protective surface treatment. Glazes have translucent color pigments, and protect wood from weathering. The quality of the finished surface is influenced by undercoat preparation and the fine sanding and polishing. The choice of coating system affects the surface's appearance: opaque or translucent, open-pored or closed, and the level of wood protection in outdoor areas. Different types of solid wood, e.g. hardwoods and softwoods, need different treatments.

VENEER
Wood veneers are manufactured with different directions of cut, creating different patterns. Depending on the manufacturing process, they are described as sliced, peeled or sawn, and are commercially available in thicknesses of 0.5 to 0.9 mm. If a different color tone is desired, veneered surfaces can be stained after fine sanding and varnished to finish.

LAMINATES/DECORATIVE COATINGS
HPL (high pressure laminate) as described by DIN EN 438 consists of cellulose, phenol and melamine resin. Decorative coatings are color-printed or impregnated papers that are covered with a melamine resin. They are firmly bonded to the surface at high temperature and high pressure, creating a sealed melamine surface with no pores that is easy to clean. For this reason, HPLs are recommended for areas with strict hygiene requirements (e.g. hospitals and food production premises). Surfaces of this kind tested according to DIN EN 438 and DIN 16926 have good resistance to wear and scratching, as well as optimal impact resistance. Color, design and structure must be described exactly with reference to the manufacturer. Available patterns include uni decors, photographically created reproductions and special effect surfaces. It is necessary to check the available patterns, as manufacturers' ranges change constantly. Laminate sheets are only available in certain sizes: this can be a limiting factor for door formats. The generally available formats are: 2180 mm x 915, 1020 or 1320 mm. For large door units, the sheets must be butt joined. Some manufactures may offer larger sizes: range and availability should be checked.

CLIMATE CLASSES
Temperature-related requirements for windows and doors vary. They often separate areas with different climates, meaning that the surfaces on either side of a door can be exposed to different humidities and temperatures. This climate imbalance can cause warping effects, which also

SPECIAL DOORS

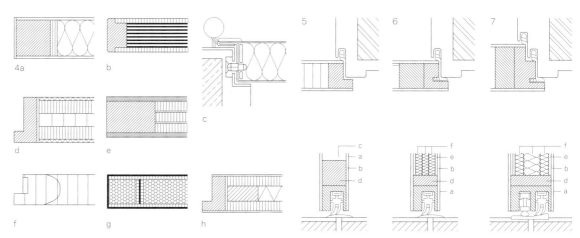

4   Flush door constructions for special doors are governed by standards, which must be complied with. Door leaf constructions for special purposes, such as intrusion protection, sound insulation, smoke containment, radiation protection, moisture protection and wet area use. These special-purpose doors often need special-fittings or seals, and can therefore only be certified as a unified construction element (e.g. fire and smoke protection).
a   flush door leaf with laminate edge
b   bulletproof door leaf
c   fire-rated door—T30-1 steel door
d   wood fire-rated door leaf—multi-layer composite door leaf
e   wood fire-rated door leaf—sandwich construction with non-combustible insert material
f   wood fire-rated door leaf—special compacted chipboard sheet
g   door leaf for damp area door
h   sound insulation door leaf

Sound insulation requirements: Construction of frame rebates/seals for simple and double rebates. The sealing tongue should be continuous, including the hinge area. The floor seal is a weak point and should have an appropriate design. Increased recommendations for airborne sound insulation may be as high as 42 dB.

5-7   Comparison of ready-to-use sound insulation doors:
5   door leaf with single-layer construction, full chipboard sheet, rebate and contact seals
6   door leaf with multi-layer construction, flexible sound insulation board, door leaf seals, rebate and contact seals
7   door leaf with multi-layer construction, flexible sound insulation board, door leaf seals, double rebate seals, contact seals and drop-down floor seals

Layer construction:
a   top veneer
b   fiberboard
c   chipboard
d   double solid wood frame
e   hardboard
f   flexible sound insulation board

Sound insulation values:
door leaf construction:
5   R_w = 34 dB
6   R_w = 42 dB
7   R_w = 45 dB
ready-to-use door:
5   R_w = 29 dB
6   R_w = 39 dB
7   R_w = 42 dB

vary from summer to winter. To ensure the right closing pressure on the seals at all points, the maximum warping from the plane must not exceed ±2 mm. Door leaf constructions are therefore divided into three climate classes. ⟶ 3 The materials used for doors also affect their temperature and humidity-related warping behavior, which is a thermal process in the case of metals and plastics and a hygrothermal process in the case of wood.

MECHANICAL STRESS GROUPS
Besides their climate class, door leaves are divided into three stress groups—(N) normal, (M) medium and (S) strong—based on their mechanical stress performance. This relates to static and dynamic deformation and hard and soft impact. Apartment entrance doors should be in stress groups N to M.

SPECIALIST DOORS/SPECIAL-PURPOSE DOORS
Fire-rated, anti-intrusion and sound insulation doors have special multi-layered, glue-laminated cores. ⟶ 4 If flush doors are constructed specially as sound-insulating doors, sound-absorbing doors and fire-rated doors, care should be taken that all of the materials, fillers and fittings meet the extra requirements. Special doors with different primary functions can be combined to create multi-functional doors: these doors, usually constructed as whole door units, can combine fire, smoke, noise and intrusion protection, as well as suitability for a wet environment. The door's appearance is affected by these requirements—and particularly by the corresponding fittings, such as automatic door-closing devices and panic locks, or sturdier frames with suitable hinges (depending on the manufacturer). If this is not to restrict design choices, the designer must have knowledge of these doors' specific requirements.

THERMAL INSULATION (EXTERNAL DOOR)
Joint gaps and thermal transmission through the door unit lead to loss of heat. In this respect, entrance doors and windows are generally the weakest parts of a building's outer skin. Using thicker components and installing insulating layers and appropriate seals (e.g. sponge strips, lip or brush seals) improves thermal insulation. The statutory energy-saving requirements should be remembered. The door leaves of an entrance door should be thicker and heavier than interior door leaves, for instance.

INTRUSION PREVENTION/SECURITY
When closed and locked, a security door should effectively resist attempts at breaking and entering, with or without tools, for a certain length of time. Six resistance classes are listed in DIN ENV 1627 (WK1-WK6). ⟶ tab 1-p. 164 The door's effectiveness in preventing break-ins is determined by testing the whole unit: door frame, door leaf and the necessary security fittings.

FIRE PROTECTION/SMOKE CONTAINMENT
According to the German model building regulations, construction systems must prevent the outbreak and spread of fire and smoke for a certain length of time, measured in minutes (for doors: T30-T120). The construction regulation DIN 4102 is valid in all German states. In terms of fire protection, it defines fire doors as barriers to the spread of fire. A fire-rated door is a unit consisting of a door frame, a door leaf and appropriate fittings. It is certified by a mark on the edge of the door leaf near the hinge, and must be self-closing. In apartment buildings, the doors between the stairwell and the cellar, to boiler rooms and to passageway airlocks must be T30 doors. Smoke containment is governed by DIN 18095 and depends on the seal type.

HINGED DOOR FITTINGS

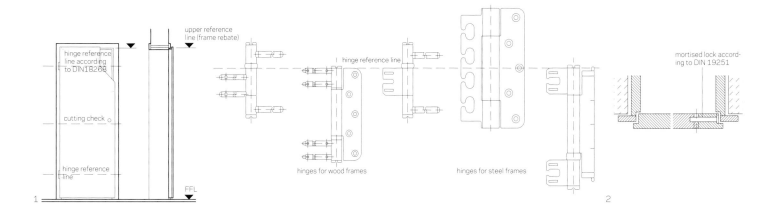

1

hinge reference line according to DIN18268

upper reference line (frame rebate)

cutting check

hinge reference line

FFL

hinge reference line

hinges for wood frames

hinges for steel frames

mortised lock according to DIN 19251

2

SOUND INSULATION

Entrance doors of apartments and spaces such as conference rooms have stricter soundproofing requirements. The heavier the door and the better the seals (particularly at floor level and around the joints—i.e. the rebates and keyholes), the better the soundproofing. Appropriate installation is important. The minimum requirements are given in DIN 4109, which specifies three different classes for the required reduction of airborne sound to protect against sound transmission (I 27 dB, II 32 dB, III 37 dB). In multi-storey residential buildings, for instance, the minimum requirement for doors that separate stair areas or entrance halls from corridors is 27 dB. A minimum noise reduction of 37 dB is required for doors that connect stair areas or entrance halls with non-circulation spaces, e.g. in hotels or consulting rooms. There are no sound insulation requirements for single family homes.

DAMP/WET AREA USE

A door requires special moisture-resistance properties wherever it is subject to damp conditions for short periods (in domestic bathrooms, for instance). This is caused partly by occasional rises in humidity, and partly by brief exposure to splashes of water. Joints with masonry or tiles at its sides, including the cut end of the door frame at floor level, must have permanent elastic seals.

Door leaves in wet areas, e.g. swimming baths, are subject to continually high levels of moisture and wetting. The whole door unit, including all fittings, must be appropriate for a wet area. For this reason, the door frame should be stainless steel, as galvanized steel frames begin to rust relatively quickly in wet areas. Wood wraparound frames cannot be used in wet areas. To prevent rust damage and corrosion, locks, hinges and handles should also be suitable for wet areas. Wet area doors should be equipped with stainless steel hinges. Damp area doors are generally less expensive than wet area doors.

FITTINGS

As with windows, the way a door moves depends on its fittings. Fittings connect the door leaf with the door frame, allowing it to be opened and closed. Pivoting fittings are described as door hinges. Specialized hinges allowing the door leaf to move in certain ways characterize the different door types: hinged doors, swing doors, lift-and-slide doors or simple sliding doors. Lock fittings allow the door to be secured. The components are the door lock on the door leaf and the corresponding strike plate on the frame. Locks are supplemented by the other door furniture: door latches, revolving knobs and door handles.

HINGE SYSTEMS

The depth of the door's rebates and the pivot point determine the choice of hinges. ➘1 Hinges should have a loadbearing capacity to match the weight and dimensions of the door. Where a third hinge is used, the loadbearing capacity is increased by approx. 10%. However, the place of use, the frequency of opening/use, the door's dimensions, the type of door, its closing action, the variety of hinge used and its material/surface qualities also influence the overall form of the hinge. Where the measurements chosen for hinges promote stability, durability is improved. Depending on manufacture, the loadbearing capacity of 2 hinges on a single door varies from 70 to 120 kg, and may be as much as 300 kg per door leaf for some hinge types. Distinctions are made between ball-tip butt hinges, pivot hinges and butt hinges, drill-in hinges and, for special requirements, system hinges or completely covered specialist hinges. The spacing for door hinges with reference to the door head is governed by the hinge reference line specified by DIN 18268; this is a fixed measurement, regardless of the hinge's type. The reference line for a third hinge (where there is one) will be 350 mm beneath the first hinge refer-

1 The hinge reference line according to DIN 18268 is an imaginary line whose distance from the upper frame rebate or door head determines the heights at which the door's hinges are fixed. This means that when ordering door leaves for door frames assembled on site, it is essential to include a dimensioned construction sheet, which is also recommended for door units that differ from the DIN measurements. In this case, the hinge reference lines for the door leaf and door frame will be recorded in the order confirmation (see below).

2 For a hinge to function properly, it must be firmly fixed to the masonry/stud construction.

Hinge construction:

Type class V:
two-dimensionally adjustable (domestic doors)

Type class VS:
with ball bearings, only two-dimensionally adjustable (frequent use)

Type class VN:
with sliding contact bearings, two or three-dimensionally adjustable depending on the hinge retainer (frequent use)

Type class VSX:
VS ball bearing hinges with three-dimensional hinge retainer (frequent use)

Type class VX:
with sliding contact bearings. A further development of the hinges mentioned above. These are used where the door is subjected to heavy use. They are always three-dimensionally adjustable

DOOR HINGES

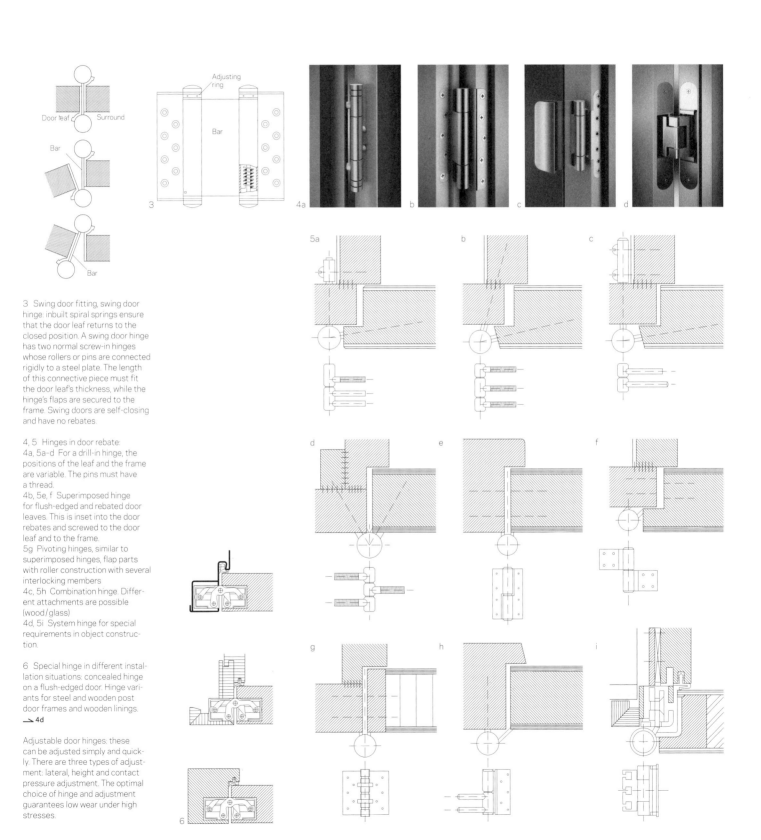

3 Swing door fitting, swing door hinge: inbuilt spiral springs ensure that the door leaf returns to the closed position. A swing door hinge has two normal screw-in hinges whose rollers or pins are connected rigidly to a steel plate. The length of this connective piece must fit the door leaf's thickness, while the hinge's flaps are secured to the frame. Swing doors are self-closing and have no rebates.

4, 5 Hinges in door rebate:
4a, 5a–d For a drill-in hinge, the positions of the leaf and the frame are variable. The pins must have a thread.
4b, 5e, f Superimposed hinge for flush-edged and rebated door leaves. This is inset into the door rebates and screwed to the door leaf and to the frame.
5g Pivoting hinges, similar to superimposed hinges, flap parts with roller construction with several interlocking members
4c, 5h Combination hinge. Different attachments are possible (wood/glass)
4d, 5i System hinge for special requirements in object construction.

6 Special hinge in different installation situations: concealed hinge on a flush-edged door. Hinge variants for steel and wooden post door frames and wooden linings.
→ 4d

Adjustable door hinges: these can be adjusted simply and quickly. There are three types of adjustment: lateral, height and contact pressure adjustment. The optimal choice of hinge and adjustment guarantees low wear under high stresses.

SLIDING DOOR FITTINGS

ence line. ◢ 1-S. 114 Door leaf sizes, the fit of hinges and locks and the relationship between these values are specified in DIN 18101(doors for residential buildings). Hinges are available with various surface treatments: galvanized, plastic-coated, stainless steel (for corrosion-prone areas), brass-plated or with standard colors.

SLIDING DOOR SYSTEMS

Sliding doors may slide to the left or right. They may have one or two leaves, and may slide in front of the wall or disappear into a pocket within the wall. Sliding door fittings consist of a track and at least two carriages per leaf, with end stops and guide cams at the bottom.

In top-mounted systems, the top rail bears the load of the suspended door leaf and must be designed accordingly. Manual sliding doors combine the grip with the latching or locking system Self-closing, automatic sliding doors used as fire protection need a tested automatic closer such as a magnetic hold-open device with smoke detector release.

Where the track is at floor level, it takes the whole weight of the sliding door. With some flooring materials, an inset track channel may require a groove to be cut. A surface-mounted rail, in contrast, projects from the finished floor. Where there is no floor guide and their weight is not enough to prevent it, the door leaves may tilt forwards. The construction of sliding doors is not completely soundproof, airtight or smoketight, so brush seals are often used. With external sliding doors, for instance, it is difficult to protect the lower frame from driving rain.

A playful, sensitive approach to sliding doors can be seen in the extension of the former vicarage of St. Gertrudis in Leuven. Architects Philippe Vander Maren and Mireille Weerts used the door surface to construct and elaborate a variation on a classic theme. The sliding door system consists of double-leaved doors that slide in front of the wall. The flush door leaves are of a typical construction, with inset edge bands, inserts and facings with different finishes: a mirror foil with simple grips on one side and a mirror motif printed on the other.

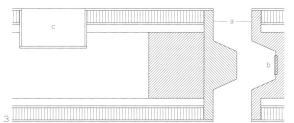

1, 2, 4 Sliding doors in former rectory, Leuven, 2008, Philippe Vander Maren and Mireille Weerts.

2 Horizontal section through sliding door, 1:2:
a solid oak
b magnet
c stainless steel recessed grip polished on all sides, 35 x 140 mm, non-welded

5 Vertical section through sliding door, 1:2:
a brushed stainless steel 100 x 6 mm
b spacer, brushed stainless steel
c ball-bearing carriage, thickness 3
d guidance rail, thickness 3, the same length as the stainless steel panels
e solid wood frame 35 mm
f fiberboard 4 mm
g zinc sheeting
h chipboard 8 mm
i enameled metal sheeting
j polished stainless steel sheeting
k stainless steel sheeting
l tubular chipboard

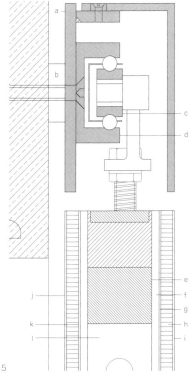

6 Sliding gear for internal doors:
roller sliding door track /
ball-bearing sliding door track
a wall fixing
b ceiling fixing
c floor guide
d wall angle bracket
e mortise sliding-bolt lock with pull
handle

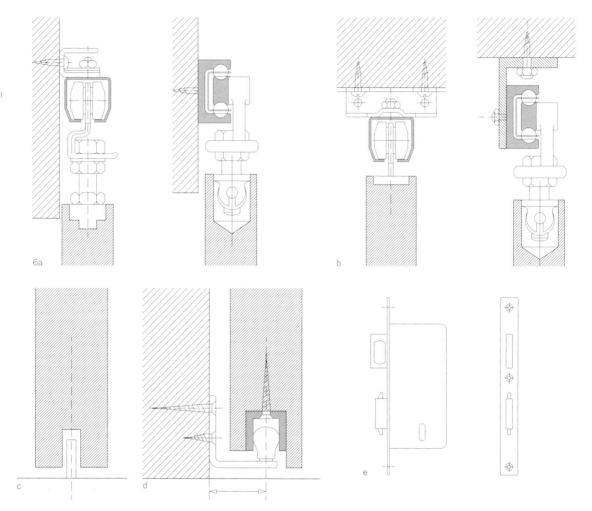

LIFT-AND-SLIDE DOOR FITTINGS
A sliding door that has to be lifted out of the frame rebate during opening and closing resists wind and driving rain better. The barrier-free threshold of a lift and slide door is constructed so that the outer and inner area are thermally decoupled, avoiding cold floor areas in front of this window / door system. The seal system guarantees maximum resistance to wind and driving rain, as well as sound insulation and intrusion resistance.

LOCKS
Historically, screwed-on case locks evolved into non-visible, integrated fittings, set into door leaves that gradually became thicker in order to accommodate all necessary functions. Consequently, locks can be divided into rim locks, metal frame locks for metal frame door panels and mortise locks for door leaves. Non-integrated case locks were once used that combined lock and handle in a single visible component. Today, the two functions are outwardly separated. Locks are mortised in and the different door handles on the door leaf are coupled by means of a square shaft.
Mortise locks with strike plates and bolts as described in DIN 18251 for latching and barring hinged doors at the frame. The latch's primary function is to keep the door

LOCK FITTINGS

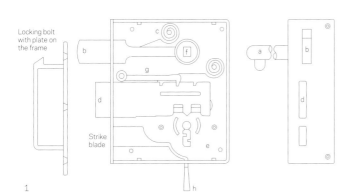

closed, while the bolt prevents unauthorized access. All mortise locks are installed in special recesses in the door leaf. The planner should bear in mind the size of the lock case and bolt, the width of the face plate and the length of the lock case, and harmonize these with the width of the door leaf. ➘ 5

Metal frame locks are therefore used for doors with narrow stiles (< 120 mm), such as solid wood frame doors. They are based on the standards observed by individual manufacturers. Mortised locks can be warded locks, profile cylinder locks or bit key locks.

WARDED LOCKS
Warded locks are found in standard interior doors and other simple doors. They can be locked with a single or double turn using differently shaped keys. They are not permitted for special doors, such as smoke-stop doors, and are also not recommended for high-performance soundproof doors. Profile cylinder locks are always used for fire protection doors, but if a warded lock-type key-hole is required, these can be manufactured with a special warded lock insert. DIN 18252 governs the installation of profiled cylinder locks. The profile cylinder lock with pin tumblers, as described in DIN 18254, is the present standard construction. The bolt is moved into locked position by a double turn of the key (dead bolt). Locks for bathrooms are single-turn and operated simply by turning a vertical pin.

REQUIREMENTS AND ADDITIONAL FUNCTIONS
The general requirements for locks are grouped in 4 classes. ➘ 4 Additional functions include action of the key on the latch bolt function, particularly for apartment entrance doors with a handle on one side (a knob/handle combination). This prevents unauthorized access when the bar is in the forward position. Another special feature is multiple locking, which is a special closing fitting

for intrusion prevention and is classified according to its resistance. Other additional functions include corrosion-proofing, radiation-proofing and panic functions.

ESCAPE DOOR SYSTEMS
Regulations for the construction of escape doors were harmonized across Europe since 2003. The lock, fittings and mounting accessories are tested together and can only be sold and installed as a certified unit. Depending on the area of use, a distinction is made between emergency exit locks and panic locks.

EMERGENCY EXITS
To permit a quick and safe exit, the escape door must be openable by a single hand grip with a maximum force of 70 newtons (7 kg approx.). Where a panic is not expected in an emergency, emergency exit locks as described in DIN EN 179 are used. This applies to non-public buildings, such as workplaces and office buildings, and this kind of system requires everyone in the building to know the escape routes and doors and how they work. The basic geometry of the handle is specified to prevent injuries.

PANIC DOORS
Panic doors as described in DIN EN 1125 are used in public buildings where visitors must operate escape doors without any instructions and without being familiar with how they work: e. g. hospitals, schools, public administration buildings, airports, meeting places and shopping centers. As people might be crushed against the escape door in the event of a panic, bar handles or push bars must be fitted instead of door handles. These must cover 60 % of the door's width and may not require a force in excess of 80 newtons (approx. 8 kg) to open them. Appropriate handles, knobs or blind plates should be mounted on the exterior face.

1 Historical surface-mounted case lock with latch and bolt for thin, solid, framed door leaves:
a grip/lever/handle
b lifting latch
c spring
d lock striker plate for warded lock key
e lock casing/plate
f socket
g pull
h additional bolt

2 Mortise lock.

3 Biometric fingerprint reading system: the finger is run over the thermal scanning strip and the door unlocks automatically. As well as providing access to the house, this system also prevents unauthorized access. As no fingerprint is left on the scanner strip, manipulation of the system is practically impossible.

Lock requirements in 4 classes:

Class 1:
low stress
Class 2:
moderate stress
Class 3:
medium-weight interior door lock used in object area, subject to regular operational checks
Class 4:
official door locks, high visitor frequency or need for intrusion prevention, subject to regular operational checks

4

LOCKS

5 Terms and measurements for face plate locks: where security requirements are low, warded locks are standard. The key bit fits into the motion link of the case lock's top so that the key can be put in and the bolt can be moved by turning the key.

6 Intrusion prevention lock system: with additional multiple locking function according to resistance class. Apart from the main mortise lock, there are two additional bolts (secondary locks).

7 Mortised lock case and mounting position: this influences the thickness of the door leaf and the corresponding lock strike plate on the frame. The lock's bolt and latch move in the recesses in the strike plate. This is inset in the door frame's rebate and screwed in. Lock strike plates are available for rebated and non-rebated doors. A distinction is made between angle strikers, normal strike plates, beveled strike plates and security strike plates.

8 Differently constructed lock cylinders:
a profile cylinder
b round cylinder
c oval cylinder

9 Differently constructed lock cylinders:
a double cylinder
b half cylinder (for thinner door leaves)
c thumb turn cylinder

10 Key types:
a warded key
b lever key
c cylinder security key
d dimple key
e three-dimensional coding

11 How the currently widespread cylinder lock, which was patented by Linus Yale in the USA in 1851, works. The key's profiled surface moves the pins in the cylinders.

Keycard systems function mechanically or electrically without physical contact, using magnetic cards, coded keys or other data carriers. They are used in hotels and other large buildings.

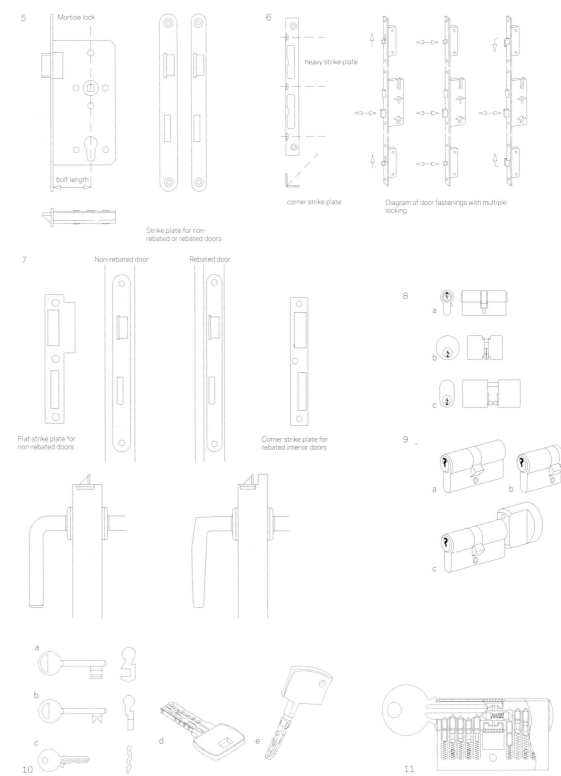

5 Mortise lock

bolt length

Strike plate for non-rebated or rebated doors

heavy strike plate

corner strike plate

Diagram of door fastenings with multiple locking

7 Non-rebated door Rebated door

Flat strike plate for non-rebated doors

Corner strike plate for rebated interior doors

8
a
b
c

9
a b
c

10
a
b
c
d
e

11

MEANS OF CLOSING DOORS

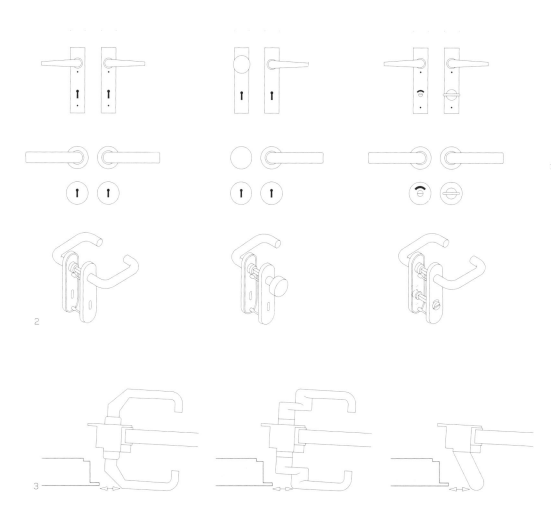

1   Emergency exit door with an emergency exit lock; panic handle.

2   "Door accessories" include the door handle and the two plates or rosettes. Plates may be long, short or broad. Door handles are made from all commonly used metals or from plastic.

3   Steel door and doorframes with strike plate.

4   Overview of automatic door closer systems:
a   integrated overhead door closer with concealed slide rail (linear action)
b   overhead door closer with visible hinged arm
c   floor spring door closer
d   coupled floor spring door closer

5   Glazed emergency exit door with panic handle and biometric finger-print reading system.

6   Integrated, inconspicuous closing systems affect a door's appearance less. Available systems include floor spring door closers and concealed door closer systems integrated into the door leaf or frame. The door leaf must be thick enough for the mechanism to fit inside it.

CLOSING DEVICES

Mortise locks for fire compartment doors and smoke-stop doors as described by DIN 18250 are a special case, as these are self-closing. Safety in case of fire is ensured either independently or as part of a comprehensive system. Choosing the right combination of regulation fittings, lock and accessories is crucial in allowing the doors to be used in accordance with standard procedure. Door closers automatically close (in a controlled way) doors that have been opened manually. This can be done by an overhead door check (which can also be used for smoke and heat extraction systems), a floor-spring door closer, or a spring hinge.

The energy created by the door opening is mechanically stored in a spring, and the closing action can be hydraulically dampened. The degree of dampening, the closing force and other details can be adjusted depending on the model. A considered choice of closing mechanism and mounting should be part of a door's design concept. Closing devices are available with different surface finishes (e.g. standard colors, stainless steel, brass etc.) to match the other door fittings.

Overhead door closers use visible scissor-action arms or runners. If there are issues concerning the appearance of the door, it is a good idea to install the overhead door closer in a concealed position. The advantage of inserting door closers into the floor lies in the system's high loadbearing capacity and reliability. This also preserves the door's appearance. The space in the floor needed for the closer's protective box is approx. 65 mm between the upper surfaces of the structural slab and the finished floor. It has to be mortared in and fixed to the structural slab. This system dispenses with projecting components that would otherwise obstruct doors when opening.

DOOR CLOSERS

4a   b   c   d

5

Automated door actuators open the door automatically when triggered by a sensor, button etc. Requirements are specified in DIN 18650 (automatic door systems). These pivoting drives open doors by moving an arm or sliding rod and are used in goods transport areas, or in areas with heavy pedestrian traffic.

SPECIAL EQUIPMENT

For doors to be automatically opened and closed, they must be connected to an electricity supply. Current consumers in the frame can be connected directly to the cable outlet on the door leaf surface, using a flexible metal tube to protect the cable. This apparatus is set above the upper hinge. If it is desirable for the run of the cable from the wall to the door leaf not to be seen, it can be concealed in the door rebate at the hinge edge.

Magnetic catches for holding fire doors open are connected to the fire alarm system. In the event of a fire hazard, the door is released and automatically closed. Magnetic hold-opens may be surface-mounted or recessed flush into the wall, floor or ceiling.

Door selectors
a   projecting arm door selector
b   projecting arm door selector with detent, concealed in transom
c/d   door selector integrated into door closer

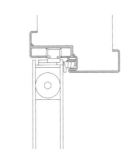

Door leaf construction with frame-mounted door closer in a wrap-around steel frame

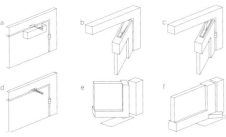

Door closer types
a   top door closer
b   frame door closer with swing function
c   frame door closer with single-side action
d   door closer mounted inside transom
e   floor spring closer with double action (for swing doors)
f   floor spring closer with single action

Door leaf construction with frame-mounted door closer behind a fascia

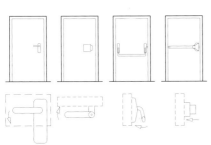

Emergency exit door locks   Panic door locks

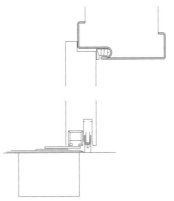

6   Door leaf construction with floor-spring closer

DOOR SEALS

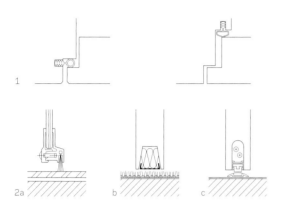

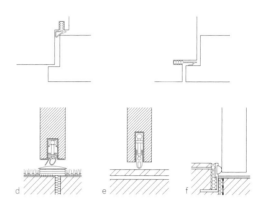

1 Rebate seals:
Side and top seals for doors. Sealing strips are inserted in a groove in the frame.

2 Floor seals:
a brush seal made from natural horsehair on a wooden door
b contact seal with height-adjustable sealing strip
c automatic drop-down door seal with elastic strip on a level flooring material
d acoustic seal (sound-absorbing chamber seal) on the lower edge of the door leaf
e automatic magnetic seal with a magnetic strip dropping to seal the gap.
f rabbetted threshold with continuous seal and thermally separated threshold joint

3 Different types of chamber seal, multiple chamber seal and lip seal.

Sealing strips are described and classified according to their properties, on the basis of the EN 12365 product standard. These components, their construction, certification and calculations are also governed by national regulations. Seals improve functionality by reducing natural air exchange, but this also leads to high levels of condensation in rooms. The planner must evaluate the expected room climate and room temperature. A distinction is made between sealing strips for exterior doors, interior doors, and special-purpose doors, as well as floor door seals.

EXTERIOR DOORS
For exterior doors, it makes sense to have separate windproof and rainproof constructions. For these two sealing levels to function optimally, the door's closing pattern (how often it is opened and closed, for instance) must be assessed. Silicon strips are often used, as the substance is soft and can compensate for warping and deviations within tolerances.

INTERIOR DOORS
A distinction is made between insulation and sealing strips. The sealant's tolerance of paint and varnish should be tested. A door with a sealing and insulating function needs sealing strips; but they can also be used on special sound insulating doors. Unlike door leaves whose pivot point does not lie over the joint, flush-edged doors need special seals, as the leaves tend to rub on them. The choice of sealing strip depends on the pivot point of the door leaf. There are profiles for use in linings, leaves and folding elements, as well as in frames. There are also special seals for steel frames and brush seals for sliding doors.

SOUND INSULATION AND SMOKE CONTAINMENT
Acoustic insulation properties are generally required for apartment doors in residential buildings. Apartment entrance doors must not warp more than 4 mm (RAL product and test specifications), and this warping must be compensated for appropriately. A design should be chosen that combines ease of closing with the greatest possible tolerance compensation. The seals must be smoke-tight: if there is a fire, they must not let any smoke through. Smoke-stop doors can save lives and are therefore an essential part of a fire protection concept: most deaths caused by fire are due to inhaling smoke. Aspects such as joint permeability and the expected level of warping play a crucial role in this. For instance, a door leaf with aluminum inset on both sides, which provides very good warping stability in wet areas, would be unsuitable in a fire protection context. High temperature stress causes aluminum to expand too much on one side. making the joint spring open and increasing leakage. Smoke-stop doors and seals are certified after a permeability inspection; the leakage rate when the door is closed must not exceed a certain level. The fitness for purpose of these special seals is ensured by ongoing functional checks. To ensure acoustic insulation and smoke containment and the reliable closing of the joints, there should be a clearly perceptible closing pressure. For special-purpose doors, an operating force of up to 20 N is acceptable (ISO 8274).

FLOOR AND DOOR SEALS
Floor seals fulfill a number of different requirements and interior doors are fitted with them as well as exterior doors. Above all, these seals close joints for acoustic insulation and smoke containment purposes. Depending on the way they operate, they are described as contact seals, recessed seals, acoustic seals, magnetic seals or threshold seals.

GATES / INDUSTRIAL DOORS

4 Diagrammatic elevation of a sectional door with transparent panels and a wicket gate. ↘ 8

5 Details of sectional door:
a guide channel
b door leaf
c guide roller

6 Diagrammatic section through a sectional door with solid lintel over the opening:
a door segment
b concrete lintel
c guide channel
d electric motor

7 Sectional door—with cladding of horizontal wood slats, and fascia in place of lintel: ↘ 9
a door segment with wood cladding
b fascia
c motor
d electric motor
e guide channel

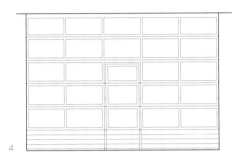

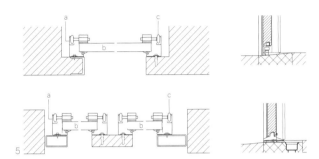

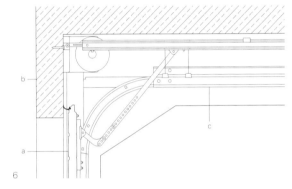

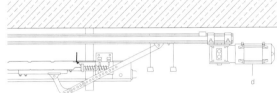

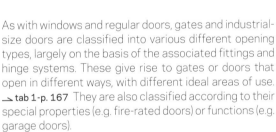

As with windows and regular doors, gates and industrial-size doors are classified into various different opening types, largely on the basis of the associated fittings and hinge systems. These give rise to gates or doors that open in different ways, with different ideal areas of use. ↘ tab 1-p. 167 They are also classified according to their special properties (e.g. fire-rated doors) or functions (e.g. garage doors).

Gates are used both by pedestrians and by vehicles. Throughout history, additional smaller integrated doors—known as wicket doors or pass doors—have been used to avoid having to open the whole hinged gate or overhead door every time.

Folding up-and-over doors, overhead coiling doors, overhead sectional doors or garage doors, as well as roller shutters, are integrated constructions, available on order from the manufacturer as finished units that only need to be installed by workmen on site.

Overhead coiling doors consist of interlocking profiled sheet steel laths or from insulated sandwich laths. The laths are made from steel or aluminum, single or double-skin. Overhead coiling doors as wide as 10 m are available for industrial premises. The door is coiled up in front of or behind the lintel, and moves along guide channels at the sides. These are integrated systems subject to official technical approval, the design of which cannot be significantly influenced.

SECTIONAL DOORS

Sectional or membered doors are doors that open vertically. The sections are raised and stowed in the open position by various means. The usual opening mechanisms stow them horizontally or vertically beneath the ceiling or at a certain angle, or fold them horizontally or vertically. ↘ p. 101 The sections are supported by guide rails at the side. The weight must be offset to make the door easy to operate; this is done by a torsion spring shaft, counterweights or a compression or tension spring system.

Opaque doors consist mainly of insulated double-skin sheet steel sections, while transparent or translucent sections are usually aluminum frame constructions filled in with glass, plastic or sandwich elements. The surfaces can be painted or coated in different colors. Doubled surfaces are also possible. For instance, wood facing can

GATES / INDUSTRIAL DOORS IN DETAIL
SCALE 1:5

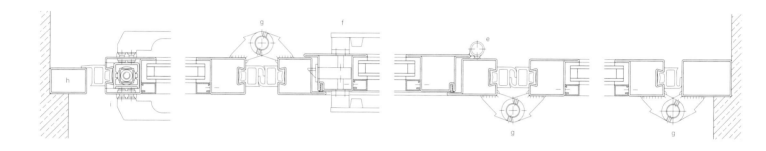

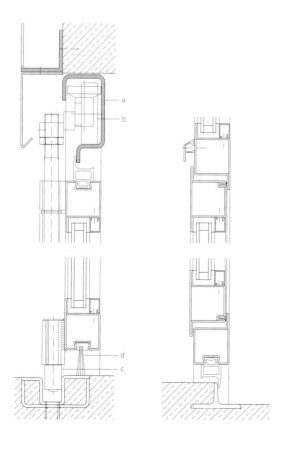

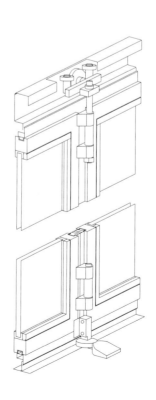

a   runner rail
b   loadbearing roller
c   guide
d   brush seal
e   pivot fitting
f   grip and lock wicket gate
g   folding hinges
h   sealing strip
i   lock using shoot bolt rod

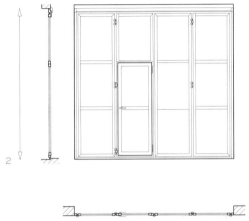

1 Simple wooden sliding gate with a wicket door / pass door. Mild steel track rail with visible rollers. All fittings mounted and visible.

2 Hinged, sliding folding door with wicket gate. ➔ 3

3

be fixed to the sections. Depending on the way the door is positioned in the opening's reveal, this can be used to create surfaces flush with the façade, effectively masking the door's principle of operation.

WORKING WITH STANDARD SYSTEM COMPONENTS
An individual gate system can be assembled using the semi-finished products provided by the manufacturer, as demonstrated in this example, a steel folding door. The variety of semi-finished products on offer—sections, fittings, locks, rails and seals—and the different ways of working with them can be used to create different designs. They are listed in a system catalogue, are compatible and freely combinable, allowing the semi-finished products to be matched and fitted to each other.
Development work in the technological systems sector involves the technical certification of the individual components and the product subsequently put together from them by the design engineer. These are usually a series of continuous sections that can be welded. The sections' shapes and dimensions can be matched to the door and window programs. This allows the planner to easily combine steel sections, and the person constructing the design to use identical accessory parts.

STEEL FOLDING GATE AND DOOR CONSTRUCTION
Tubular steel sections are an ideal material for gate and door construction. Their good static properties allow the use of small diameter sections. This means that large format elements with slender frames, resistant to distortion, are possible. Folding doors, sliding doors and

folding / sliding doors can be manufactured using the same systems. Folding doors have several leaves, which when opened are folded together at one side. These doors are usually hung on rails and guided by a rail or trolley on the floor. The door panels of the folding door can be sheet steel, sandwich panels or glazed frames welded together with special hinges.

Their construction allows the leaf weight to be reduced below that of wider-opening hinged doors, whose weight can cause problems with the hinges and with hanging the doors. As sliding doors put less stress on the hinges and the door hanging, they make very large door openings possible (hangar doors). The dimensions are affected by wind load and the maximum permissible deflection. Large expanses of insulating glass increase the leaf's weight, requiring a more rigid construction. The commonest approach to this is to use the same measurements as with a façade construction. Sliding and folding systems are either manually operated or automatically controlled.

OPEN | CLOSE
CASE STUDIES

CHAPTER 5

SCHOOL AND MULTI-PURPOSE HALL IN
RÜSCHLIKON, SWITZERLAND
RAMSER SCHMID, ZURICH

———————

The Rüschlikon school complex consists of several build-ings in different historical styles. The centrally placed primary school building is the main unit, while the other structures relate to the small houses of the neighbor-hood. To preserve the village's appearance, the new multi-purpose hall was dug into the hillside. From the outside, the only sign that it is there at all are the retaining walls, out of which, to the east, the extension to the school develops. On the roof of the sports hall is a school play-ground, on a level of its own between the upper and lower levels of the school play area. The architects developed skylights shaped like small play houses to light the sports hall beneath the playground. Together with a grove of trees, these structure the playground space and make the outside area more varied and interesting, while the visual connection and natural lighting they provide make the low-lying hall space a more pleasant place to be. At night, the skylight structures are illuminated from within, thus lighting up the playground area. Curtains allow day-light to be excluded from the hall so it can be lit entirely with artificial light if desired.

Daylight source, peep box and demarcating object—while using standard windows, the artists have developed an original approach to the skylight, combining function-alism with an architectural form that adds to the char-acter of the location. The rather whimsical shape and positioning of the play houses combine with an almost archaic simplicity. The same window system was used for the whole of the school extension: simple, two-part, white-glazed wooden windows subtly emphasized by pale concrete frames. The materials harmonize perfectly with the whitewashed masonry of the walls.
The facing masonry of the building's double-leaf wall is coated with a light-colored lime wash. Seen from a dis-tance, this gives the elements of the complex a homog-enous appearance, helping it to fit into its surroundings. Seen close to, the masonry's texture gives the building a lively quality and matches the retaining walls.

The "play house" skylights divide the playground on the gym hall roof into several areas and are illumi-nated at night.

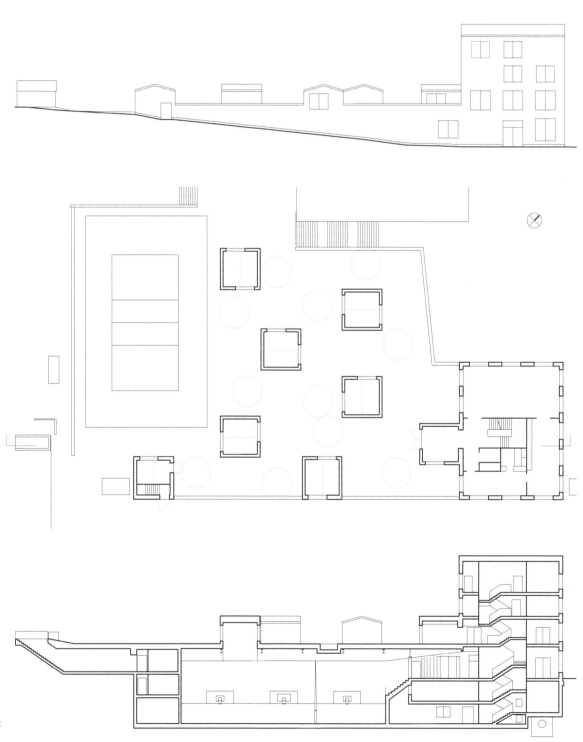

Drawings 1:500
Elevation, floor plan of playground
level. Longitudinal section throught
sports hall and extension building.

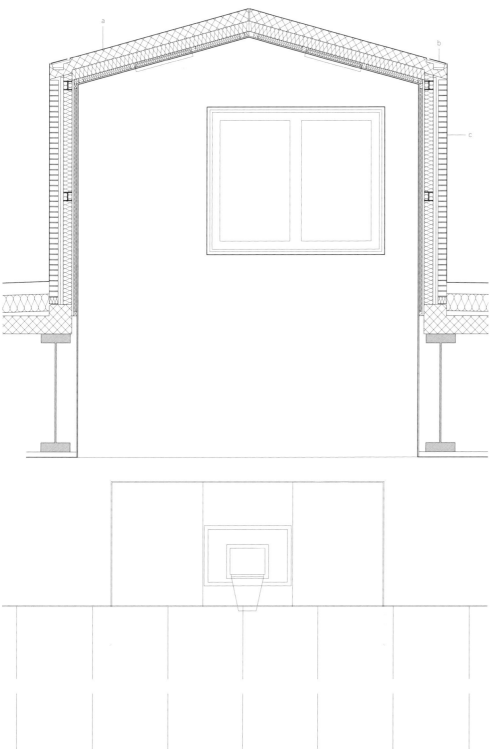

Sports hall/skylight. Vertical section 1:50

a   Roof construction:
Liquid synthetic roof sealant with sand
Prefabricated concrete element with gutter section
in drip area. Gutter fall, 40 mm
Extruded polystyrene insulation 120 mm, glued all
over and mechanically fastened
Wooden substructure/mineral insulation 60 mm
Plasterboard 12.5 mm, filled and painted

b   Gutter cover, secured with metal brackets glued
to the synthetic sealant coat

c   Wall construction:
Lime wash
Brick 120 mm
Back ventilation 30 mm
Water and wind repellent layer
Soft fiberboard 35 mm
Steel section HE-A 120, L-shaped steel section
as bracing
Thermal insulation 120 mm
Three-ply laminated board 25 mm
Vapor barrier
Wooden substructure/mineral insulation 40 mm
Plasterboard 12.5 mm, smoothed and painted

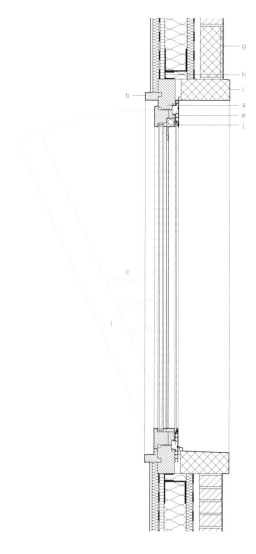

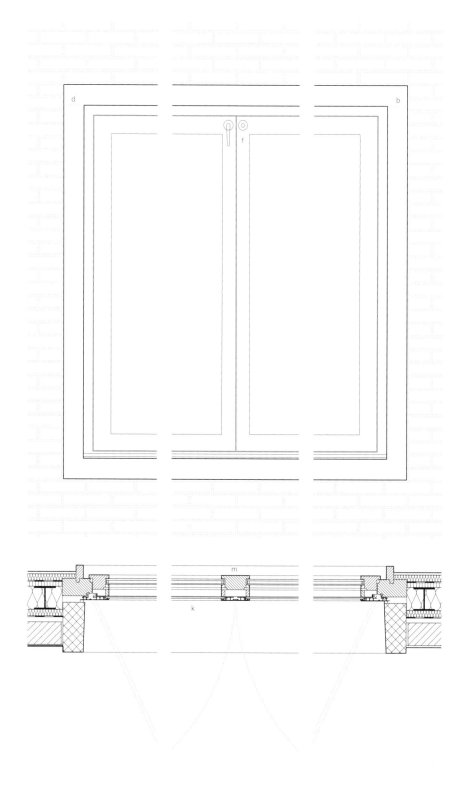

Skylight window. Vertical section, elevation,
horizontal section 1:20

a Wood and aluminum window, oak, 2 pivoting casements
b Oak inner wooden frame / oak reveal lining
c Side-mounted stays arms as fall protection
d Butt joint
e Aluminum casement frame
f Lock with handle for fire brigade (to release tilt function
   of the whole window)
g Prefabricated concrete lintel with facing stones affixed
   (irregular pattern)
h Steel section as window frame fastening
   (point fastening)
i Cladding / window surrounds, prefabricated concrete
   parts
j Slat blinds integrated into the casements
k Coupled window with single glazing on the outside and
   double glazing on the inside
l Tilting casement, travel approx. 600 mm
m Wooden window post

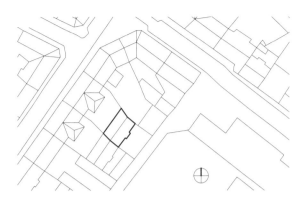

LOFT CONVERSION IN MUNICH, GERMANY
ANDREAS MECK WITH SUSANNE FRANK, MUNICH

The brief was to extend and upgrade an existing attic apartment by converting the roof space above it. This is located in the rear block of listed building from the Wilhelmine period between Munich's inner city and the River Isar.

The double pitch and structural peculiarities of the mansard roof gave the existing space a potential that has been exploited by extending it upwards to the ridge.

The challenge was to convert the low, dark upper attic into a living space within the limits permitted for a listed building.

Using conventional roof window units, several raised skylights were inserted into the roofspace. Their frames project above the roof, providing greater headroom beneath them. This opens up previously unusable spaces under the slope of the roof for uses such as the bathroom. The reveals, which are sometimes angled, face either to the east or the west, allowing light to penetrate deep into the space throughout the day. The window frames and casings are made of pine.

Black fitted furniture incorporating an en suite bathroom structures the otherwise open studio space, creating a surprise effect against the otherwise pale surfaces. The materials used are minimalist and based around the contrast between the bright white walls and larchwood floorboards, on the one hand, and the black fitted furnishings on the other. Subdued, smooth surfaces interact with a lively structure.

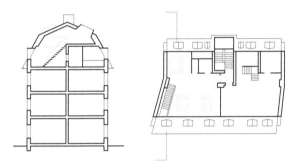

Site plan 1:1000
Floor plan of roof space,
section 1:500.

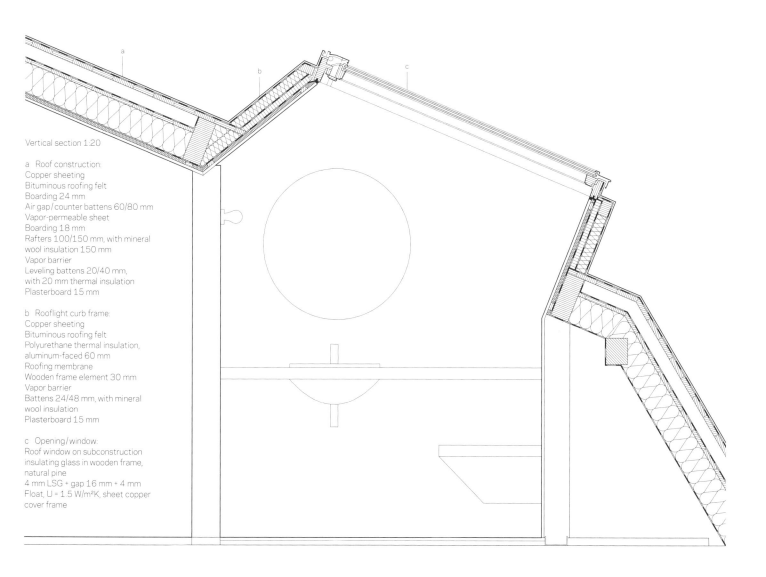

Vertical section 1:20

a   Roof construction:
Copper sheeting
Bituminous roofing felt
Boarding 24 mm
Air gap / counter battens 60/80 mm
Vapor-permeable sheet
Boarding 18 mm
Rafters 100/150 mm, with mineral
wool insulation 150 mm
Vapor barrier
Leveling battens 20/40 mm,
with 20 mm thermal insulation
Plasterboard 15 mm

b   Rooflight curb frame:
Copper sheeting
Bituminous roofing felt
Polyurethane thermal insulation,
aluminum-faced 60 mm
Roofing membrane
Wooden frame element 30 mm
Vapor barrier
Battens 24/48 mm, with mineral
wool insulation
Plasterboard 15 mm

c   Opening / window:
Roof window on subconstruction
insulating glass in wooden frame,
natural pine
4 mm LSG + gap 16 mm + 4 mm
Float, U = 1.5 W/m²K, sheet copper
cover frame

RENOVATION/CONVERSION OF MORITZBURG IN HALLE, GERMANY
NIETO SOBEJANO, MADRID

The Moritzburg in Halle was built in the fifteenth century. Since 1904, the former castle has housed a museum with a remarkable collection of modern art, chiefly German Expressionist works.

The donation of a private collection containing major works by artists from the "Die Brücke" group to the Moritzburg foundation created a need for more space, and resulted in a new, expressive roof extension being added to the exhibition space. Folds and kinks in the pitched roof create various different kinds of skylight. These conical projections and depressions change the shape of the building while providing the new exhibition spaces with daylight. The openings have glare protection and darkening systems on their inner side, allowing for controlled and even lighting.

The suspension of the new exhibition areas from the roof structure keeps the ruined building's existing spaces free of any fittings that might interrupt them, allowing them to be used and divided in a variety of ways. This precise, angular superstructure made from gleaming sheet metal contrasts with the irregular shape and aged masonry of the ruin. At the same time, the conical skylights combine with the steep gable roof of the chapel to create an effective ensemble.

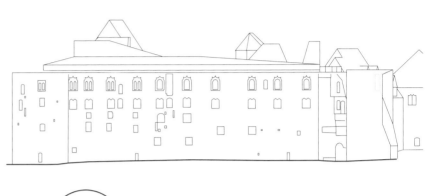

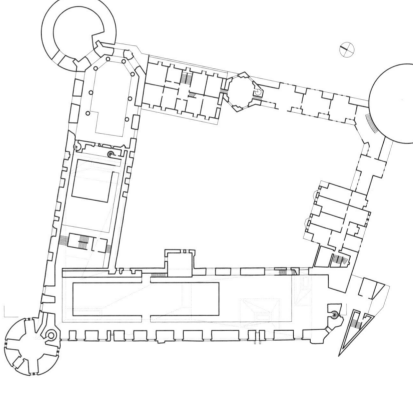

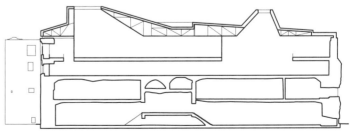

East elevation, floor plan and longitudinal section through new exhibition area 1:1000.

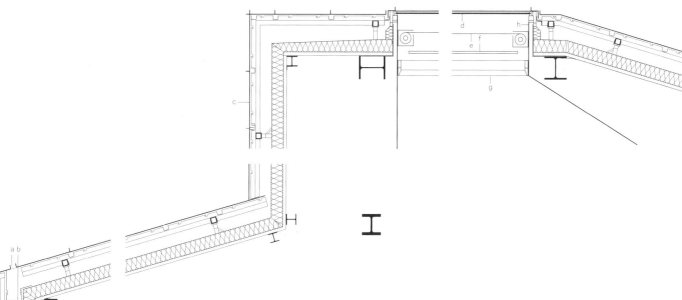

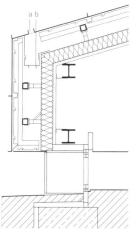

Vertical section 1:20.

a Aluminum grating to catch leaves, reversible
b Aluminum box gutter, NG 500, with sound deadening coating on the reverse side

c Roof construction:
Cast aluminum plates 8 mm, joint 5 mm
Suspended bolts 10 mm
EPDM foil seal
Insulation 160 mm
Vapor barrier
Aluminum section with punched suspension points.
Drainage parallel to slope 60/60 mm
Aluminum section. Drainage perpendicular to direction of section
Corrugated sheeting 40 mm

d Structural glazing system, overhead glazing, 2° angle
e Darkening system
f Lighting; illuminated ceiling
g Tensile membrane on folding frame, pull cord mechanism
h Exhaust air, perforated aluminum sheet with square holes

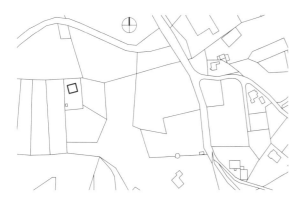

HOLIDAY HOME IN FURX, AUSTRIA
MARTE MARTE, WEILER

———————

The building stands in an exposed position on the brow of a hill with views in all directions, as far as the distant Lake Constance. The house was constructed from pre-fabricated wooden elements around a concrete core with a fireplace. A few carefully positioned openings create a clear pattern of open and closed surfaces. Their depth makes them especially visible from a distance, giving the building a striking appearance.

The ground floor is divided into four different areas. For each of these, a floor-to-ceiling opening is cut into the outer walls, bringing the surrounding landscape into the interior. Some of these openings, situated at the interface between the interior and exterior, have been constructed as niches of different depths, allowing them to be experienced as spaces in their own right—some with a specific purpose, depending on the function of the room they are associated with. While the openings for the kitchen and the entrance area to the south, which is fronted by a terrace, are only slightly recessed, the living area, to the west, has a deep loggia. The openings for the ground floor have three different closure mechanisms: full-height sliding elements that allow the opening to be closed completely, fabric roller blinds and the window itself. The windows and doors are made of solid larch wood; oiled, matt larch wood is also used as a veneer for the interior.

The use of openings that create spaces extends to the strip windows in the roof storey, which are also recessed, creating storage space beneath the windows. Glazed panels between the ceiling and free-standing interior walls preserve the roof's spatial effect, despite the compact room layout.

Site plan, not to scale

Deep, sharply demarcated cut-aways in the facade, such as the loggia to the west, structure the building's facade.

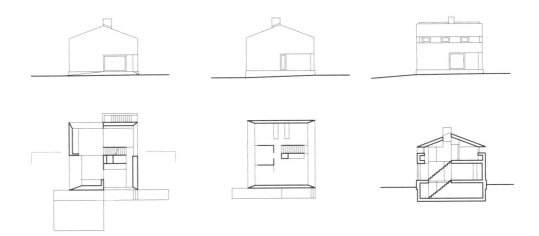

North, east and south elevations.
Plans of ground floor and upper
floor, section 1:500.

A view of the entrance, on the
south side of the building.

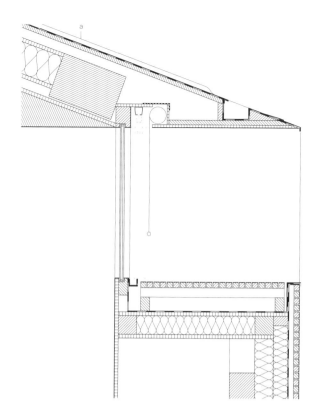

Photograph taken from the southwest
Strip window, upper floor. Vertical section, elevation,
horizontal section 1:20

a   Roof construction:
Sheet metal strips with standing seam, stainless steel
Underlay, bitumen sheet 4 mm
Wooden boarding 24 mm
Counter battens 50 mm
Three-ply laminated board 20 mm
Wooden beam with mineral wool insulation 160 mm
Three-ply laminated board 20 mm
Battens (angled) with mineral wool insulation 50 mm
Plywood sheet, larchwood veneer 15 mm

b   Wall construction, upper storey:
Horizontal planking, larch 30/30 mm
Vertical planking, larch
Air gap 100 mm
Wind barrier (UV resistant)
Three-ply laminated board 20 mm
Wooden section with mineral wool insulation 100 mm
Three-ply laminated board 20 mm
Battens with mineral wool insulation 50 mm
Vapor barrier

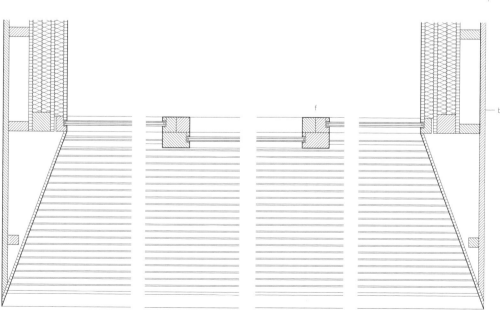

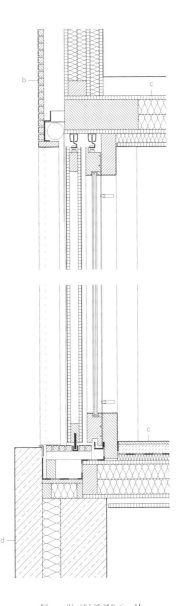

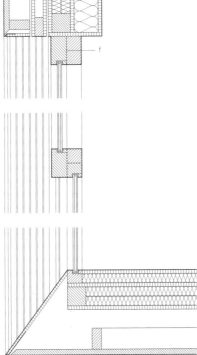

French door (ground floor): Vertical section, horizontal section 1:20

c Floor structure: ground floor and upper floor:
Wood block flooring, larch 15 mm
Underfloor heating screed 65 mm
Vapor barrier
Impact sound insulation 20 mm
Three-ply laminated board 20 mm
Wooden joist with mineral wool insulation 160 mm
Three-ply laminated board 20 mm
Wooden battens (angled) 35 mm
Plywood sheet, perforated, larchwood veneer 15 mm

d Wall of basement (above-ground):
Exposed concrete facing wall 150 mm
Insulation XPS 100 mm
Reinforced concrete (waterproof) 250 mm

e Wall construction of ground floor:
Horizontal battens, larch 30/30 mm
Vertical battens, larch
Air gap, 100 mm
Cavity for sliding doors 110 mm
Wind barrier (UV resistant)
Three-ply laminated board 20 mm
Wooden section with mineral wool insulation 100 mm
Three-ply laminated board 20 mm
Battens with mineral wool insulation 50 mm
Vapor barrier
Plywood sheet with larch veneer 15 mm

f Window:
Window and casement frames in larch 70 mm
Double glazing (U-value = 11 W/m²K), 24 mm

VILLA GARBALD IN CASTASEGNA, SWITZERLAND
MILLER MARANTA, BASEL

———————

The densely clustered settlement of the village of Castasegna runs along the Passstrasse, which slopes downward to the west. The settlement is characterized by houses given a Mediterranean urbanity by substantial facades directly on the street.

Gottfried Semper's Villa Garbald, on the other hand, is more like an Italian country house. Its narrow gable facade faces towards the valley. When the villa was converted to accommodate guests of the ETH Zurich, it was repaired and a new residential building was added on the site of the former barn. The richly furnished rooms in the main part of the existing villa were extensively restored and carefully adapted to the needs of its modern users. The new windows were constructed to match the original windows—made from spruce wood, with antique glass single glazing, and using the old handles.

The amorphous form of the exposed concrete extension owes nothing to the villa or to the valley's building traditions. Its simple, rocklike materials and shape give it an autonomy deeply rooted in its location. It evokes the North Italian bird-catching towers, or roccoli. Seen from the outside, the arrangement of the square openings cut into this structure shows no apparent order, although it does reveal the unusual arrangement of the storeys. Both the complex shape and the arrangement of the openings evoke design motifs from the old Engadine houses.

The windows are made from solid larch wood, which contrasts pleasantly with the exposed concrete. Their inner frames are an important design element and impart a warmth to the otherwise austere interior. Sun shading is provided by vertical sliding shutters with larch slats. They are pulled downwards, running along guide rails at the sides of the opening. The lower shutter can be folded outward and hung at the side to provide ventilation.

Semper's Villa Garbald, from the 19th century

"Roccolo": The tower-like new construction evokes the North Italian bird-catching towers. Its geometry and materials make it look like a rock projecting from the earth.

South elevation, section, plans 1:500. Ground floor (with surrounding) 1st–4th upper storeys.

Historical building
Vertical section, elevation, horizontal section 1:20

a   Window:
Wooden window with two side-hung casements:
Wooden surround and window casements: spruce
Glazing: single glazing with antique glass

b   Gathered slats, larchwood, coated
c   Wooden fascia, spruce
b   Granite window sill

e   Wall construction:
Plaster
Masonry (existing)
Solid spruce wood with coating

f   Ceiling construction:
Wood floorboards, larch on subconstruction
Wooden beam ceiling with pugging
Plaster, stucco

g   Panel shutter, spruce with coating

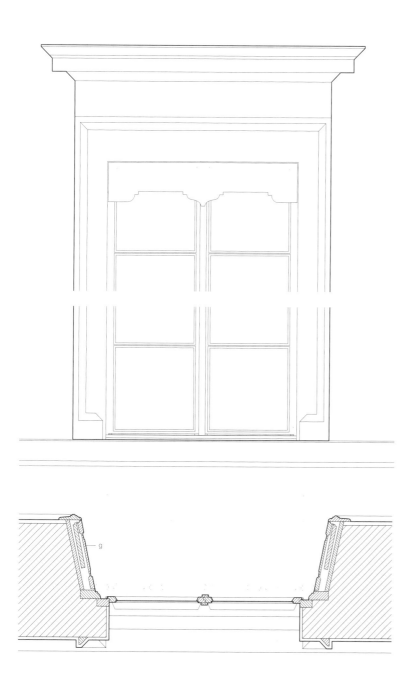

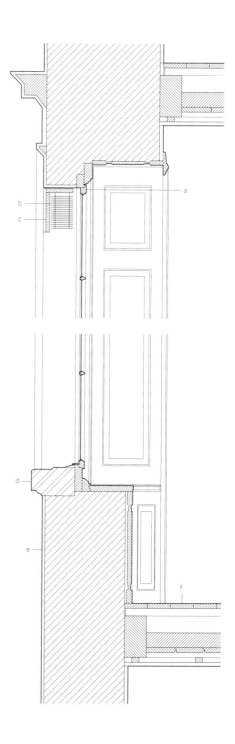

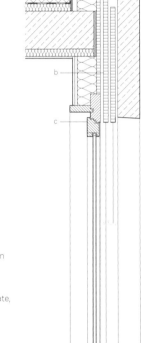

New building
Vertical section, elevation,
horizontal section 1:20

a Ceiling construction:
Granolithic concrete with
underfloor heating, 110 mm
Impact sound insulation, 40 mm
Reinforced concrete ceiling
240 mm, 200 mm in edge area
Ceiling insert, insulation 40 mm in
edge area
Gypsum plaster 5 mm

b Panel shutter, three-ply laminate,
larch, two-part, 24 mm, faced on
both sides with larchwood slab
board

c Window:
Window casement, natural larchwood 90/65 mm
Glazing: insulating glass, U-value
1.1 W/m²K
Glazing bead flush with surface,
square-edged
Surround, larchwood, natural finish
150/54 mm
inlay, larchwood
Glazing bead flush with surface,
square-edged

d Larch window sill

e Solid wall construction:
Exposed concrete, pressure-
washed 200 mm
Cellular glass 140 mm
Plasterboard sheet 15 mm
Gypsum plaster 5 mm

f Counterweight of sliding shutter
in wall niche

HAUS W IN HOMBURG / SAAR, GERMANY
BAYER STROBEL, KAISERSLAUTERN

———————

This building is on the edge of the city of Homburg, where, to the east, a view of the reed flats that fringe the Landstuhler Bruch opens up. This compact building accommodates two apartments, an additional 'granny flat' as well as a double garage. The ground plan is arranged in a way that allows the building to adapt to the changing needs of users without needing extensions. The building's clearly defined "block" shape with openings in all four walls and the roof characterize its external appearance. Carefully positioned cutaways (such as the loggia on the ground floor and the patio on the upper floor) give the interior a light and varied spatial structure within a subdued outer shell. The clinker masonry combines aesthetic quality with durability, while the bonding pattern references the Saarland's industrial traditions. Frame windows specially developed for the building permit fixed glazing flush with the surface of the facade alongside recessed opening casements. The change in glazing planes creates a niche inside the building and a sculptural sense of depth on the outside, expressing the dual nature of the space inherent in the depth of an opening. The window frames have a black coating on the outside and a milky glaze on the inside. The interior plaster is smoothed and painted white, in contrast to the exterior. The cement screed flooring is ground, glazed in a dark color tone and sealed. The use of wood can also be seen in the fitted cupboards.

Large-format openings to the rear of the building provide a view of the Landstuhler Bruch.

Vertical section, elevation, horizontal section 1:20

a   Roof construction:
Loose gravel 50 mm
EPDM rubber roof membrane
Sloped insulation rigid polystyrene sheet
100-220 mm, avg. 160 mm
Bitumen vapor barrier
Reinforced concrete slab 220 mm
Gypsum plaster 10 mm

b   Window construction:
Outer and inner frame: moabi wood,
black on outside with milky white glaze on inside
Glazing: thermal glazing, largest pane
approx. 2.70 x 4.40 m (east facade)
Fittings: Aluminum

c   Regular wall construction:
Clinker facing wall 115 mm
Air gap 50 mm
Mineral wool 100 mm
Sealant
Sand-lime blocks (LMUs) 175 mm
Gypsum plaster 15 mm

d   Floor construction:
Screed 70 mm with underfloor heating
Impact sound insulation 25 mm
Reinforced concrete 220 mm
Gypsum plaster 10 mm

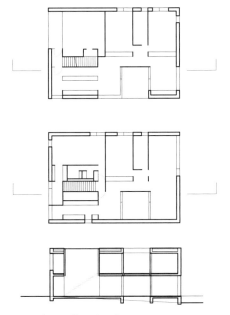

Plan of ground floor, plan of upper
floor, longitudinal section 1:500.

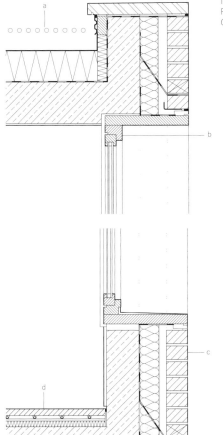

SCHOOL IN VELLA, SWITZERLAND
BEARTH & DEPLAZES, CHUR

———————————

Four buildings—the existing primary school, the assembly hall, the new sixth form building and the multi-purpose hall—are grouped around a shared square in an ensemble that extends into open terrain and anchors itself there.

The school's playground provides the school with a sporting venue and the community of Vella with a site for open-air events. The theatre stage of the hall can be opened up to the square by means of four large folding/sliding elements. Like a "wallpapered door", the surfaces of these elements are plastered in the same way as the rest of the building, and are barely noticeable when closed. Instead, the openings that really characterize the facade are the openings for the classrooms. The series of identical openings reflect the floor plan on the outside of the building and make it recognizable as a school building. The funneled window reveals are painted an opaque white. They make the glazed ochre-colored plaster appear as a thin skin, while together creating a relief effect that gives depth to the facades. The windows are constructed from wood. In the hall, they have a cross-bar, owing to their size. While sun protection and darkening are provided by white roller blinds, interior blinds provide additional glare protection.

For economic reasons, emphasis was placed on the "multi-purpose use" of rooms and components, as well as the use of identical window elements. For instance, the characteristic ribbed ceilings combine a simple load-bearing structure with acoustic, lighting and heat storage systems, all of which go towards making them an aesthetically successful ceiling.

The entrance with the new sixth form building.

View of the north facade, which faces the lake, with large openings with fixed glazing and wooden opening vents.
The openings of the sixth form building have deep reveals and can be darkened using roller blinds.

Elevation and ground floor plan 1:750.

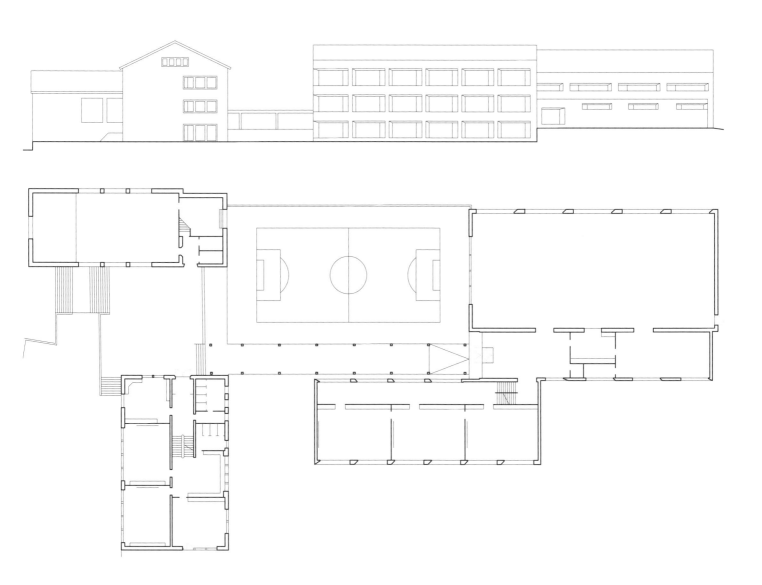

Vertical section, elevations, horizontal section (sixth form building) 1:20

a   Wall construction:
Finishing compound 10 mm
Base and final rendering 20 mm
Insulation 125 mm
Reinforced concrete 320 mm

b   Internal gathering blind
c   Sun blind
d   Wooden window
e   Weatherboard: aluminum section 56 mm
f   Fiber cement sill

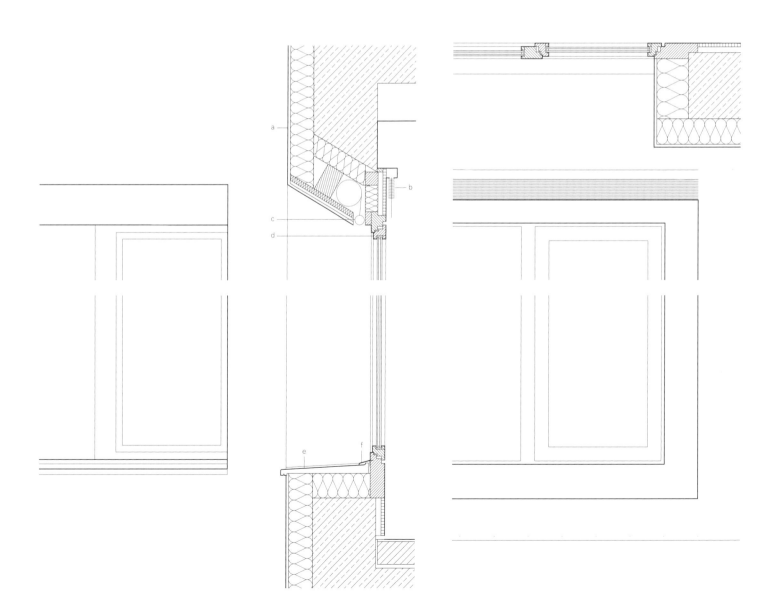

Vertical section, elevations, horizontal section (assembly hall) 1:20

a   Wall construction:
Rendering 20 mm
Insulation 120 mm
Reinforced concrete 300 mm

b   Protective cover solid wood 20 mm
c   Roller with ball-bearing, dia. = 40 mm
d   Internal roller blind; front tube, dia. = 40 mm, weighted with rollers
at sides dia. = 50 mm
e   Wooden window

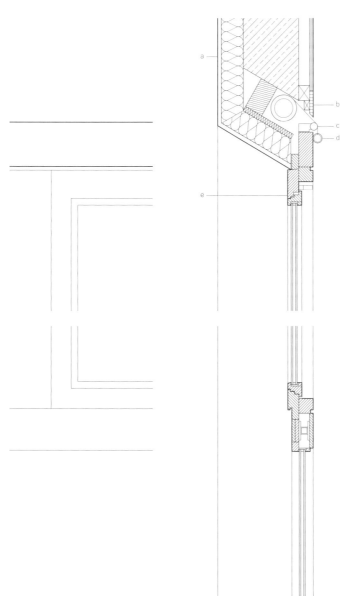

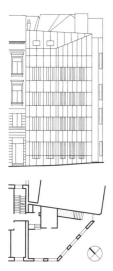

Floor plan, elevation 1:500.

In line with the monolithic design principle, the openings can be "veiled" by perforated steel folding blinds.

RESIDENTIAL/COMMERCIAL BUILDING IN BRUSSELS, BELGIUM
MARIO GARZANITI, LIÈGE

This building is located in Brabant, a district that was created during the expansion of Brussels in the nineteenth century. The main landmarks dating from this time, such as the station, the ring road and the botanical gardens, contrast with the district's internal structure, which is a jumble of streets. This quarter is inhabited by people of many different nationalities, and it features very different buildings standing side by side. Brabantstraat is a lively shopping area. Since the Second World War, there has been a small, irregular gap in the built fabric at the junction of Brabantstraat and Liedtstraat, which is now occupied by a building with a shop on the ground floor and two apartments on the upper floor.

The design of the building and its openings was inspired by Brabant's ethnic diversity: a building with a freestanding facade that is nonetheless integrated into the city's structure. This confident gesture is reinforced by the Corten steel sheeting. The coming and going of shoppers in the square can be filtered, acoustically and visually, by panel window shutters made of perforated steel. Like the Arabic mashrabiya, they place a veil before the opening to separate the public and private space. When they are closed, they turn the building into a monolithic structure; the occupants can observe the outside world undisturbed and can choose how open they want the building to be, thereby changing its appearance. In the interior, the perforations interact with the red-colored reveals and the superimposed wooden frames (doussie or more specifically afzelia wood) to create a warm, almost oriental atmosphere.

The perforations allow a certain amount of daylight to fall on the red-colored reveals. They interact with the wooden window and casement frames to give the interior an unexpectedly warm atmosphere.

Vertical section, exterior and interior elevation, horizontal section 1:20

a Window panel shutter, sheet steel, perforated, patinated, 4 mm

b Wall construction:
Sheet steel with patina 4 mm
Substructure steel sections, back ventilation
Facade membrane, permitting diffusion
Substructure battens 50/60 mm, with thermal insulation 60 mm in between
Masonry 190 mm
Internal plaster 14 mm

c Sheet stainless steel, sand-blasted 3 mm

d Latching

e Wooden window, afzelia

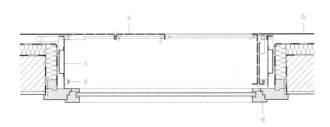

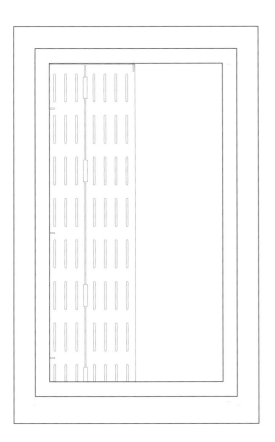

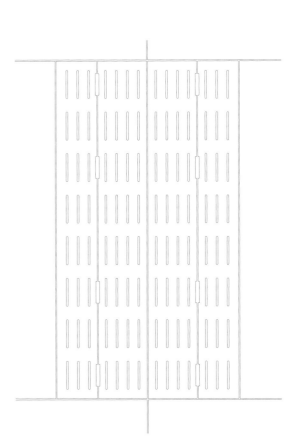

VERA RÖHM'S STUDIOS IN DARMSTADT, GERMANY
SCHAUER VOLHARD, DARMSTADT

Studios and exhibition spaces need glare-free, even lighting. A different type of opening, therefore, was chosen individually for each hall. Sometimes existing openings were used for lighting, sometimes new ones were created. The consistent use of matted glass filtered the incoming daylight, avoiding heavy shadows. Since the aim was not just to preserve the characteristic industrial architecture, but to show its alterations, an existing facade within the hall with the arched windows was opened up again. The original subdivision of the existing window openings was recreated by hand using narrow steel sections and new glass panes. This hall is lit by a strip window in the roof. The "light corridor" this creates can also be used as an exhibition space. To light the hall adjoining the sculpture garden, the brick infills of the steel framework construction were removed. A matted glass facade was constructed in front of them like a bay window, with enough space in between for ventilation to be provided at the sides through slatted shutters. This opening reveals the new role of the old factory hall to the outside world without allowing people to look in and without changing the existing structure.

The sun protection is adapted to the different needs of the different types of opening. The south facade has a fixed horizontal grille construction over the window strips. The east and west facades and the rooflights have external textile sun protection systems which can move automatically to provide cooling in summer (together with a night-time ventilation system).

All windows and glass facades have thermally insulating glazing. The brick facades have been cleaned and repaired, while bricks have also been used for the new building and the wall. The materials help to preserve the organic character of the complex. The design of the interior is restrained, providing both the creative process and the finished artworks with an appropriate setting: white predominates, combined with shades of gray.

Many superfluous welded elements were removed from the existing steel frame construction, and some roof trusses were reinforced. With the exception of the ceiling belonging to the oldest hall, all the suspended ceilings were replaced. Insulation was applied to the outer skin to make the buildings more economic to heat; the walls were given core insulation and inner shells, and the roofs were renewed using wooden box elements. The new building is also a steel frame structure filled in with masonry, with core insulation and a clinker facing wall.

The studios, workshops and exhibition spaces belonging to sculptor Vera Röhm are located in an old factory complex in Darmstadt. The buildings on this site, which is just over 4000 m² in size, are heterogeneous, and have gone through a process of extensive repairs and restructuring measures to reach the state they are in today. Building a new studio and extending the boundary wall has created a kind of court in front of the old buildings at the center of the site. The flexible interior plan allows the individual areas to be altered at any time to adapt to new uses. At present, the halls contain workshops, studios, exhibition spaces and storage and archive rooms. The three older buildings are used as studios and for exhibitions, owing to their height. The newly inserted levels can be reached via a central access core using a freight elevator (a pallet loader) with no steps between levels.

View of a bay window on the old building with the new building. The bay window is in front of the old steel frame. Louvers at the sides provide ventilation.

Cross section, longitudinal section, floor plan 1:500.

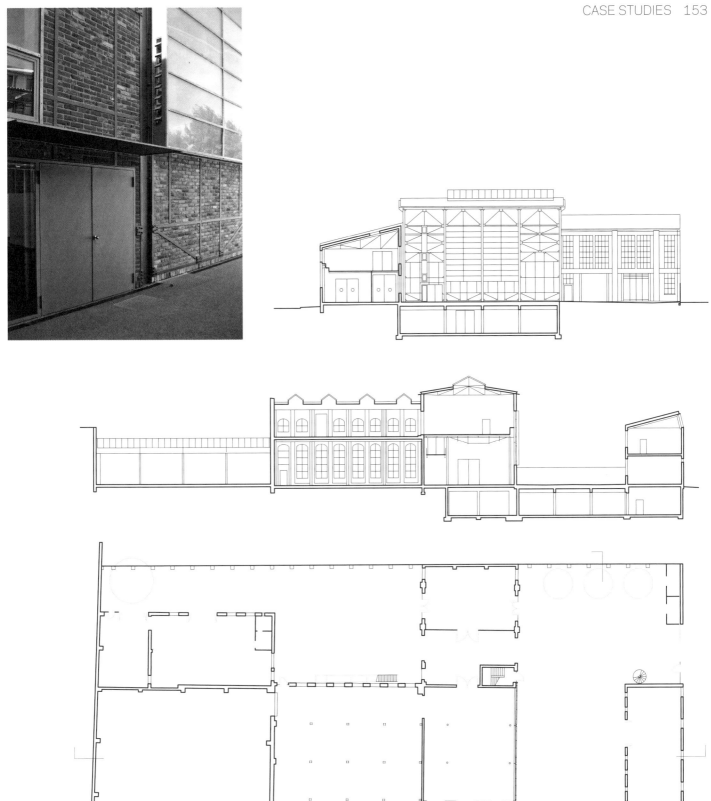

Floor plan and section through windows in light corridor 1:5, elevation 1:50

a Single glazing, with matt finish on one side
b Steel section window frame
c Existing masonry

Right side:
Sections, elevations of bay window 1:20

a Crimped sheet aluminum 2 mm, secured with screws and seals
b Steel sheet 10 mm
c Rectangular hollow section 50/30/3 mm
d Motor
e Hollow square section 50/50/3 mm
f Insulation glazing k = 1.8 W/m²K, inside pane of frosted glass
g Galvanized cover strips, 50 x 6 mm, visible
h Facade screws: stainless steel socket cap screws
i Slatted window with closed, thermally insulated aluminum slats; sheet aluminum external cladding, crimped, coated
j Screwed to subconstruction; the subconstruction is welded to the steel framework; steel parts of inner construction primed and painted; cavities insulated with mineral wool

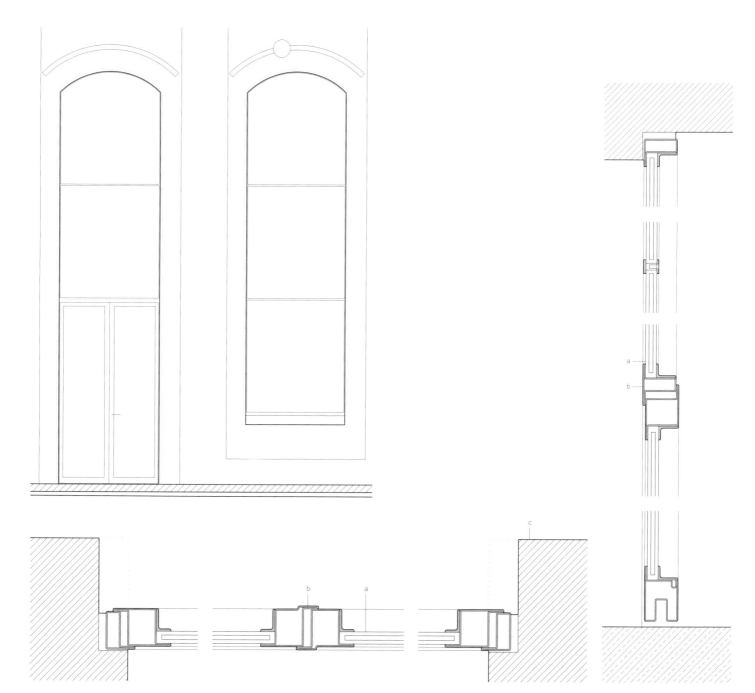

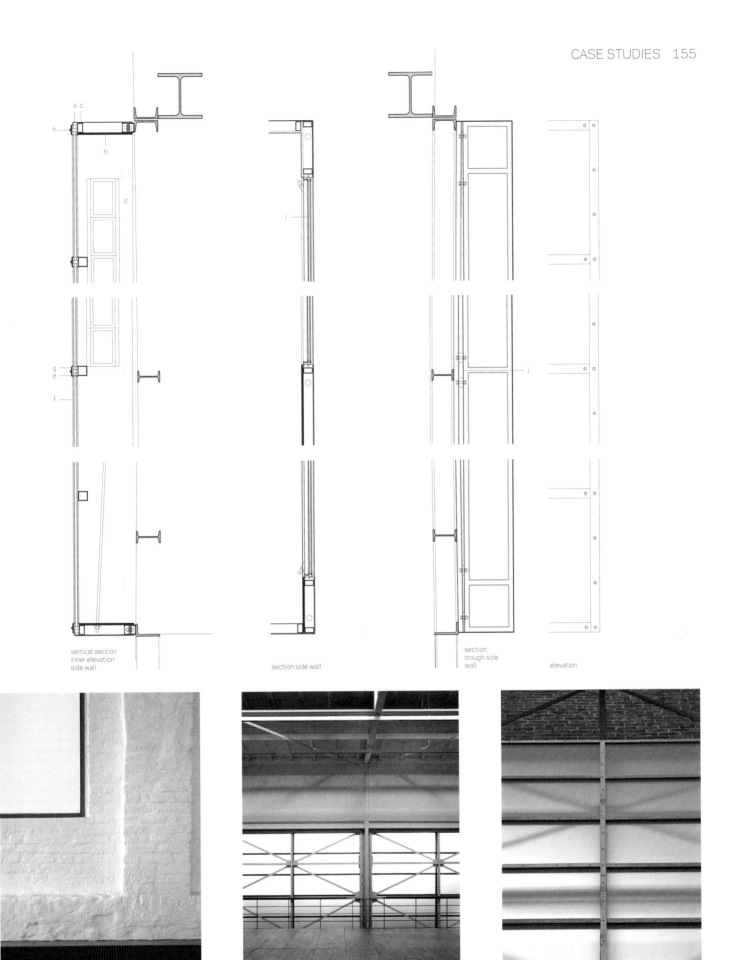

a c
h
b
d

g
e
f

vertical section
inner elevation
side wall

i

section side wall

j

j

section
trough side
wall

elevation

OPEN | CLOSE
APPENDIX

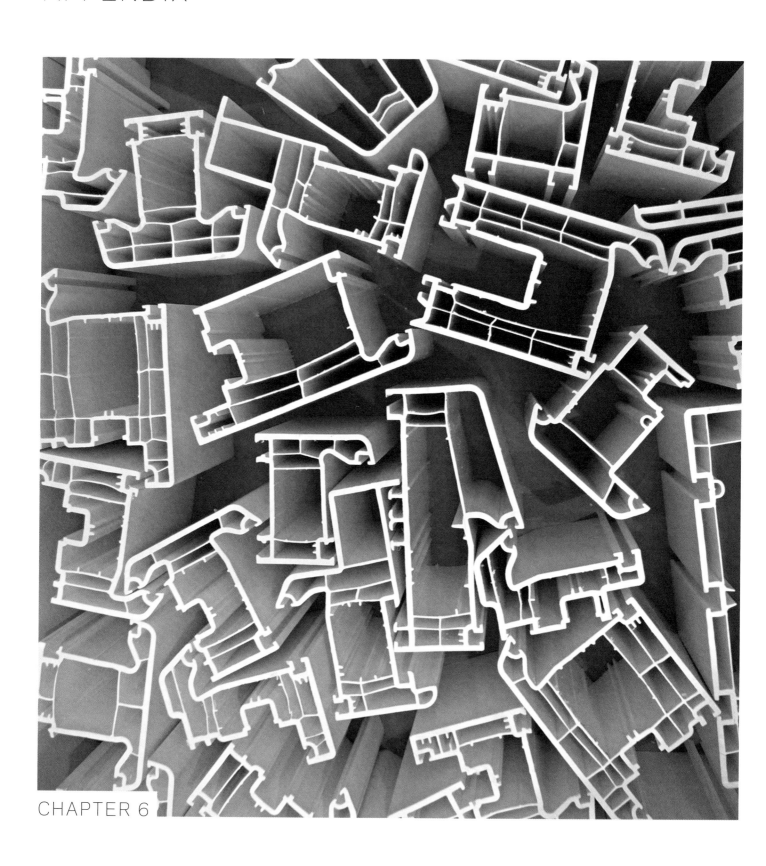

WINDOWS, FILTERS
TABLES AND INFORMATION

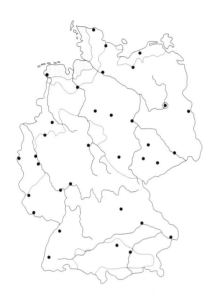

	Wind load zone 1:	22 m/s
	Wind load zone 2:	25 m/s
	Wind load zone 3:	27.5 m/s
	Wind load zone 4:	30 m/s

1   The load for different building locations classified by wind zones named in DIN 1955-4.

The weathering load of wooden windows is given by 4 factors:

1, 2 Building location/terrain categories: The load associated with the building location is given by wind zones and terrain categories. DIN 1955-4 distinguishes four different wind zones, while ENV 1991-2-4 (Eurocode 1) distinguishes four terrain categories.

3 Facade orientation: Load dependent on the orientation of the installed components. Stress calculated according to DIN EN 927-1. The stress on the coating is given by climatic conditions und by the construction. → 4, 5-p. 161

4 Installation point: This too affects the level of structural wood protection needed. Installation points are divided into four groups depending on the installation point in the external wall and on the form of the building (projecting areas, recessed areas). → 1, 2

Terrain category I		open areas of water; lakes with at least 5 km of water in the prevailing wind direction; flat land without barriers
Terrain category II		agricultural land with boundary hedges, individual farms, houses and trees
Terrain category III		suburbs, industrial and commercial areas; woods
Terrain category IV		urban areas where at least 15 % of the surface area is covered by buildings with an average eaves height of over 15 m

2 Terrain category acc. ENV 1991-2-4 (Eurocode 1).

MAINTENANCE INTERVALS

BFS fact sheet 18 recommends planning initial maintenance intervals:
If coatings are not renewed at regular intervals, moisture and other environmental influences will cause the familiar forms of damage. For this reason, regular monitoring, care and maintenance are necessary.
Thick coat glazes without UV blockers and with insufficient pigments have a limited effect in reducing the breakdown of wood through photochemical processes, resulting in breakdown and destruction of the coating.
Generally, water-based acrylic paints and water-based or solvent-based alkyd resin paints are superior in terms of material properties such as resistance to ageing, elasticity, UV protection, diffusion (dimensional stability) and blocking strength.
Historical window constructions often have solvent-containing alkyd resin coatings or oil-based paints that have already been heavily broken down and made brittle by ageing processes. These coatings have lost their ability to cover cracks, behave elastically and reduce diffusion. Blistering may result if oil-based paints are painted over using non-oil-based compounds.

SWELLING AND SHRINKAGE MEASUREMENTS OF DIFFERENT WOOD TYPES → tab 3

Swelling and shrinkage measurements depend on the type of wood and on the direction of cut. The hygroscopic qualities of wood are ultimately what causes it to split. Wood has the property of absorbing water from the air, or from direct contact with moisture, and releasing it again in dry conditions.
The end use moisture content of wood products that are in constant contact with outdoor air is approx. 10–15 %, provided that no water can come into contact with the wood in liquid form.
Swelling processes in wooden window components are caused by humidity, weather stress caused by precipitation, relative humidity stress on the inside of the building, construction moisture and the transfer of moisture from the adjacent structure.
Shrinkage processes are caused by alternating low and high humidity (related to temperature change) and by sunlight heating and drying the wood moldings. Growth-related variations in the wood can lead to inconsistent swelling and shrinkage behavior within a section, causing localized warping such as twisting, cupping and bowing. These changes in shape also contribute to splits and cracks appearing.

2 Wood surface temperatures from BFS fact sheet no. 18.

Opaque coatings Possible wood surface temperatures depending on the color tone				Glazed coatings / thick coat glazes Possible wood surface temperatures depending on the color tone			
Color tone	Temperature			Color tone	Temperature		
light tone RAL 9001 white RAL 1015 light ivory RAL 1004 yellow	40 °C 49 °C 50 °C			light tone natural oak	50 °C 60 °C		
medium tone RAL 3003 ruby red		67 °C		medium tone medium red teal		60 °C 70 °C	
dark tone RAL 7011 iron gray RAL 5007 brilliant blue RAL 9005 black			71 °C 75 °C 80 °C	dark tone walnut anthracite			70 °C 80 °C

3 Swelling and shrinkage measurements of different wood types.

Wood type	Wood fiber moisture saturation [%]	Volumetric shrinkage longitudinal [%]	Volumetric shrinkage radial [%]	Volumetric shrinkage tangential [%]	Oven-dry density— bulk density of dry wood with 0 % wood moisture
Softwood					
Pine	26–28	0.2–0.4	3.7–4.0	7.7–8.3	0.49
Fir	30–34	0.1	3.3	7.0	0.39
European larch	26–28	9.1–0.3	3.4–3.8	7.8–8.5	0.55
Spruce	30–34	0.2–0.4	3.6–3.7	7.9–8.5	0.43
Douglas fir	26–28	0.1–0.3	4.8–5.0	7.6–8.0	0.48
Hemlock		0.6	in diameter 7.4	in diameter 10.75	0.43
Pitch pine		0.2	in diameter 4.6	in diameter 7.4	in diameter 0.65
W. Red cedar		0.2–0.6	in diameter 2.1–2.5	in diameter 4.75–5.3	in diameter 0.35
Hardwood					
Oak	22–24	0.3–0.6	4.6	10.9	0.65
Teak		0.2–0.3	in diameter 2.7	in diameter 4.8	0.63
Eucalyptus			9.8	20.6	in diameter 0.72
Sweet chestnut	22–24	0.6	in diameter 3.8	in diameter 6.5	in diameter 0.56
Afzelia			in diameter 2.6	in diameter 4.0	in diameter 0.77
Afromosia					0.65
Framire			in diameter 1.23	in diameter 5.2	in diameter 0.47
Iroko / Kambala		0.2–0.7	in diameter 3.5	in diameter 5.5	in diameter 0.59
Khaya / Mahogany		in diameter 0.19	in diameter 5.5	in diameter 5.67	in diameter 0.49
Sipo / Mahogany		0.2–0.3	in diameter 4.9	in diameter 6.7	in diameter 0.58
Makore / Douka		in diameter 0.27	in diameter 0.8	in diameter 6.7	in diameter 0.59
Merbau			in diameter 0.19	in diameter 1.65	in diameter 0.79
Niangon			in diameter 3.7	in diameter 8.43	in diameter 0.58
Robinia	22–24	0.1	in diameter 3.9	in diameter 6.3	in diameter 0.72

Weathering stress caused by solar radiation: in addition to humidity and precipitation, windows are affected by other climatic factors such as solar radiation. This causes the wood surface to heat up.
The differences in temperature profile between the inside and the outside areas produce greater variations in moisture. This can cause the wood to split internally and at joints.
The choice of color and coating/ glaze for dimensionally stable wood components can be crucial to longevity and crack prevention. Light colors can prevent excessive tension building up.

moderate	usually on the north side of buildings (NW to NE). The weather stress on the north side of a building is relatively weak.
severe	usually on the east side of buildings (NE to SE). For south-facing surfaces (i.e. between east and west) increased solar radiation stress must be taken into account.
extreme	usually on the south, southwest and west sides of buildings (SE to NW). West-facing surfaces (i.e. from south to north) face the prevailing weather, with correspondingly high driving rain stress.

1

protected wooden components	Windows are not subject to direct stress from driving rain. Stress from solar radiation is low. Components are largely sheltered from direct solar radiation, precipitation and wind by adequately sized roof cover, e.g. recessed windows and external doors with deep reveals, or in balconies, loggias or external corridors.
partially protected wooden components	Windows installed in buildings of up to three storeys. There is a small degree of structural shelter from projecting components or recessed installation within reveals. Stress through driving rain and solar radiation is at a normal level. This applies in sheltered locations beneath small roof structures and for recessed windows or exterior doors with the usual reveals.
partially protected wooden components	Either there is no effective protection or the windows are installed at a height above 3 storeys. These windows are under high stress from driving rain and solar radiation. The effects of solar radiation, precipitation and wind cannot be mitigated. This applies to particularly exposed locations and particularly to windows or external doors that are flush with the facade or project from it (without structural protection) on all storeys.
exposed wooden components	Windows are completely exposed to weather stress, owing to a projecting construction in an exposed building location (e.g. on a slope) or are being used for a high-rise building. The windows are under extreme stress from driving rain and solar radiation.

2

1 Facade orientation and place of installation: DIN EN 927-1—coating materials and coating systems for exterior wood—distinguishes between three different climatic situations.

2 Place of installation of wood components.

Noise level category	Exterior ambient noise level [dB] (A)	Bedrooms in hospital wards and sanitariums	Living rooms in residences, sleeping areas in hostels, classrooms etc.	Office spaces etc.*
		required $R'_{w,res}$ of exterior component [dB]		
I	up to 55	35	30	—
II	56–60	35	30	30
III	61–65	40	35	30
IV	66–70	45	40	35
V	71–75	50	45	40
VI	76–80	**	50	45
VII	>80	**	**	50

3

3 Requirements for the resulting sound insulation of exterior components.

* There are no requirements for exterior components of rooms for which the sound of traffic makes only a minor contribution to the interior noise level, owing to the activities that take place there.

** Requirements must be established on the basis of the specific onsite situation.

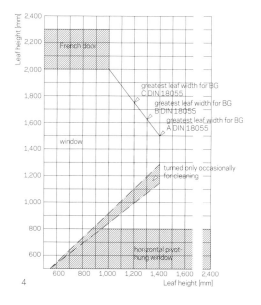

4

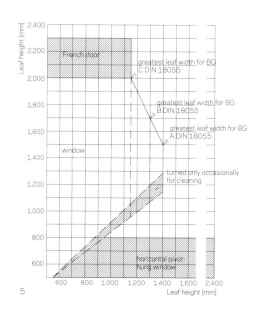

5

Sizes of elements:
Depending on the type of opening, the material and the size of the sections affect the maximum leaf width. For instance, the leaf of a French window should not be wider than 1.00 m if the wood members of the frame have a cross-section of 56/78 mm, due to the weight of the leaf itself and the strain on the hinges. For a cross-section of 56/92 mm, the maximum width is 1.15 m.

4 Leaf measurements for section group IV 56/78 (leaf timber width 78 mm).

5 Leaf measurements for section group IV 56/92 (leaf timber width) 92 mm.

6   Dry layer thickness of coating systems (BFS fact sheet).

Construction	Coating system	Technique of application	Coating total dry layer thickness**, surface	Systems dry layer thickness** acc. DIN EN 927-1	Glaze total dry layer thickness**, surface	Systems dry layer thickness** acc. DIN EN 927-1
industrial coating (usually first coat)	impregnation	dipping, flooding*	> 100 μm, wood structure generally no longer visible	high	> 80 μm, usually pore-filling / structure-filling	high
	priming	dipping, flooding				
	intermediate coat	dipping, flooding				
	alternative	spraying (Airless, AirMix)				
	final coat	spraying (Airless, AirMix)				
semi-industrial coating (usually first coat)	impregnation	dipping, flooding	60–100 μm	high	40–80 μm	medium to high
	priming	dipping, flooding				
	intermediate coat	dipping, flooding				
	alternative	spraying (Airless, AirMix)				
	alternative	spreading (with a brush)*				
	final coat	spreading (with a brush)*				
brush coating (usually during maintenance, rarely first coat)	impregnation	spreading (with a brush)*	60–100 μm	high	30–50 μm, non pore-filling / non-structure-filling	medium
	priming	spreading (with a brush)*				
	intermediate coat	spreading (with a brush)*				
	final coat	spreading (with a brush)*				

*   Individual coats can also be applied by rolling or spraying.
**   Particular attention should be paid to the manufacturer's information on the composition of the coating in this case.

6

7   Table for determining stress groups for window glazing (acc. ift-Rosenheim).

A coat's thickness is determined in part by the coating substance, product-specifically. For manufacturers' product information, DIN EN 927-1 classifies the dry layer thickness in four different categories:

Category	Coating thickness range	
minimal	average coating thickness	below 5 μm
low	average coating thickness	5–20 μm
medium	average coating thickness	20–60 μm
high	average coating thickness	over 60 μm

7

Coatings for dimensionally stable exterior wood components (windows and external doors) Source: BFS fact sheet 18:
The durability of coatings depends on the construction, the choice of suitable wood types / qualities, acceptable preparation of the wood components, the choice of a suitable coating system and the coat thickness.
Physical protective measures such as hydrophobic impregnation, glazes and opaque and non-opaque coatings on wooden surfaces prevent water in drip and vapor form, as well as UV and thermal radiation and other harmful environmental influences, from reaching the wood's surface in spite of constructive measures and damaging it.
There are three different kinds of coat: primer, intermediate coat and final coat. These can be colorless, have glazed or opaque pigments, contain solvents or be water-based. The water uptake and water vapor permeability (sd value) of a coating depends on the type of coating material used and the coat thickness.
For this, a suitable, uninterrupted, uniform film of the specified minimum thickness is required. This should likewise cover edges, joints and end grain areas.
There are various coating systems, depending on the application technique. The formula and end result of coating materials for dipping and spray application are different from those of products that are applied with a brush (manual coating).

Stress groups for window glazing

Stress groups	1	2	3	4	5
Glazing systems acc. DIN 18545 Part 3	Single glazing with exposed bevel edge sealant	Double glazing with glazing bead, filled rebate space	Va 3: Glazing with filled rebate space Vf 3: Glazing with no sealant compound in rebate space	Va 4: Glazing with filled rebate space Vf 4: Glazing with no sealant compound in rebate space	Va 5: Glazing with filled rebate space Vf 5: Glazing with no sealant compound in rebate space
Diagrammatic section					
Abbreviation	Va 1	Va 2	Va 3 Vf 3	Va 4 Vf 4	Va 5 Vf 5

Stress from operation					
	Classification by opening mechanism				
	fixed glazing, casement windows, tilt-and-turn windows				
	horizontally pivoted sash windows, vertical sliding sash windows and windows subjected to comparable stress				

Classification of pane size according to frame material, edge length and sealant

Frame material	Sealant	Color tone	Edge length		
aluminum	3 mm	pale	up to 0.80 m	up to 1.00 m	up to 1.50 m
aluminum-wood	3 mm	dark	up to 0.80 m	up to 1.00 m	up to 1.50 m
steel	4 mm	pale	up to 1.50 m	up to 2.00 m	up to 2.50 m
	4 mm	dark	up to 1.25 m	up to 1.50 m	up to 2.00 m
	5 mm	pale	up to 1.75 m	up to 2.25 m	up to 3.00 m
	5 mm	dark	up to 1.50 m	up to 2.00 m	up to 2.75 m
wood	3 mm	edge length up to 0.80 m	up to 1.00 m	up to 1.50 m	up to 1.75 m	up to 2.00 m
	4 mm			up to 1.75 m	up to 2.50 m	up to 3.00 m
	5 mm			up to 2.00 m	up to 3.00 m	up to 4.00 m
plastic	4 mm	pale	up to 0.80 m	up to 1.00 m	up to 1.50 m
	4 mm	dark	up to 0.80 m	up to 1.00 m	up to 1.50 m
	5 mm	pale	up to 1.50 m	up to 2.00 m	up to 2.50 m
	5 mm	dark	up to 1.25 m	up to 1.50 m	up to 2.00 m
	6 mm	dark	up to 1.50 m	up to 2.00 m	up to 2.50 m

Load on glass layer in relation to building height

Building height	Assumed load	Pane size up to 0.5 m²	Pane size up to 0.8 m²	Pane size up to 1.8 m²	Pane size up to 6.0 m²	Pane size up to 9.0 m²
8 m	0.60 kN/m²	Load: up to 0.16 N/mm	up to 0.22 N/mm	up to 0.35 N/mm	up to 0.70 N/mm	up to 0.90 N/mm
20 m	0.96 kN/m²	up to 0.25 N/mm	up to 0.35 N/mm	up to 0.55 N/mm	up to 1.10 N/mm	up to 1.40 N/mm
100 m	1.32 kN/m²	up to 0.35 N/mm	up to 0.50 N/mm	up to 0.75 N/mm	up to 1.50 N/mm	up to 1.90 N/mm

1   Stress groups (BG) for window glazing:

Criteria for glazing that is technically correct and fit for its purpose:

1   The frame construction must have adequate dimensions.

2   The dimensions of the glazing rebates are determined by DIN 18545 Part 1. The insulation glass manufacturer's installation guidelines must also be taken into account.

3   Glazing elements with no sealant in the rebate space must have openings on the outer side to equalize vapor pressure (slits or drilled holes).

4   Padding of the glass panes should conform to the guidelines of the relevant professional institute.

5   Glazing elements with glazing beads should be installed on the side facing into the building.

Stress groups are calculated from:
– operation (way of opening)
– environmental influences (moisture impact on the glazing seal on the inner side)
– pane size (sealant type depends on frame material, glazing edge length and thickness of sealant strip)

If the stress group is known, the glazing system can be identified (DIN 18545 Part 3). The different groups are:

Va 1:
Glazing system with exposed sealing compound

Va 2–Va 5:
Glazing systems with glazing beads and filled rebate space

Vf 3–Vf 5:
Glazing systems with glazing beads and no sealing material in rebate space

V glazing system
a filled rebate space
f no sealing material in rebate space

1–5 Stress groups for glazing windows

2 Construction requirements for different types of window.

R'$_{w,res}$ in dB	Construction features	Single-glazed window	Multiple-glazed window		Box window
		with insulation glass	with two single panes	with 1 single pane and 1 insulation glass pane	2 single / single insulation glass pane
25	total glass thickness	double ≥ 6 mm	≥ 6 mm	none	none
	space between panes	≥ 8 mm	none	none	none
	R$_{w,P.GLASS/GLAZING}$	≥ 27 dB	—	—	—
	rebate seal	not required	not required	not required	not required
30	total glass thickness	double ≥ 6 mm	≥ 6 mm	≥ 6 mm	none
	space between panes	≥ 12 mm	≥ 30 mm	≥ 30 mm	none
	R$_{w,P.GLASS/GLAZING}$	≥ 30 dB	—	—	—
	rebate seal	[1] required	[1] required	[1] required	not required
32	total glass thickness	double ≥ 8 mm	≥ 8 mm	≥ 4 mm + 4/12/4	none
	space between panes	≥ 16 mm	≥ 30 mm	≥ 30 mm	none
	R$_{w,P.GLASS/GLAZING}$	≥ 32 dB	—	—	—
	rebate seal	[1] required	[1] required	[1] required	[1] required
35	total glass thickness	double ≥ 10 mm	≥ 8 mm	≥ 6 mm + 4/12/4	none
	space between panes	≥ 16 mm	≥ 40 mm	≥ 40 mm	none
	R$_{w,P.GLASS/GLAZING}$	≥ 35 dB	—	—	—
	rebate seal	[1] required	[1] required	[1] required	[1] required
37	total glass thickness	≥ 14 mm	≥ 10 mm	≥ 6 mm + 6/12/4	≥ 8 mm or ≥ 4 mm + 4/12/4
	space between panes	≥ 20 mm	≥ 40 mm	≥ 40 mm	≥ 100 mm
	R$_{w,P.GLASS/GLAZING}$	≥ 39 dB	—	—	—
	rebate seal	[1] required	[1] required	[1] required	[1] required
40	total glass thickness	—	≥ 14 mm	≥ 8 mm + 6/12/4	≥ 8 mm or ≥ 6 mm + 4/12/4
	space between panes	—	≥ 50 mm	≥ 50 mm	≥ 100 mm
	R$_{w,P.GLASS/GLAZING}$	≥ 44 dB	—	—	—
	rebate seal	[1,2] required	[1,2] required	[1,2] required	[1,2] required
42	total glass thickness	—	≥ 16 mm	≥ 8 mm + 8/12/4	≥ 10 mm or ≥ 8 mm + 4/12/4
	space between panes	—	≥ 50 mm	≥ 50 mm	≥ 100 mm
	R$_{w,P.GLASS/GLAZING}$	≥ 49 dB	—	—	—
	rebate seal	[1,2] required	[1,2] required	[1,2] required	[1,2] required
45	total glass thickness	—	≥ 18 mm	≥ 8 mm + 8/12/4	≥ 12 mm or ≥ 8 mm + 6/12/4
	space between panes	—	≥ 60 mm	≥ 60 mm	≥ 100 mm
	R$_{w,P.GLASS/GLAZING}$	—	—	—	—
	rebate seal	—	[1,2] required	[1,2] required	[1,2] required
48	Generally applicable values are possible. Sole means of proof: suitability tests specified by DIN 52210				

R$_w$, P. glass = test value of a standard format pane (1.23 m x 1.48 m) in laboratory
1) at least one continuous elastic seal, usually in consisting of a middle seal
2) two continuous elastic seals, usually consisting of a middle seal and inner seals, or else of an outer and inner seal

DOORS
TABLES AND INFORMATION

Component resistance class (DIN V ENV 1627)	WK1	WK2	WK3	WK4	WK5	WK6
Component resistance class (DIN V 18103)	—	ET 1	ET 2	ET 3	—	—
Resistance time	no manual test	3 minutes	5 minutes	10 minutes	15 minutes	20 minutes
	Component provides basic protection against break-in attempts using physical force.	Component provides additional protection against break-ins using simple tools, such as screwdrivers.	Component provides additional protection against break-ins with a second screwdriver or a crowbar.	Component provides additional protection against break-ins with saws and striking tools—sledgehammer, pry bar, hammer and chisel or battery-powered drill.	Component provides additional protection against break-ins using power tools, e.g. power drills, pad saws or saber saws and anglegrinders with a disc of 125 diameter max.	Component provides additional protection against break-ins using high-performance power tools, e.g. power drills, pad saws or saber saws and anglegrinders.
Requirements for enclosing masonry walls acc. DIN 1053 Part 1						
Min. nominal thickness	≥ 115 mm	≥ 115 mm	≥ 115 mm	≥ 240 mm	—	—
Compressive strength class of masonry units	≥ 12	≥ 12	≥ 12	≥ 12	—	—
Mortar group	II	II	II	II	—	—
Requirements for enclosing walls of reinforced concrete walls						
Min. nominal thickness	≥ 100 mm	≥ 100 mm	≥ 120 mm	≥ 140 mm	≥ 140 mm	≥ 140 mm
Min. strength class	B15	B15	B15	B15	B15	B15

1 Break-in protection (acc. DIN V ENV 1627), specifications and requirements.

Climate class		DIN EN 1121				
		Testing climate	Temperature differences [°C]		Humidity differences [%]	
I		a	18 ± 2	23 ± 2	50 ± 5	30 ± 5
II	Doors in heated apartments; rooms opposite hallways of buildings or stair spaces	b	13 ± 2	23 ± 2	65 ± 5	30 ± 5
III	Doors separating an apartment from non-heated hallways of buildings or stair spaces; doors in public buildings, doors between residences and garages; doors to non-habitable attic storeys; cellar doors	c	3 ± 2	23 ± 2	85 ± 5	30 ± 5
IV	Doors in external passageways; external doors	d	-15 ± 2	23 ± 2	no requirement	30 ± 5

2 Door climate classes.

3 Minimum airborne sound insulation requirements for doors (extract from DIN 4109).

Building type	Areas and spaces between which a door is installed			$R'_{w,R}$ [dB]	$R_{w,P}$ [dB]
Multi-storey building with apartments and workspaces	building hallways and stair spaces	<–>	hallways, corridors	27 (37)	32 (42)
	building hallways and stair spaces	<–>	living rooms in residences	37	42
Schools and teaching buildings	hallways	<–>	classrooms and similar spaces	32	37
	hallways	<–>	sleeping areas	32 (37)	37 (42)
Hospitals and sanatoriums	examination rooms and consulting rooms	<–>	examination rooms and consulting rooms	37	42
	hallways	<–>	examination rooms and consulting rooms	37	42
	hallways	<–>	wards / patients' rooms	32 (37)	37 (42)
	operating theatres and wards / patients' rooms	<–>	operating theatres and wards / patients' rooms	32	37
	hallways	<–>	operating theatres and wards / patients' rooms	32	37

4 Door leaf constructions:
For single-shell constructions, the sound insulation measure (R_w) depends on bending stiffness and mass per unit area. Materials to increase the bulk density or the door leaf weight, include homogeneous solid chipboard inserts and plywood boards. Higher door leaf weights place heavier loads on fittings, which must be made thicker. Multi-layer door leaf constructions are a further development of decoupled single-layer door leaves. Materials with different bulk densities are used as fillings. Heavy materials such as sheet steel, laminated wood veneer boards should be used for the cover layers, while a further option is weighting with lead, sheet metal or sand. Sound insulation values (R_w) of up to 48 dB can easily be achieved with such methods, although they also result in thicknesses of up to 90 mm.

		Description	Door leaf thickness [mm]	Mass per unit area [kg/m²]	Sound insulation measurement [dB]
single-shell		with strip core	40	12.3	27
		with tubular chipboard core	4	15.4	32
		with chipboard solid core	40	24.8	34
		with inserts made from multiple chipboard plates – 2 three-ply boards – 3 extruded boards (spot glued) – 3 extruded boards (nailed) – 5 extruded boards (nailed)	42 41 40 68	18.0 25.0 25.0 33.0	29 39 40 41
multiple shell		with veneered facing and mineral wool	60	20	35
		with veneered facing, sheet lead and mineral wool	85	46	45
		with chipboard, fire-resistant board, mineral wool and soft fiberboard	85	64	44

Softwoods						
Wood type	Abbreviation	Geographical distribution	Color	Typical properties	Moisture content equalization rate	Basic density range at 12-15% wood moisture content
Spruce	PCAB (FI)	Europe	yellowish-white or reddish-white	resin pockets	medium	0.40-0.50
Hemlock	TSHT (HEM)	Northwest of North America	whitish-gray to light gray-brown	somewhat brittle	medium	0.44-0.51
Pine	PNSY (KI)	Europe	heart: yellow to red-brown sapwood: light yellow	resinous	heart: medium sapwood: high	0.44-0.60
Larch	LAER (LA)	Central and eastern Europe, North America, northeast Asia	heart: red-brown. Darkens heavily over time sapwood: yellowish	resinous. somewhat brittle	heart: low sapwood: high	0.47-0.62
Pitch pine	PNOO (PIP)	North and Central America	heart: reddish Sapwood: yellowish-white	easy to work, resinous, good weather resistance	rapid	0.49-0.70

Hardwoods						
Wood type	Abbreviation	Geographical distribution	Color	Typical properties	Moisture content equalization rate	Basic density range at 12-15% wood moisture content
Afzelia	AFXX (AFZ)	West Africa	heart: yellowish to light brown sapwood: gray	hard, difficult to dry	very low	0.73-0.88
Oak	QXCE, QXCA (EI, EIW)	Europe, North America	heart: grayish-yellow to light brown to dark brown sapwood: gray	darkens on contact with iron due to tannic acid	low	0.67-0.77
Meranti	SHDR, SHLR (MER)	Southeast Asia	heart: light pinkish-brown to dark reddish-brown sapwood: yellowish to pinkish-gray	different parts have different properties	low to medium	0.36-0.60
Ash	FXEX	Europe	yellowish to white		low	0.41-0.82
Mahogany	ENUT (MAU)	West, Central and East Africa	reddish, darkens over time	very easy to work, weather-resistant	medium	0.55-0.76
Elm	ULCP, ULCL (UL)	Europe	light brown to dark brown	very easy to work, good stability	low	0.56-0.77

1 Wood types for constructing doors:

The properties of products from processed wood materials have been improved by larger cross-sections and weather-resistant, low-warping (dimensional stability) and durable construction. Apart from laminated timber blockboards and plywoods, chipboards and MDF boards are used for door construction. The surface construction and finish, however, is also important. There are two types: exposed and covered surfaces.

	DIN EN 1192			
Stress group	Vertical load	Static torsion	Soft impact	Hard impact
N	400 N	200 N	30 J	1.5 J
M	600 N	250 N	60 J	3.0 J
S	800 N	300 N	120 J	5.0 J

2 Stress groups.

Stress group N
normal stress, e.g.
- interior doors in residences

Stress group M
medium stress, e.g.
- offices and other commercially used spaces

Stress group S
heavy stress, e.g.
- hotels, schools, kindergartens, hospitals

GATES / INDUSTRIAL DOORS
TABLES AND INFORMATION

3 Selection criteria for gates/
industrial doors, sorted by
construction type.

Construction type	Manual operation	Power-assisted operation	Usual speed of main closing edge [m/s]	Restricted usability in pivoting area	High-performance sealing possible	Thermal insulation possible	Glazing possible	Affected by wind and snow	Wicket door in main leaf possible	Remarks
Hinged door	low frequency, adequate traverse	high frequency, difficult to protect against accidents	0.2–0.3	yes	yes	yes	yes	yes	yes	—
Hinged door	normal for pedestrian traffic	pedestrian transport with heavy traffic	≤ 0.5	yes	yes	yes	yes	yes	—	automatic doors that open in the opposite direction to the direction of travel should be particularly clearly marked
Swing door	frequently used indoor transit areas	frequently used indoor circulation areas. Full transit width clearance advisable	0.5–1.0	yes	limited	limited	yes	yes	no	an additional barrier is advisable for outdoor areas
Flap door	low frequency, restricted traverse	—	—	yes	yes	yes	yes	yes	yes	—
Folding sliding door, accordion door	large openings with low frequency	large openings with high use frequency	0.2–0.3	yes	yes	yes	yes	yes	yes	small traverse area required
Sliding door	low use frequency	large openings with large leaf measurements	≤ 0.3	no	limited	yes	yes	limited	yes	requires plenty of space at the sides
Vertical lift gate	not common	low-frequency use	0.1–0.2	no	yes	yes	yes	no	yes	space needed above and below the gate
Sectional overhead door	low use frequency	high use frequency	≤ 0.3	no	yes	yes	yes	no	yes	small leaf measurements and lower space requirements
Coiling overhead door	not common	for large openings	0.1–0.2	no	limited	limited	limited	no	no	—
High-speed door	—	frequently used transit areas	≤ 1.5	no	limited	no	yes	limited	no	alternative to swing gate
Up-and-over door	small garages	small garages	≤ 0.2	limeted	yes	yes	yes	limited	yes	difficult to prevent accidents

3

STANDARDS AND GUIDELINES (EXTRACTS)

WINDOWS

Planning in general
– DIN 107   Left and right designation in construction engineering.

Wind loads
– DIN 1055   Design loads for buildings, especially Part 3 + 4.
– DIN EN 12210   Windows and doors – Resistance to wind load; (replaces DIN 18055).
– DIN 18056   Window walls; dimensioning and implementation; partially updated by: Technische Regeln für die Verwendung von linienförmig gelagerten Vertikalverglasungen (Technical Rules for the Use of Glazing with Linear Supports).
– Institut für Fenstertechnik e. V.; Stress groups for glazing of windows

Thermal insulation
– DIN 4108   Thermal insulation in buildings.
– WschVO   Thermal Insulation Ordinance.
– EnEV   Energy Saving Ordinance.
– DIN EN 673   Glass in building – Determination of thermal transmittance (U value) – Calculation method.
– Certification for different types of glazing and constructions.
– Calculation values published in the Bundesanzeiger (the Federal Gazette).
– DIN EN 15010077-1   Thermotechnical behavior of windows, doors and shutters – calculation of thermal transfer coefficients – Simplified method.

Joint permeability
– DIN EN 12207   Windows and doors – Air permeability; (replaces DIN 18055).

Resistance to driving rain
– DIN EN 12208   Windows and doors – Watertightness; (replaces DIN 18055).

Sound insulation
– DIN 18005   Noise abatement in town planning.
– DIN 4109   Sound insulation in buildings.
– VDI-Guideline 2719   Sound isolation of windows and their auxiliary equipment, Certification for different types of glazing and constructions
– Calculation values published in the Bundesanzeiger (the Federal Gazette).

Lighting, ventilation
– LBO   Land building regulations, implementation ordinances.
– DIN 5034   Daylight in interiors.
– DIN 5035   Artificial light in interiors.
– DIN EN 410   Glass in building – Determination of luminous and solar characteristics of glazing.

Fire protection
– DIN 4102   Fire behavior of building materials and building components.
– DIN EN 357   Fire resistant glazed elements with transparent or translucent glass products – Classification of fire resistance.
– LBO   Landesbauordnungen, implementation ordinances.
– Manufacturers' information on permitted glazing systems.
– RAL-GZ 975/2 Fire protection in construction; fire protection glazing; quality assurance.

Intrusion protection
– DIN V 18054   Burglar-resistant windows.
– DIN ENV 1627   Windows, doors, shutters – Burglar resistance – Requirements and classification.
– DIN 52290   Attack-resistant glazing, Part 1–5.
– DIN 18104-1   Additional burglar resistant products Part 1: screw-on additional burglar resistant products for windows and doors;
– requirements and test methods.

– DIN EN 1063   Glass in building – Security glazing – Testing and classification of resistance against bullet attack.
– DIN EN 1522   Windows, doors, shutters and blinds – Bullet resistance – Requirements and classification.
– Manufacturers' information on different types of glass.
– Information from property insurers' association.

Sill heights
– LBO   Land building regulations, implementation ordinances.

Dimensions
– DIN 4172   Dimensions in buildings.
– DIN 18000   Modular coordination in building construction.

Wood, wooden windows
– DIN 68360   Wood for joinery works.
– DIN 4076   Terms and symbols in the field of wood.
– RAL-GZ 424/1   Wood windows, construction and mounting – Quality assurance.
– DIN 68121   Timber profiles for windows and window doors.
– DIN 68800   Protection of timber used in buildings.
– DIN V ENV 972-2   Varnishes and application materials, coating materials and coating systems for wood in outdoor areas.
– DIN 68805   Protection of wood for windows and exterior doors;
– Institut für Fenstertechnik e. V.: application groups for wood for outdoor use.
– Manufacturers' information.
– DIN 68602   Assessment of adhesives for joining wood and wood-based products.

Wood and aluminum windows
– RAL-GZ 424/2   wood and aluminum window – construction and mounting
– Quality assurance.

Concrete windows
– DIN 18057   Concrete windows; windows with concrete frames, concrete window areas; dimensioning, requirements, tests.

PVC profiles, plastic windows
– DIN 7748   Plastic molding compounds.
– DIN 16830   High impact polyvinyl chloride (PVC-HI) window profiles.
– DIN EN 477-479, 513, 514   Unplasticized polyvinylchloride (PVC-U) profiles.
– RAL-GZ 716/1   Plastic window profile systems – Quality assurance – Section I, Plastic window profiles; Section II, Plastic windows – Extruded sealing profiles; Section III Plastic windows – Quality assurance – Proof of suitability for plastic window systems.

Aluminum profiles, aluminum windows
– DIN 1748   Extruded aluminum sections.
– DIN 1745   Sheet and strip aluminum.
– DIN 17615   AlMgSi 0.5 precision profiles
– RAL-RG 636/1   aluminum windows; quality assurance.
– Manufacturer information on application materials and systems.

Fittings
– RAL-RO 607/3   Tilt and turn hardware; quality assurance.
– RAL-RG 607/9   Opening window handles and lockable opening window handles; quality assurance.

Glass, glazing
– DIN 1249   Sheet glass in construction engineering.
– DIN 1259   Glass, terms.
– DIN EN 673-675   Glass in building.
– DIN 11525   Horticultural glass; horticultural sheet glass and horticultural cast glass.
– DIN 1286-1   Insulating glass units; air filled; aging behavior.

- DIN 1286-2   Multiple walled insulation glazing units; gas-filled; aging behavior – Limiting deviations.
- RAL-GZ 520   Multiple walled insulation glazing units – quality assurance.
- Institut für Fenstertechnik e. V.: Stress groups for glazing of windows.

Seals
- DIN 18545   Glazing with sealants; rebates.
- DIN 52460   Sealing and glazing – Terms.
- DIN EN 12365-1 (draft)   Building hardware - Gaskets and weather-stripping for doors, windows, shutters and curtain walling.
- Technische Regeln für die Verwendung von linienförmig gelagerten Vertikalverglasungen (Technical Rules for the Use of Glazing with Linear Supports).

Construction standards
- DIN 18355, VOB   (German Construction Contract Procedures) General technical specifications for building works, Part C; Joinery works.
- DIN 18357   Mounting of fittings.
- DIN 18358   Rolling shutters works.
- DIN 18361   Glazing works.
- Documents of the Institut des Glaserhandwerks für Verglasungstechnik, Hadamer.
- Manufacturers' guidelines.
- Publications of the Institut für Fenstertechnik e. V.
- DIN 18540   Sealing of exterior wall joints in building using joint sealants.
- DIN 18056   Window walls, measuring and construction; partially updated by the
- Technische Regeln für die Verwendung von linienförmig gelagerten Vertikalverglasungen (Technical Rules for the Use of Glazing with Linear Supports).

FILTER

Roller shutters, sun blinds, external slatted blinds, swing, panel and sliding shutters
- DIN EN 13561   Sun blinds.
- DIN EN 13659   Roller shutters.
- DIN EN 12833   Skylight and conservatory roller shutters - Resistance to snow load – Test method.
- DIN 18073   Roller end covers, sunshades and screens in building construction; terms, requirements.
- DIN 18358   VOB (German Construction Contract Procedures) – Part C: General technical specifications for building works (ATV); Rolling shutters works.
- DIN EN 1932   External blinds and shutters - Resistance to wind loads - Test method.
- DIN EN 1933   Exterior blinds - Resistance to load due to water accumulation – Test method.
- DIN EN 12045   Shutters and blinds power operated - Safety in use - Measurement and testing of the transmitted force.
- DIN EN 12194   Shutters, external and internal blinds - Misuse - Test method.
- DIN EN 12216   Shutters, external blinds, internal blinds - Terminology, glossary and definitions.
- DIN EN 13120   Internal blinds - Performance requirements including safety.
- DIN EN 14500   Blinds and shutters - Thermal and visual comfort - Test method.
- DIN EN 14501   Blinds and shutters - Thermal and visual comfort - Performance characteristics and classification.
- DIN EN 13363-1   Solar protection devices combined with glazing - Calculation of solar and light transmittance - Part 1: Simplified method.
- DIN EN 13363-2   Solar protection devices combined with glazing - Calculation of total solar energy transmittance and light transmittance - Part 2: Detailed calculation method.

- DIN EN 60335-2-97/A1; VDE 0700-97/A4: 2004-04 draft standard Household and similar electrical appliances - Safety - Part 2-97: Particular requirements for drives for rolling shutters, awnings, blinds and similar equipment (IEC 61/2543/CDV:2003);
- German version prEN 60335-2-97:2003/prA1:2003.

DOORS

Door leaves, climatic and mechanical load
- DIN EN 130   Methods of testing doors; test for change in stiffness of the door leaves by repeated torsion.
- DIN EN 950   Door leaves - Determination of the resistance to hard body impact.
- ISO 8270   Doorsets; Soft heavy body impact test
- DIN EN 952   Door leaves - General and local flatness - Measurement method.
- DIN EN 1294   Door leaves - Determination of the behavior under humidity variations in successive uniform climates.
- DIN EN 1529   Height, width, thickness and squareness - Tolerance classes.
- DIN EN 1530   Door leaves - General and local flatness - Tolerance classes.
- DIN EN 12219   Doors - Climatic influences - Requirements and classification.

Thermal insulation
- DIN 4108   Thermal insulation in buildings.
- EnEV   Energy Saving Ordinance.
- DIN EN 12219   Doors - Climatic influences.
- DIN EN 12207   Windows and doors - Air permeability.
- DIN EN 12208   Windows and doors - Watertightness.
- DIN EN 12210   Windows and doors - Resistance to wind load.

Sound insulation
- DIN 4109   Sound insulation in buildings, especially Part 2, Minimum thermal insulation requirements.
- Certification of manufacturing firms.
- Calculation values published in the Bundesanzeiger (the Federal Gazette).

Fire protection, fire-rated and smoke-stop doors, emergency exit doors
- DIN 4102   Ignitability of building products.
- DIN EN 1634-1   Fire resistance and smoke control tests for door, shutter and openable … shutters and openable windows.
- DIN 18082   Fire barriers, steel doors T30.
- DIN 18091   Lifts; lift landing sliding doors for lift wells with walls of the fire resistance class F90
- DIN 18093   Fire barriers; installation of fire doors in fireproof masonry or concrete walls
- DIN 18095-1   Anchorage shape, anchorage position, installation.
- DIN 18250   Mortise locks for fire protection barriers.
- DIN 18272   Hinges for fire doors.
- DIN 18273   Lever handle units for fire doors and smoke control doors.
- DIN 4066   Information signs for fire brigade.
- RAL-RG 611   Fire barriers; quality assurance.
- RAL-GZ 612   Smoke barriers; quality assurance.
- RAL-GZ 975/2   Fire protection in interior construction; fire protection glass; quality assurance.
- LBO   Land building regulations and implementation ordinances.
- Certification of manufacturing firms.
- DIN EN 179   Emergency exit devices operated by a lever handle or push pad.
- DIN EN 1125   Panic exit devices operated by a horizontal bar.

Intrusion protection
- DIN V ENV 1627   Windows, doors, shutters - Burglar resistance - Requirements and classification.
- DIN 18103   Burglar-resistant doors.
- DIN 52290   Burglar-resistant glass, Part 1–5.
- DIN 18104-1   Additional burglar-resistant products, Part 1: screw-on additional products for windows and doors; requirements and test methods.
- DIN EN 1522   Windows, doors, shutters and blinds – Bullet resistance – Requirements and classification.
- DIN EN 13123-1 (draft)   Windows, doors and shutters – Explosion resistance; Requirements and classification.
- RAL-RG 611/3   Gates, doors, frames; Burglar-resistant steel doors; quality assurance.

Radiation protection
- DIN 6834   Radiation protection doors for medical locations.

Residential closure doors
- DIN 18101   Doors; doors for residential buildings; sizes of door leaves, position of hinges and lock, interdependence of dimensions.
- DIN 18105   Residential closure doors.
- RAL-GZ 996   Building doors; quality assurance.

Internal doors
- DIN 18101   Doors; doors for residential buildings; sizes of door leaves, position of hinges and lock, interdependence of dimensions.
- DIN 68706-1 (draft)   Interior doors made from wood and wood-based panels – Door leaves.
- DIN 68706-2 (draft)   Interior doors made from wood and wood-based panels – Door frames
- DIN 67706   Flush doors; terms, preferred dimensions and construction characteristics for interior doors.
- RAL-RG 426   Quality and test requirements for interior doors made from wood and wood-based panels.

Dimension
- DIN 4172   Dimensional coordination in buildings.
- DIN 18000   Modular coordination in building.
- DIN 18100   Doors; wall openings for doors with dimensions in accordance with DIN 4172.
- DIN 18101   Doors; doors for residential buildings; sizes of door leaves, position of hinges and lock.

Component standards
- DIN 18111   Door frames – Steel door frames – Part 1: Standard door frames for rebated doors in masonry.
- DIN 68706-2 (draft)   Interior doors made from wood and wood-based panels; Door frames; Definitions, dimensions, installation.
- DIN EN 1529   Door leaves – Height, width, thickness and squareness – Tolerance classes.
- DIN EN 1530   Door leaves – General and local flatness – Tolerance classes.
- DIN EN 1154   Locks and hardware – Controlled door closing devices
- DIN 18251   Locks – Mortise locks for doors; Regulations for different hardware.
- DIN 18252   Profile cylinders for door locks – Definitions, dimensions, requirements and marking.
- DIN 18255   Building hardware – Door lever handles, backplates and escutcheons – Definitions, dimensions, requirements.
- DIN 18257   Building hardware – Security plates – Definitions, measurements, requirements, tests and marking
- DIN 18263   Controlled door closing devices with hydraulic damping.
- DIN 18268   Hinges for doors – Reference-lines for hinges
- DIN EN 12365-1 (draft)   Hardware – Seals and seal profiles for windows, doors and other closing elements, as well as curtain facades; requirements and classifications.

Construction standards
- VOB, Part C   General technical specifications in construction contracts
- DIN 18355   Joinery work.
- DIN 18357   Mounting of hardware.
- DIN 18360   Metal construction and locksmith works.

GATES/INDUSTRIAL DOORS
- DIN EN 12433 Part 1 and 2   Gates – Terminology – Types of gates and parts of gates.
- DIN EN 13241-1   Gate product standard; Machine regulations EG 98/37.
- DIN EN 12453   Gates – Safety in use of power operated gates – Requirements.
- DIN EN 12445   Gates – Safety in use of power operated gates – Test methods.
- DIN EN 12978   Doors and gates – Safety devices for power operated doors and gates – Requirements and testing methods.
- DIN EN 12604   Gates – Mechanical aspects – Requirements.
- DIN EN 12605   Gates – Mechanical aspects – Testing process.
- DIN EN 12433-1   Gates – Terminology – Part 1: Types of gates.
- DIN EN 12433-2   Gates – Terminology – Part 2: Components of gates.
- DIN EN 12635   Gates – Installation and use.
- DIN EN 12426   Gates – Air permeability – Classification.
- DIN EN 12444   Gates – Resistance to wind load – Test and calculation method.
- DIN EN 12489   Gates – Resistance to water penetration – testing process.
- DIN EN 12428   Gates – Heat transfer coefficient – Requirements for the calculation.
- DIN EN 1634-1   Fire resistance tests for door and shutter assemblies – Part 1: Fire protection shutters.
- DIN EN 1634-3   Fire resistance and smoke control tests for door and shutter assemblies, openable windows and elements of building hardware– Part 3: Smoke protection cover.
- DIN EN ISO 717-1   Acoustics – measurement of sound insulation in buildings and of building elements– Part 1: Airborne sound reduction (ISO 717-1:1996).

ASSOCIATIONS AND MANUFACTURERS

Associations

Absatzförderungsfonds der
deutschen Forst- und Holz-
wirtschaft
Godesberger Allee 142–148
D-53175 Bonn
Tel. +49 (0) 228 – 308380
www.holzabsatzfonds.de

A/U/F Aluminum und Umwelt im
Fenster- und Fassadenbau
Bockenheimer Anlage 13
D-60322 Frankfurt am Main
Tel. +49 (0) 69 – 95505413
www.a-u-f.com

Arbeitskreis bauakustische
Prüfstellen
www.schall-pruefstellen.de

BINE Informationsdienst
Kaiserstraße 185–19
D-53113 Bonn
Tel. +49 (0) 228 – 923790
www.bine.info

Bundesverband Flachglas e. V.
Mülheimer Straße 1
D-53840 Troisdorf
Tel. +49 (0) 2241 – 87270
www.bundesverband-flachglas.de

Bundesverband
Rolladen + Sonnenschutz e. V.
Hopmannstraße 2
D-53177 Bonn
Tel. +49 (0) 228 – 952100
www.rs-fachverband.de

BVT – Verband Tore
An der Pönt 48
D-40885 Ratingen
Tel. +49 (0) 2102 – 186200
www.bvt-tore.de

Fachgruppe Holz-Aluminum-
Fenster des Verbandes der Fens-
ter- und Fassadenhersteller e. V.
Bockenheimer Anlage 13
60322 Frankfurt am Main
Tel. +49 (0) 69 – 9550540
www.holzalu-fenster.de

Fachverband Lichtkuppel,
Lichtband und RWA e. V.
Ernst-Hilker-Straße 2
D-32758 Detmold
Tel. +49 (0) 5231 – 309590
www.fvlr.de

Fachverband Schloß- und
Beschlagindustrie e. V.
Offerstraße 12
D-42551 Velbert

Flachglas MarkenKreis GmbH
Auf der Reihe 2
D-45884 Gelsenkirchen
Tel. +49 (0) 209 – 913290
www.flachglas-markenkreis.de

Förderkreis Holz-Aluminum-
Fenster
Saarburger-Ring 7
D-68229 Mannheim
Fax +49 (0) 621 – 4839841
www.das-holzalu-fenster.de

ift – Institut für Fenstertechnik e. V.
Theodor-Gietl-Straße 7–9
D-83026 Rosenheim
Tel. +49 (0) 8031 – 2610
www.ift-rosenheim.de

Initiative Furnier + Natur e. V.
Unterer Lichtenbergweg 5
D-76229 Karlsruhe
www.furnier.de, www.infoholz.de

Initiative ProHolzfenster e. V.
Am Herscheid 12
D-59846 Sundern
Tel. +49 (0) 2393 – 911092
www.proholzfenster.de

Institut des Glashandwerks für Ver-
glasungstechnik und Fensterbau
An der Glasfachschule 6
D-65589 Hadamar
Tel. +49 (0) 6433 – 913315
www.glaserhandwerk.de

Prüfzentrum für Bauelemente PfB
Dipl.-Ing. (FH) Rüdiger Müller
Lackermannweg 24
D-83071 Stephanskirchen/Kragling
Tel. +49 (0) 8036 – 6749470
www.pfb-rosenheim.de

PU-Schaumdosen Recycling
Deutsche Umwelthilfe
Hackescher Markt 4
D-10178 Berlin
Tel. +49 (0)30 – 240086741
www.duh.de

RAL-Gütegemeinschaften
Fenster und Haustüren e. V.
Bockenheimer Anlage 13
D-60322 Frankfurt am Main
Tel. +49 (0) 69 – 9550540
www.window.de

Technisches Kompetenzzentrum
des Glaserhandwerks
An der Glasfachschule 6
D-65589 Hadamar
www.glaserhandwerk.de

Verband der Fenster- und
Fassadenhersteller e. V.
Walter-Kolb-Straße 1–7
D-60594 Frankfurt am Main
Tel. +49 (0) 69 – 9550540
www.window.de

Verband für Fassadentechnik VFT
Ziegelhüttenstraße 67
D-64832 Babenhausen
Tel. +49 (0) 6073 – 712650
www.v-f-t.de

Verband
Schließ- und Sicherungstechnik
Ruhrallee 12
D-45138 Essen
Tel. +49 (0) 201 – 896190
www.metallhandwerk.de

Manufacturers

air-lux Fenstertechnik AG
Breitschachenstrasse 52
CH-9032 Engelburg
Tel. +41 (0) 71 – 2722600
www.air-lux.ch

Akzo Nobel Deco GmbH
Geschäftsbereich Holzbau
Werner-von-Siemens-Straße 11
D-31515 Wunstorf
Tel. +49 (0) 5031 – 9610
www.akzonobel.com

Aluprof, Aluminumprofile
Bielsko – Biała
ul. Warszawska 153
PL-43-300 Bielsko-Biała
Tel. +48 (0) 33 – 8195300
www.aluprof.eu

Annen GmbH
Sternfelder Straße 1
D-54317 Farschweiler
Tel. +49 (0) 6500 – 666
www.annen.de

Athmer, Dichtungen Türen / Tore
Sophienhammer
D-59757 Arnsberg-Müschede
Tel. +49 (0) 2932 – 477500
www.athmer.de

Baumgartner Fenster AG
Flurstrasse 41
CH-6332 Hagendorn, Cham
Tel. +41 (0) 78 – 58585
www.baumgartnerfenster.ch

BOS GmbH, Stahlzargen
Lütkenfelde 4
D-48282 Emsdetten
Tel. +49 (0) 2572 – 2030
www.bos-gmbh.com

BUG-Alutechnik GmbH
Bergstraße 17
D-88267 Vogt
Tel. +49 (0) 7529 – 9990
www.bug.de

CAPAROL GmbH
Roßdörfer Straße 50
Industriegebiet 1
D-64372 Ober-Ramstadt
Tel. +49 (0) 6154 – 710

Deventer Profile GmbH & Co. KG
Rauchstraße 38–42
D-13587 Berlin
Tel. +49 (0) 30 – 3559070
www.deventer-profile.com

Dichtungs-Specht GmbH
Industriestraße 15
D-74912 Kirchardt
Tel. +49 (0) 7266 – 91590
www.dichtungs-specht.de

Dollex, Dichtungen für Fenster
und Türen
Insterburger Str. 12
D-28207 Bremen
Tel. +49 (0) 421 – 37941660
www.dollex.de

Dorma GmbH + Co. KG
Dorma-Platz 1
D-58256 Ennepetal
Tel. +49 (0) 2333 – 7930
www.dorma.de

DÖRR Histoglas,
Raimund Dörr Glasermeister
Prof.-Schumacherstraße 1
D-74706 Osterburken
Tel. +49 (0) 6291 – 8101
www.histoglas.de

Duco, Ventilation & Sun Control
Handelsstraat 19
B-8630 Veurne
Tel. +32 (0) 58 – 330033
www.duco.eu

Dyrup GmbH
Klosterhofweg 64
D-41199 Mönchengladbach
Tel. +49 (0) 2166 – 9646
www.dyrup.de

EHRET GmbH (Alufensterläden)
Bahnhofstraße 14–18
D-77972 Mahlberg
Tel. +49 (0) 7822 – 4390
www.ehret.com

esco Metallbausysteme GmbH
Dieselstraße 2
D-71254 Ditzingen
Tel. +49 (0) 7156 – 30080
www.esco-online.de

frovin Fenster
Breite Straße 23
D-40670 Meerbusch-Osterath
Tel. +49 (0) 2159 – 91670
www.frovin.de

FSB, Franz Schneider Brakel
GmbH + Co KG
Nieheimer Straße 38
D-33034 Brakel
Tel. +49 (0) 5272 – 6080
www.fsb.de

Gegg Fensterbau GmbH
Innerer Graben 8
D-77716 Haslach
Tel. +49 (0) 7832 – 2021
www.gegg.com

GEZE GmbH
Reinhold-Vöster-Straße 21–29
D-71229 Leonberg
Tel. +49 (0) 7152 – 2030
www.geze.com

Glasid AG
Daniel-Eckhardt-Straße 22
D-45356 Essen
Tel. +49 (0) 201 – 369040
www.glasid.com

Glas Marte GmbH
Brachsenweg 39
A-6900 Bregenz
Tel. +43 (0) 5574 – 67220
www.glasmarte.at

Hahn Lamellenfenster
Hafenstraße 5–7
D-63811 Stockstadt am Main
Tel. +49 (0) 6027 – 41620
www.glasbau-hahn.de

Halu, Rolladen / Sonnenschutz
Hassinger GmbH & Co KG
Dürkheimerstraße 234
D-67071 Ludwigshafen
Tel. +49 (0) 621 – 67140
www.hassinger-sonnenschutz.de

Hanno-Werk GmbH & Co. KG
Fugenabdichtungen
Hanno-Ring 5
D-30880 Laatzen
Tel. +49 (0) 5102 – 70000
www.hanno.com

Hawa AG
Schiebebeschlagsysteme
Untere Fischbachstrasse 4
CH-8932 Mettmenstetten
Tel. +41 (0) 44 – 7679191
www.hawa.ch

Heinzmann GmbH
Rollladen und Fenster
Rudolf-Diesel-Straße 19
D-97318 Kitzingen
Tel. +49 (0) 9321 – 9360-35
www.heinzmann.eu

Hoba Brandschutzelemente
Holzbau Schmid GmbH & Co. KG
Ziegelhau 1–4
D-73099 Adelberg
Tel. +49 (0) 7166 – 5777
www.hoba.de

Holz Schiller GmbH
Pointenstraße 24–28
D-94209 Regen
Tel. +49 (0) 9921 – 94420
www.holz-schiller.de

Internorm Fenster AG
Gewerbegasse 5
CH-6330 Cham
Tel. +41 (0) 800 – 910920
www.internorm.ch

ip-company GmbH
Visbeker Damm 34
D-49429 Visbek
Tel. +49 (0) 4445 – 988990
www.ipcompany.de

Kindt Fensterladen AG
Bahnhofstrasse 60
CH-8112 Otelfingen
Tel. +41 (0) 848 – 833080
www.kindt.ch

KlimaFlex
Hohenstaufenstraße 16
D-73557 Mutlangen
Tel. +49 (0) 7171 – 976140
www.klimaflex.de

Kneer GmbH, Fenster und Türen
Riedstraße 45
D-72589 Westerheim
Tel. +49 (0) 7333 – 830
www.kneer.de

Kömmerling Kunststoffe
Zweibrücker Straße 200
66954 Pirmasens
Tel. + 49 (0) 6331 – 560
www.profine-group.com

G. Kramp GmbH
Werkstraße 3
32657 Lemgo-Lieme
Tel. +49 (0) 5261 – 968810
www.kramp-lemgo.de

Lacker AG
Schellenbergstraße 1
72178 Waldachtal-Lützenhardt
Tel: +49 (0) 7443 – 96220
www.lacker.de

La Florida S.R.L., Beschläge
Via Foscarini 12
I-31040 Nerveda Della Battaglia
Tel. +39 (0) 422 – 725543
www.lafloridasrl.it

LEHR Rollladen-Kastensysteme
Talstraße 20
D-71546 Aspach
Tel. +49 (0)7191 – 20505
www.helmut-lehr.de

Metaglas B.V.Het Eek 5
4004 LM Tiel, PF 270
NL-4000 AG Tiel
Tel. +31 (0) 344 – 750400
www.metaglas.nl

PaX AG
Neuweg 7
D-55218 Ingelheim
Tel. +49 (0) 6132 – 791110
www.pax.de

Pfeifer Beschläge GmbH + Co. KG
In der Neuen Welt 2
D-87700 Memmingen
Tel. +49 (0) 8331 – 83930
www.pfeifer-beschlaege.de

Pilkington AG
Hegestraße
D-45966 Gladbeck
Tel. +49 (0) 180 – 3020100
www.pilkington.com

RAICO Bautechnik GmbH
Gewerbegebiet Nord 2
D-87772 Pfaffenhausen
Tel. +49 (0) 8265 – 9110
www.raico.de

RENSON VENTILATION,
SUNPROTECTION
Industriezone 2 Vijverdam
Maalbeekstraat 10
B-8790 WAREGEM
Tel. +32 (0) 56 – 627111
www.renson.be

Reynaers GmbH
Aluminum Systeme
Franzstraße 25
D-45968 Gladbeck
Tel. +49 (0) 2043 – 96400
www.reynaers.com

ROMA Rollladensysteme GmbH
Ostpreußenstraße 9
D-89331 Burgau
Tel. +49 (0) 8222 – 40000
www.roma.de

Roto Frank AG
Wilhelm-Frank-Platz 1
D-70771 Leinfelden-Echterdingen
Tel +49 (0) 711 – 75980
www.roto-frank.com

Roth AG / SIROL Sicherheits-
anlagen
CH-6403 Küssnacht am Rigi
Tel. +41 (0) 41 – 8503642
www.roth-sirol.ch

RP Technik GmbH Profilsysteme
Edisonstraße 4
D-59199 Bönen
Tel. +49 (0) 2383 – 91490
www.rp-technik.com
www.welser.com

Saint-Gobain Glass France
18 avenue d'Alsace
F-92400 Courbevoie
Tel. +33 (0) 147 – 624841
www.saint-gobain.com

Schäfer Fensterbau GmbH
Opelstraße 14
D-64646 Heppenheim
Tel. +49 (0) 6252 – 77521
www.schaefer-fensterbau.de

SCHOTT AG
Restaurierungsgläser
Hattenbergstraße 10
D-55122 Mainz
Tel. +49 (0) 6131 – 660
www.schott.com

Schörghuber Spezialtüren KG
Neuhaus 3
D-84539 Ampfing
Tel. +49 (0)8636 – 5030
www.schoerghuber.de

Schüco – Jansen International KG
Karolinenstraße 1–15
D-33609 Bielefeld
Tel. +49 (0) 521 – 7830
www.schueco.com

Secco Sistemi S.p.A.
Via Terraglios 195
I-31022 Preganziol (TV)
Tel. +39 (0) 422 – 497700
www.seccosistemi.it

Silent Gliss GmbH
Rebgartenweg 5
D-79576 Weil am Rhein
Tel. +49 (0) 7621 – 66070
www.silentgliss.de

Simonswerk GmbH
Bosfelder Weg 5
D-33378 Rheda-Wiedenbrück
Tel. +49 (0) 5242 – 4130
www.simonswerk.de

Sky-Frame, R & G Metallbau AG
Bergwisstrasse 2
CH-8548 Ellikon a. Thur
Tel. +41 (0) 52 – 3690230
www.rg-metallbau.ch

Tremco illbruck GmbH & Co. KG
Fensterabdichtungssysteme,
Schäume
Von-der-Wettern-Straße 27
D-51149 Köln
Tel. +49 (0) 2203 – 575500
www.tremco-illbruck.com

Velfac A/S
Bygholm Søpark 23
DK-8700 Horsens
Tel. +45 (0) 7628 – 8555
www.velfac.de

Warema Renkhoff GmbH
Hans-Wilhelm-Renkhoff-Straße 2
D-97828 Marktheidenfeld
Tel. +49 (0) 9391 – 200
www.warema.de

Weinig AG, Profiliermaschinen
Weinigstraße 2/4
D-97941 Tauberbischofsheim
Tel. +49 (0) 9341 – 860
www.weinig.de

Westag & Getalit AG
Hellweg 15
D-33378 Rheda-Wiedenbrück
Tel. +49 (0)5242 – 170
www.westag-getalit.de

BIBLIOGRAPHY / PICTURE CREDITS

Baus, Ursula; Siegele, Klaus: Öffnungen, Stuttgart 2006

Belz, Walter: Zusammenhänge, Bemerkungen zur Baukonstruktion und dergleichen, Cologne 1993

Blaser, Werner: Mies van der Rohe, Basel 1997

Deplazes, Andrea (Ed.): Constructing Architecture, Basel 2005

Dierks, Klaus; Schneider, Klaus-Jürgen; Wormuth, Rüdiger: Baukonstruktion, Düsseldorf 2006

Dürr, Herrmann Rupprecht: Das Stahlfenster in der Bauwirtschaft, Berlin 1940

Frank, Hartmut: Die Augen der Häuser; in archithese 5.97, Sulgen 1997

Gropius, Walter; Moholy-Nagy, Laszlo: Internationale Architektur, Munich 1925

Hasler, Thomas: Das Fenster und seine Gestik auf den Raum – Zur Beziehung von Öffnung und Innenraum; in archithese 5.97, Sulgen 1997

Häuser, Karl; Kramer, Bernd; Schmid, Rainer W; Walk, Rainer: Gestalten mit Glas. Interpane; Lauenförde 1994

Hegger, Manfred; Fuchs, Matthias; Stark, Thomas; Zeumer, Martin: Energy Manual, Munich 2007

Herzog, Thomas; Krippner, Roland; Lang, Werner: Facade Construction Manual, Basel 2004

Huber, B.; J. C. Steinegger: Jean Prouvé: Architektur aus der Fabrik, Zurich 1971

Institut für Fenstertechnik e.V, Rosenheim: Einbau und Anschluss von Fenstern und Fenstertüren mit Anwendungsbeispielen, Düsseldorf 2002

Institut für Fenstertechnik e.V, Rosenheim: Nr. 20 – Einbau und Anschluss von Fenstern und Fenstertüren mit Anwendungsbeispielen, Düsseldorf 2002

Janser, Andres: Das grosse Fenster; in: archithese 5.97, Sulgen 1997

Krippner, Roland; Musso, Florian: Basics Facade Apertures, Basel 2008

Künzel, Helmut: Fensterlüftung und Raumklima, Stuttgart 2003

Langenbeck, Florian; Schrader, Mila: Türen, Schlösser und Beschläge als historisches Baumaterial, Suderberg-Hösseringen 2002

Le Corbusier: Feststellungen zu Architektur und Städtebau, Basel 2001

Leitner, Bernhard: The Wittgenstein House, New York City 2000

Mäckler, Christoph: Vielfalt der Fenster; in: Werk, Bauen und Wohnen 9/2007, Zurich 2007

Meiss von, Pierre: Elements of Architecture: From Form to Place, Basel 1994

Meyer-Bohe, Walter: Fenster Elemente des Bauens, Stuttgart 1973

Mittag, Martin: Baukonstruktionslehre, Gütersloh 1952

Moravánsky, Ákos: Nur Umrisse im Glas – Die Opazität des Fensters; in archithese 5.97, Sulgen 1997

Neumann, Dietrich; Weinbrenner, Ulrich: Frick/Knöll: Baukonstruktionslehre Teil 1, Stuttgart 2006

Neumann, Dietrich; Weinbrenner, Ulrich: Frick/Knöll: Baukonstruktionslehre Teil 2, Stuttgart 2008

Neumann, Hans-Rudolf; Hinz, Dietrich; Müller, Rüdiger; Schulze, Jörg: Fenster im Bestand, Renningen 2003

Neumeyer, Fritz: Die Augen des Hauses – Das Fenster als architektonische Form; in Werk, Bauen und Wohnen 9/2007, Zurich 2007

Oberbach, Karl: Plastic Handbook, Munich 2001

Pech, Anton; Pommer, Georg; Zeininger, Johannes: Baukonstruktionen, Band 11: Fenster, Vienna 2005

Pech, Anton; Pommer, Georg; Zeininger, Johannes: Baukonstruktionen, Band 12: Türen und Tore, Vienna 2007

Pech, Anton; Pommer, Georg; Zeininger, Johannes: Baukonstruktionen, Band 13: Fassaden, Vienna 2009

RAL-Gütegemeinschaften Fenster und Türen: Der Einbau von Fenstern, Fassaden und Haustüren mit Qualitätskontrolle durch das RAL-Gütezeichen. RAL-Gütegemeinschaften Fenster und Türen, Frankfurt/Main

Reichel, Alexander; Hochberg, Anette; Köpke, Christine: Plaster, Render, Paint and Coatings, Munich 2004

Reitmayer, Ulrich: Holzfenster, Stuttgart 1980

Reitmayer, Ulrich: Holztüren und Holztore, Stuttgart 1970

Riccabona, Christof: Baukonstruktionslehre 2 – Stiegen, Dächer, Fenster, Türen, Vienna 2005

Rolf, Olaf: Moderne Fenstertechnik, Landsberg 1993

Ronner, Heinz: Öffnungen, Baukonstruktion im Kontext des architektonischen Entwerfens, Basel 1991

Scheck: Fenster aus Holz und Metall: Die Bauelemente, Band 1, Stuttgart 1953

Schittich,Christian; Staib, Gerald; Balkow, Dieter; Schuler, Matthias; Sobek, Werner: Glass Construction Manual, Basel 2006

Schmitt, Heinrich; Heene, Andreas: Hochbau Konstruktionen, Braunschweig 1977

Schrader, Mila: Fenster, Glas und Beschläge als historisches Baumaterial, Suderberg-Hösseringen 2001

Spannagel, Fritz: Das große Türenbuch für Schreiner, Architekten und Lehrer, Hannover 2001

Tschanz, Martin: Bildhaftigkeit oder räumliche Verschränkung – Wie Fenster innen und aussen trennen oder verbinden; in: Werk, Bauen und Wohnen 9/2007, Zurich 2007

Wagner, Andreas: Energieeffiziente Fenster und Verglasungen, Cologne 2000

Abache, Ludwig: p. 33 6

air-lux Fenstertechnik AG: p. 69 3

archinoah.de: p. 44 1

Archive Olgiati: p. 11 4, 5; p. 13 7; p. 98 1, 2

Bayer, Stefan: p. 109

BeluTec GmbH: p. 123 9

BINE Informationsdienst: p.58 3

Bluguia, Pablo: p. 33 5

Bryant, Richard: p. 25 5, 6

Bucher, Hanns-Hermann: p. 73 5

Bühler, Beat: p. 28 1, 2

Caulfield, Allie: p. 15 8

Darpa, Josef: p. 12 1, 2; p. 22 2

Delonga, Lucia: p. 18 3

Dorma GmbH: p. 118 2; p. 120 4

Dörr Histoglas: p. 72 2

Drewniak, Frans: p. 32 1

Eid-Sabbagh, Yasmine: p. 29 3, 4

Fano, Tomás: p. 96

Feiner, Ralph: p. 43 3; p. 102 1; p. 146–149

Flachglas MarkenKreis: p. 61 6

Fondation Le Corbusier © 2009 FLC/ProLitteris, Zürich: p. 80 2

Frei, Roger: p. 128–130

Fundación Miguel Fisac: p. 22 5

G. Kramp GmbH: p. 70 1, 2, 3

Galuzi, Luca: p. 12 3

GEZE GmbH: p. 100 1, 5, p. 108

Glasid AG: p. 61 7

Gutmann, Horst: p. 44 3

Hagen, Marcel: p. 44 4

Halbe, Roland: p. 31 4; p. 134–135

Heinrich, Michael: p. 132–133

Heinzmann GmbH: p. 93 7

Helfenstein, Heinrich: p. 25 3, 4; p. 102 2

Henz, Hannes: p. 16 2, 3

Hirai, Hiroyuki: p. 20 1

Hörmann KG: p. 101 4, 5; p. 123 8

Janssens, Alain: p. 150–151

Jara, Viktor: p. 30 1

Jeck, Valentin: p. 36 1, 2; p. 126

Kindt Fensterladen AG: p. 89 2

Kirchner; G.G.:   p. 144

Knapp, Jan Kristian: p. 42 1, 3, 5; p. 44 5; p. 86 1, 2, 3, 5; p. 87 6; p. 100 2, 3; p. 101 2

Kneer GmbH: p. 53 4; p. 57 5, 6

Köpke, Christine: p. 6; p. 30 2

Koslowski, Paul © 2009 FLC/ProLitteris, Zürich: p. 10 2

Krutzenbichler, Michael: p. 101 1

Lacker AG: p. 44 2

Letterman, Doug: p. 8 2

Levers, Andreas: p. 15 9

Lichtenberg, Christian: p. 12 4

Lintner, Linus: p. 27 3

Lord, John: p. 8 1

Malagamba, Duccio: p. 22 3, p. 78, p. 83 4

Marte Marte Architekten: p. 136–139

Mayer, Thomas: p. 15 7; p. 33 7

Mudford, Grant: p. 18 2

ninara/Flickr: p. 14 2

oscartdesign/Flickr: p. 19 6

Ott, Paul: p. 13 8, 9; p. 80 1

Padget, Laura: p. 83 5; p. 98 3

Padura, Sergio: p. 21 3

Palma, Cristobal: p. 25 1, 2

PaX AG: p. 63 4

Prof. Christoph Mäckler Architekten/Christoph Lison: p. 18 4

Roma GmbH: p. 92 2; p.158 1

Romberg, Helen: p. 22 4

Rommel, Klaus: p. 10 1

Roth, Lukas: p. 31 5

Ryberg, Bent: p. 14 5

Saint-Gobain Rigips GmbH: p. 110 4

Schauer Volhard Architekten: p. 152–155

Scheffler, Ingrid: p. 101 3

Schittich, Christian: p. 32 2; p. 43 6

Schüco International KG: p. 43 7, 9, 10; p. 57 3, 4; p. 67 8; p. 87 10; p. 93 5, 6; p. 118 3; p. 120 1; p. 121 5; p. 125 3

Schulz-Dornburg, Ursula: p. 23 7

seier+seier+seier/Flickr: p. 14 3

Silent Gliss GmbH: p. 94 1, 2, 3; p. 95 4, 5

Simonetti, Filippo: p. 16 1

Simonswerk GmbH: p. 115 4

Staufer & Hasler Architekten/Heinrich Helfenstein: p. 42 4

Strobel, Peter: p. 145

Testa, Daniele: p. 14 4

Tremco illbruck GmbH: p. 65 6–8

Tschanz, Martin: p. 18 1

Vander Maren Weerts Architechts: p. 74 1, 2; p. 75 3; p. 116 1, 2, 4

Velfac A/S: p. 68 2

Walti, Ruedi: p. 86 4; p. 102 1; p. 140–143

Warema GmbH: p. 87 7–9

Zucchi, Zino: p. 9 3, 4

INDEX

PUBLISHING INFORMATION

Edited by Alexander Reichel, Kerstin Schultz
Concept: Alexander Reichel, Kerstin Schultz, Andrea Wiegelmann
Authors: Jan-Henrik Hafke, Anette Hochberg, Joachim Raab

Drawings: Anna-Katharina Tomm, Anna Rauch, Inga Scholz
Picture editors: Jan K. Knapp, Odine Oßwald

Translation into English: Michael Robinson (chapters 1, 3–6), Raymond Peat (chapter 2)
English editing and proof-reading: Richard Toovey

Layout und cover design: Nadine Rinderer
Typesetting: Jan K. Knapp, Amelie Solbrig, Lena Ebert

The technical and construction recommendations contained in this book are based on the present state of technical knowledge. They should be checked in each case against the relevant instructions, standards, laws etc. as well as local regulations before applying them. No liability is accepted.

Library of Congress Control Number: 2009925057

Bibliographic information published by the German National Library
The German National Library lists this publication in the Deutsche Nationalbibliografie; detailed bibliographic data are available on the Internet at http://dnb.d-nb.de.

This book is also available in a German language edition (ISBN 978-3-7643-9960-3).

© 2010 Birkhäuser Verlag AG
Basel · Boston · Berlin
P.O. Box 133, CH-4010 Basel, Switzerland
Part of Springer Science+Business Media

Printed on acid-free paper produced from chlorine-free pulp. TCF ∞

Printed in Germany

ISBN 978-3-7643-9961-0

9 8 7 6 5 4 3 2 1   www.birkhauser.ch